FIRST EDITION

INTERNATIONAL RELATIONS (GS-2) & INTERNAL SECURITY (GS-3)

ARIHANT PUBLICATIONS (INDIA) LIMITED

Administrative & Production Offices

Regd. Office

'Ramchhaya' 4577/15, Agarwal Road, Darya Ganj, New Delhi -110002
Tele: 011- 47630600, 43518550

Head Office

Kalindi, TP Nagar, Meerut (UP) - 250002
Tel: 0121-7156203, 7156204

Sales & Support Offices

Agra, Ahmedabad, Bengaluru, Bareilly, Chennai, Delhi, Guwahati, Hyderabad, Jaipur, Jhansi, Kolkata, Lucknow, Nagpur & Pune.

PRICE ₹ 325.00

PO No : TXT-59-T064054-03-25

Published by Arihant Publications (India) Ltd.

For further information about the books published by Arihant, log on to www.arihantbooks.com or e-mail at info@arihantbooks.com

Follow us on    

Few Words
to the Budding UPSC Aspirants

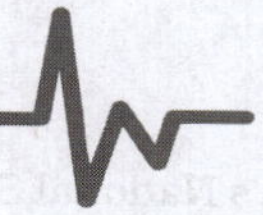

UPSC Mains Exam is **the most crucial stage on your path to becoming a civil servant.** But conquering it isn't a walk in the park - it's a strategic game. You need the right arsenal (effective study materials) and honed tactics (answer writing skills) to succeed. **PULSE Mains Series** equips you for every challenge, a one-stop solution for your Mains preparation.

Forget about sifting through mountains of irrelevant information. **PULSE Mains books are meticulously organized, packed with dynamic analysis and updated with the latest developments.**

These books provide only exam-relevant content and removing the cluttered content available in the market, thus bringing time-optimised notes for the students.

Following are the salient features of Pulse Mains books:

- **Comprehensive and Exam-oriented content** covering all relevant topics in depth.
- **Content Enrichment with** the help of current examples, data & facts, case studies and supreme court judgements.
- **Innovative exam-ready frameworks** (PESTEL, Stakeholder, Life-cycle, etc) to meet evolving answer writing demands.
- **Visually appealing presentation** by incorporating flowcharts, timelines, mindmaps, hand-drawn diagrams, tables and maps.
- **Integration of PYQs** at the end of each chapter to align the content with the recent exam trends.
- **Easy for multiple revision of the syllabus** which can help in improving the Mains score.

On behalf of **MentorsHut**, I would like to express our deepest gratitude to each and every student for placing your trust in Pulse Books. Thanks to your incredible support, Pulse Books have become best-sellers!

We are also incredibly thankful to **Arihant Publications** for partnering with us and providing the opportunity to develop the **PULSE series for the UPSC Mains examination.**

The creation of these masterpiece Mains books wouldn't have been possible without the tireless, combined efforts of the entire MentorsHut family, who dedicated thousands of hours to the project. Our sincere thanks go to **Ashutosh Bansal, Tarun Sahu, Vishal Anand, Vishal Singh, Shefali, Shadab Ahmad and Avinish Kumar** for their exceptional contributions. Their creativity in content presentation, clear handwriting and unwavering support for each other were instrumental in this success.

We also want to express my **deepest gratitude to my daughter, Prisha Mangtani.** While we poured our heart into these books, we know the sacrifices this meant for you. You are truly special!

We at MentorsHut are dedicated to continuous improvement. While we believe Pulse Books represent our best effort, we recognize the possibility of human error. We welcome any suggestions for improvement to the content. Please feel free to share your thoughts at info@mentorshut.com

Amit Mangtani
CA Shalini Wadhwani
Founders, MentorsHut

Let's Begin Our Journey

Part-A Internal Security

Part-B International Relations

Note: The book covers current developments till May 2024. Recent current developments and some peripheral issues will be given as Value Addition Material (Online). Scan the QR Code to get access of current issues.

Part-A Internal Security

National Security

CHAPTER 01

NATIONAL SECURITY

National Security is a state or condition where a nation's most cherished values and beliefs, its way of life, its institutions of governance and its unity, welfare and well being as a nation and people are permanently protected and continuously enhanced.

Objectives of National Security

01 **Defense of National Territory**- Protection over land, sea and air. Ensuring the inviolability of land borders, land territories, offshore assets and maritime trade routes.

02 **Internal Security**- Addressing threats to unity or progress arising from religious, language, ethnic or socio-economic conflict

03 **Regional influence**- Influencing other regional countries to promote harmonious relationships that support Indian national interests.

04 **Out of area operations**- Executing operations beyond national borders to contribute to international stability.

05 **Global Recognition**- Promoting India's rise to its rightful place in international affairs

06 **Peace for citizens**- Creating a climate for our citizens that is just, equitable, prosperous and shields them from risks to life and livelihood.

Law and order, public order and security of State in India

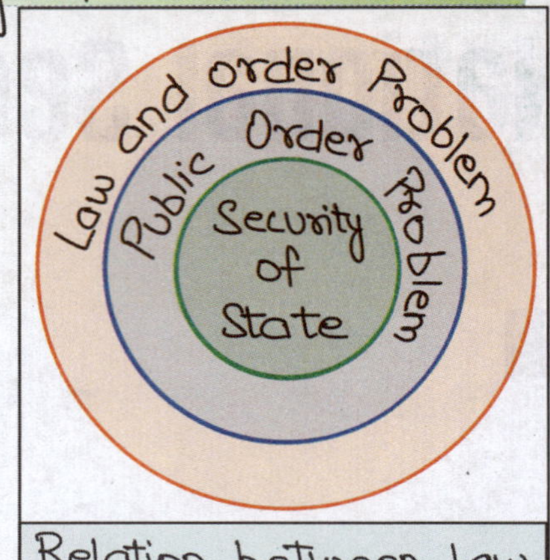

Relation between law and order, public order and security of state

- **Law and order**- General state of peace and tranquility in society
  - Encompass all violations of law, from minor traffic offenses to serious crimes.
  - Maintained by police and legal system
- **Public order**
  - A subset of law and order specifically focussed on maintaining peace and safety in public spaces.
  - Includes situations that disrupt daily life and cause public inconvenience or fear
  - eg-riots, protests that turn violent, hate speech that incites violence.

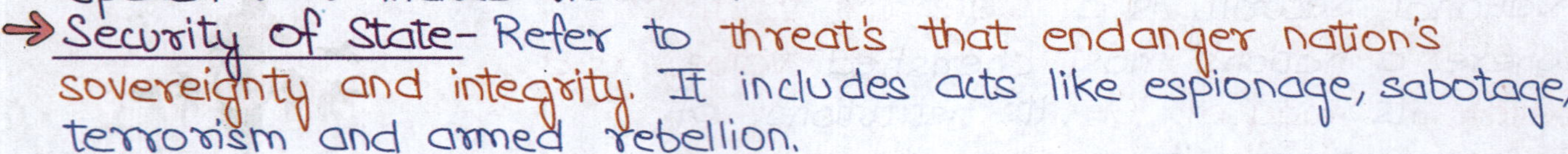

- **Security of State**- Refer to threat's that endanger nation's sovereignty and integrity. It includes acts like espionage, sabotage, terrorism and armed rebellion.

Threats faced by State

Arthashashtra by Kautilya identifies four main categories of threats a state can face:

01 **External Threats**- These originate from outside the country's borders and can include- terrorism, foreign intelligence activities.

02 **Internal Threats**- These arise from within the country itself and can encompass- Naxalism (communist insurgency), communal violence, riots

03 **Internally aided external threats**- Support provided by extremist or separatist groups within a country to foreign nations with the intent to destabilize their own nation

04 **Externally aided internal threats**- Acts funded or supported by international terror organisations within a country.
eg- 2008 Mumbai terror attacks by Lashkar-e-Taiba, a militant organisation

EVOLUTION OF NATIONAL SECURITY

Traditional Dimensions
- Territorial Defense
- Military Preparedness
- Border security

Non-military Dimensions
- Terrorism
- Cybersecurity
- Security (economic, energy, environment, food, health)
- Social Stability

Emerging Dimensions
- Cyberspace
- Geopolitical shifts
- Climate Change
- Resource Scarcity
- Technological Advancement

Major Threat to India's National Security

Internal Threats

Insurgency and extremism

- **Left Wing Extremism (LWE):** The ongoing Maoist insurgency in Central India, particularly affecting states like Chattisgarh, Jharkhand, Odisha.
  Maoist violence resulted in over 10,000 fatalities between 2010-2020.
- **Separatist movements:** Militant groups advocating for independence in regions like Jammu and Kashmir and the North-east
  Kashmir insurgency has claimed over 40,000 lives since 1989.
- **Religious Extremism:** Rise of radical religious ideologies that could incite violence and social unrest
  NCRB (2021) shows a rise in communal crimes in India.
- **Ethno-nationalist conflicts:** Tensions between different ethnic groups within India.
  Manipur ethnic conflict since 2023 has claimed more than 220 lives and displayed 67,000 others.

Socio-economic Challenges

- **Poverty and inequality:** Large sections of the population living in poverty can create fertile ground for extremism and unrest.
  World Bank (2022), 12.92% of India's population still lives below national poverty line.
- **Unemployment:** High youth employment rates can lead to frustration and social instability.
  CMIE: Unemployment rate in India rose to 8.1% in April 2024.
- **Resource Scarcity:** Issues like water scarcity and food insecurity can exacerbate social tensions
  India is ranked 13th globally on water stress index (2023)
- **Cybercrime:** Growing dependence on technology increases vulnerability to online fraud, data theft and cyberattacks on critical infrastructure.
  Lok Sabha: Around 1.1 million financial fraud cases registered in 2023

Organised crime

- **Mafia activities:** Operation of criminal syndicates involved in smuggling, extortion and trafficking.
  eg- D-Company, a Mumbai-based organised crime syndicate
- **Drug Trafficking:** flow of illegal drugs through India, impacting public health and fueling criminal activity.
  India's Golden Drug Silk Route- Transit route for heroin and other drug from Afghanistan and South-east Asia.
- **Human Trafficking:** Exploitation of vulnerable individuals for forced labour, prostitution or organ trade.
  India recorded 10,659 cases of human trafficking between 2018-2022

External Threats

Border Tensions

- **Pakistan-** Long standing territorial disputes in Kashmir and history of cross border terrorism → ceasefire violations on Line of control.
- **China-** Rising assertiveness on border and competition for regional influence.
  eg- 2020 Doklam standoff.
- **Maritime security-** Threats to India's shipping lanes and coastal infrastructure.
  eg- piracy off the coast of Somalia.
- **Porous borders** and tough terrain are used for smuggling (arms, drugs, illegal migrants), destabilisizng nations internally.

External Threats

- **Instability in Afghanistan and Pakistan-** Potential spillover effects of regional conflicts on India's security.
  eg- Taliban's takeover of Afghanistan in 2021
- **Proxy warfare-** Involvement of external powers in supporting non-state actors against India's interests.
  eg- Pakistan's alleged support for militant groups.
- **Terrorist networks-** Global terrorist organisations using India as a target or base for operations.
  eg- 2008 Mumbai attacks

Emerging Threats

- **Cyber Warfare**- Potential for cyberattacks on critical infrastructure like power grids or communication systems.
  eg- major cyberattack on its power grid in 2021
- **Information Warfare**- Use of propaganda and disinformation campaigns to manipulate public opinion and destabilize the Indian government.
  eg- alleged mistreatment of Indian minority community
- **Climate Change**- Impact of climate change on India's water resources, food security and potential for mass displacement.
  India experienced 123 consecutive days of extreme weather events between June and September 2023.
- **External interference**- They try to halt developmental work in the guise of environmental protection.

Dimensions of National Security

01 **Internal Security**- Act of preserving and maintaining the unity and integrity of the state, maintaining law and order, and upholding the sovereignty of the country within its territory from disruptive and anti-national forces.

- **Focus**- Maintaining peace within a country's border
- **Threats**- Issues arising from within the nation itself, eg- Naxalite Movement in India.
- **Management**- Responsibilities lies with institutions like Ministry of Home Affairs which uses established mechanisms to address internal threats.

02 **External Security**- Act of protecting a country against any external threat from a foreign country such as terrorism, war, etc.

- **focus**- Protecting a country from threats originating outside borders
- **Threats**- Issues arising from neighbouring countries or geographically distant regions that can impact a nation's security.
  - Direct neighbourhood- Countries with shared borders that may pose a threat due to political tensions or conflicting interests.
    eg- India's concerns regarding Pakistan and China
  - Extended neighbourhood- Countries that may not share a direct border that may pose threat due to proximity to direct neighbours. eg- Developments in Central Asia impacting India's security
- **Management**- Domain of Armed forces under Ministry of Defence

Importance of Maintaining National Security

01 **Maintaining law and Order**- A secure environment fosters respect for the law, allowing legal systems to function effectively.
eg- Naxalite insurgency in some regions disrupts law enforcement and hinders development initiatives.

02 **Rule of Law**- Upholding the rule of law ensures justice, fairness and equal treatment for all citizens. Internal security measures prevent subversion of legal processes.
- Secure state → legal principles apply equally to all citizens, fostering trust and social cohesion.

eg- India's crime rate has shown a decline in recent years (NCRB 2021)

03 **Maintain Peace**- A peaceful environment promotes social harmony, facilitates dialogue and fosters national unity.
eg- Communal clashes in India disrupt daily life, create fear and impede economic activity.
- Community policing initiatives in Kerala promote trust, cooperation

04 **Securing Territorial Integrity, Unity and Sovereignty**- Protecting borders ensures national integrity and sovereignty, unity among diverse regions strengthens the nation.
eg- 2020 Doklam Standoff highlighted the importance of securing territorial integrity.

05 **Economic and Social Development**- A secure environment attract foreign investment, facilitates trade and allow business to operate uninterruptedly.
eg- political instability and violence are major impediments to economic growth

06 **Protecting Individual freedoms**- freedoms like speech and assembly can only be exercised freely in a secure environment without fear of repression or violence.
eg- Terrorist attacks and riots create atmosphere of fear leading to restrictions on movement and assembly.

Evolution of India's National Security Policy

- India's national security strategy has undergone a significant shift in recent years, transitioning from cautious and defensive approach to more proactive and assertive one.
- This evolution reflects India's growing confidence as regional power and its determination to address security challenges emanating from its neighbourhood and the wider world.

Phase I: During Cold War

→ India's security strategy emphasized non-alignment and peaceful conflict resolution, influenced by factors like:
- Legacy of colonialism and desire to avoid great power rivalries
- focus on nation-building and economic development

Post Cold War till 2014: Restraint and strategic Hesitation

→ **Focus on diplomacy**- India's security strategy relied heavily on diplomatic solutions and displayed reluctance to use military force

→ **Strategic uncertainity**- India may have lacked a clear understanding of regional and global security dynamics leading to an unwillingness to take decisive action.

→ **Shortcomings of Defensive Approach**
- Ineffective against cross-border terrorism- Pakistan's use of unconventional warfare tactics like terrorism exposed limitations of India's purely defensive strategy.
- Perceived weakness- India's restraint may have been misconstrued as weakness by adversaries, emboldening them to exploit perceived gaps in Indian security.
  eg- 2008 Mumbai Terror attacks, India opted for diplomatic channels instead of immediate counter attacks against Pakistan.

Since 2014: Doval Doctrine of National Security

→ **Shift towards assertiveness**- Recognising the shortcomings of previous strategy, India adopted a more assertive approach under Nation Security Advisor Ajit Doval.
- Offensive Defense- Taking preemptive actions to neutralise threats before they materialize.
  eg- surgical strikes (2016) against terrorist havens in Pakistan occupied Kashmir (PoK)
- Defensive offense- Countering adversaries through diplomatic isolation, sanctions and offensive deterrance.
  eg- Balakot Airstrikes (2019) in response to the Pulwama terror attack, India launched airstrikes on Jaish-e-Mohammed (JeM) training camp.

Indian Military Doctrine related to Pakistan

01 Sundarji Doctrine (1984-2004)

- **Deployment**- Seven defensive "holding corps" stationed near Pakistan border.
  Three offensive "strike corps" located in Central India.

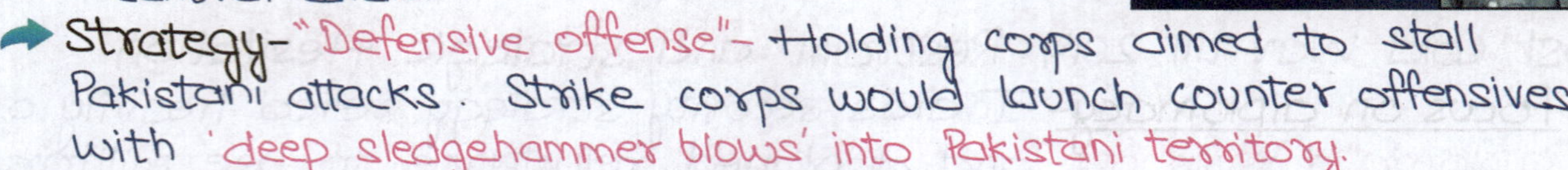

- **Strategy**- "Defensive offense"- Holding corps aimed to stall Pakistani attacks. Strike corps would launch counter offensives with 'deep sledgehammer blows' into Pakistani territory.
- **Limitations of Sundarji Doctrine**
  - Operation Parakram (2001)- Doctrine failed due to slow mobilisation (3 weeks) of strike corps from Central India.
  - International Pressure- By the time forces mobilized, international intervention prevented a full-scale response.

02 Cold Start Doctrine (CSD)

- **Aim**- Swift retaliation to inflict significant damage on Pakistan before international intervention
  focuses on calibrated action to avoid triggering nuclear response
- **Evolution**- Developed after shortcomings of Sundarji Doctrine
- **Strategy**- 'Offensive Defense'- a more proactive approach
- **Key elements**:
  - Enhanced offensive capabilities- Upgrading "holding corps" (now called Pivot corps) to conduct offensive operations with minimal mobilization.
  - Relocating Strike Corps- Moving them closer to border for faster deployment.
  - Integrated battlegrounds- forming specialized units for swift, limited offensives into Pakistan
  - Territorial Leverage- Captured territory to be used as bargaining chip to pressure Pakistan against supporting terrorism

NATIONAL SECURITY STRATEGY (NSS)

- **About**- NSS is a document outlining a country's security objectives and the methods to achieve them. It encompasses both traditional threats to the state and non-traditional threats that can impact individuals and even humanity as whole.
- **Key Components of NSS**
  - Threat Assessment- Evaluation of potential security threats faced by the country.

- Resource Allocation- Strategic allocation of resources to address identified threats.
- Diplomatic and Military Actions- Outline of diplomatic and military strategies to counter threats.
- Security related policies- Policies related to intelligence gathering, defense and other security domains

- Countries with National Security Strategy (NSS)- United States, United Kingdom, Russia, China (Comprehensive National Security Strategy), Pakistan (National Security Policy 2022-2026)
- India lacks a formally documented and publicly available National Security Strategy. Currently, it is guided by Raksha Mantri's Operational Directive of 2009.
- Recommendations for NSS
  - Multiple Committees- The Kargil Review Committee, Naresh Chandra Committee, Shekatkar Committee and government think tanks all advocate for formal NSS.
  - Government Initiative (2018)- By restructuring Defense Planning Committee led by NSA Ajit Doval to prepare a NSS in April 2018
  - Military Leaderships- Gen. Bipin Rawat's (then Chief of Defence Staff) stand during Doklam standoff.
- Steps taken towards NSS in India
  - Kargil Review Committee Report (2000)- following Kargil War, it offered recommendations on national security, though it did not directly translate into an NSS.
  - Naresh Chandra Task force on Security (2012)- It addressed national security aspects like defense and intelligence reforms, but no formal NSS was established.
  - Gen. D.S. Hooda's Report (2019)- It marked a significant step towards NSS for India.

Significance of National Security Strategy (NSS) in India

- Comprehensive Approach- Addresses various security challenges (eg- border disputes with China, cyber attacks)
- Clear Objectives- Defines critical infrastructure (eg- power grids) and potential threats (eg- terrorist attacks)
- Policy guidance- Informs counter terrorism strategies (eg- de-radicalization programs)
- Prioritisation- Guides resource allocation (eg- cybersecurity infrastructure)

- Resource allocation- Optimizes military spending (eg- modernizing equipment)
- Deterrence- Strengthens military presence to deter adversaries (eg-naval developments)
- Whole of Government Approach-Enhances collaboration between intelligence agencies (eg- RAW) and defense forces (eg-Indian Army)
- Public Awareness- Raises awareness about maritime security threats (eg- piracy)
- International Engagement- fosters partnerships for counter-terrorism cooperation (eg- Quadrilateral Security Dialogue)

Need of National Security Strategy (NSS) in India

01 Changing global dynamics

- End of cold war's Era of strategic uncertainity- The global landscape is increasingly complex with emerging threats and a growing number of potential adversaries.
- Countering Modern Threats- Terrorism + ethnic conflict + Proliferation of small arms + Drug Trafficking + Religious extremism.
- Shifting Power Dynamics- Balance of power is tilting towards the Indo-Pacific region, making it new strategic focal point.
  An emerging security framework envisions a balance between "competitive cooperation" and broader "cooperative security" within the region.
- Geopolitical Tensions- Rising geopolitical tensions (eg- Israel-Hamas conflict, Russia-Ukraine war) highlight the need for a strategy to address future uncertainities.

02 Armed forces Governance

- Traditional Threats Persist- Porous borders, terrorism, internal conflicts (naxalism), tense relations with neighbours like China and Pakistan necessitates a robust security strategy
- Military Reform and Modernisation- NSS can guide critical military reforms like theaterization and modernisation efforts, similar to those undertaken by US (Goldwater-Nicholas Act), UK and China (PLA Reforms)
- Clear Direction- Outdated 2009 Raksha Mantri directive needs replacing. NSS would provide clear political direction for the armed forces
- fixing Accountability- A defined strategy can enhance accountability of political class in managing national security and defense forces

- Defined Roles- The NSS would clarify the roles and responsibilities of national security institutions like National Security Council (NSC), National Security Advisor (NSA), Chief of Defense Staff (CDS) and Chiefs of Staff Committee.
- Enhanced Cooperation- An NSS can foster better cooperation between national security establishments at the central and state levels, improving inter-ministerial coordination in tackling threats.

03 New Challenges

- Technological Advancements- Armed forces face expanding missions beyond traditional warfare.
- Environmental Security Concerns- Ecological degradation, including glacier melting and rising of sea level, poses security risks.

Challenges in implementing India's National Security Strategy (NSS)

- Dynamic Threat Landscape- Ever-evolving nature of security threats, including cyber-attacks and crypto-terrorism, necessitates a constantly updated NSS. eg- Wanna Cry ransomeware attack
- Resource constraints- Efficient allocation of financial and human resources for effective NSS implementation is crucial (Pension bill vs Modernisation budget)
- Public perception- Lack of public awareness regarding the importance of a comprehensive NSS can hinder public support and government action.

National Security Strategy(NSS): Defines broad security goals and objectives
Eg-Protecting India's territorial integrity, countering terrorism

National Defence Policy(NDP): Translates that direction into actionable plans for the military.
Eg-Modernizing the armed forces,developing specific military capabilities

National Military Strategy(NMS): Operational level plans to achieve goals set out in the NSS and NDP
Eg-Deployment strategies for border security,response plans for specific purpose.

- Additional Challenges
  - Divergent Leadership Views- The Ministry of Defence and other agencies may hold differing options on the NSS format
  - Reactive Approach- Kargil War (1999) exposed vulnerabilities in border management, highlighting the need for a more proactive approach
  - Building a National Security Culture- fostering a national consciousness that prioritizes NSS and strategic thinking about security is an ongoing process.
- Government Apprehensions
  - Reduced flexibility in decision making- NSS might limit its ability to respond dynamically to new threats

- Declared NSS might strain relations with adversaries (China, Pakistan)- These countries already engage in "grey zone warfare" and territorial disputes.
- Compromise Strategic Autonomy- NSS might raise concerns about future commitments on military alliance
- Increased accountability-NSS might expose shortcomings in defense preparedness, territorial security and counter-terrorism efforts.

➜ Reaching consensus among diverse stakeholders with varying interests and ideologies (government, policymakers, security agencies) can be challenging.

Pathways to enhance India's National Security Strategy (NSS) framework (Hooda Committee (2019))

01 Assuming Our Rightful Place in Global Affairs

- Promote international cooperation- Champion equitable digital development and provide intellectual leadership
- Engage with major powers- Confidently assert India's national interests in dealings with US, Russia and China.
- focus on Middle East- Pursue shared interests in energy, trade and security.

02 Achieving a secure neighbourhood

- Strengthen regional ties- foster good relations with neighbours through soft power, improved connectivity and regional trade.
- Navigate the India-Pakistan dynamic- Implement a sustained strategy to pressure Pakistan against terrorism using diplomacy, economic isolation and potentially limited military actions. Address nuclear concerns through dialogue.
- Manage China's rise- Seek a peaceful relationship while safeguarding core interests like border security and counter-terrorism efforts.

03 Peaceful Resolution of Internal Conflicts

- Jammu and Kashmir- Counter radicalisation and eliminate terrorists while offering a clear political path to mainstream the region and replace fear with hope.
- North-east- Prioritize development and integration alongside efforts to resolve the Naga insurgency.
- Left Wing Extremism (LWE)- Address root causes like tribal deprivation while combating the insurgency.

04 **Protecting people from Global and Domestic Risks**- Develop strategies to address threats from climate change, cyber threats, demographics, urbanization and inequalities.

05 **Strengthening Capabilities**

- Border Security- Enhance land and maritime border protection capabilities
- Indigenous Defense- Support research and development for domestic defense technologies
- Cybersecurity- Established a dedicated cyber command.

INDIA'S NUCLEAR DOCTRINE

India's Nuclear Doctrine is a strategic framework that outlines how a nuclear armed state would employ its nuclear weapons during both peace and conflict

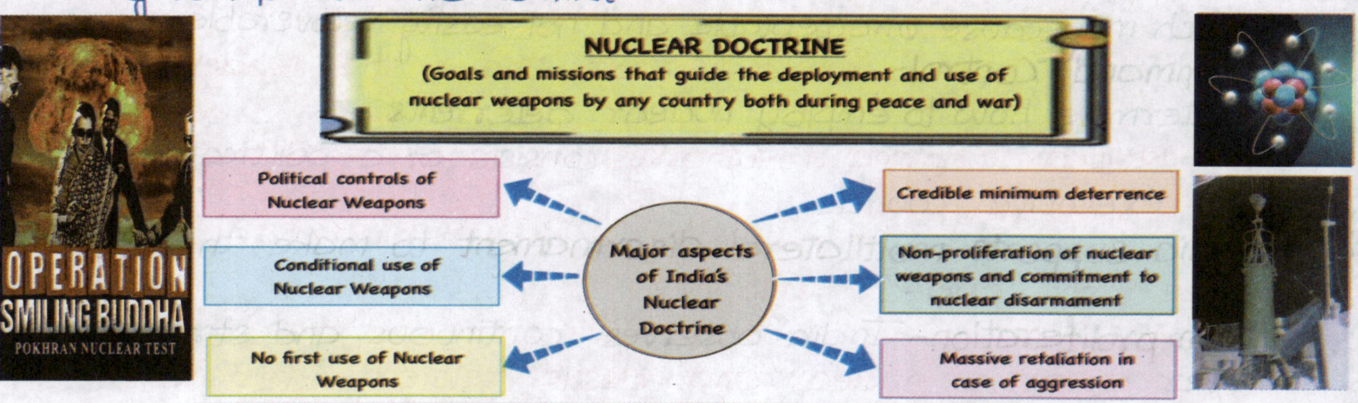

Evolution of India's Nuclear Doctrine

Pokhran Test (1974)

- India conducted its first nuclear test in 1974, downplaying it as a "peaceful nuclear explosion"
- No formal nuclear doctrine existed at this time

Pokhran Test II (1998-1999)

- India conducted second nuclear test in 1998, openly declaring itself a nuclear weapon state.
- In 1999, the National Security Advisory Board (NSAB) released a Draft Nuclear Doctrine
  - No first Use (NFU)- India pledged not to initiate the use of nuclear weapons in a conflict

- Retaliatory Policy- Nuclear weapons would only be used in response to a nuclear attack on India or its forces

Official Nuclear Doctrine (2003)

- Credible minimum deterrence- Maintaining a minimum level of nuclear force to deter potential adversaries.
- Reiterated NFU- The "No first Use" Policy was reaffirmed
- Non-nuclear weapon states- India declared it would not use nuclear weapons against states without nuclear weapons.
- Nuclear Deterrence of CBW (Chemical/ Biological Warfare)- Option to Indian decision makers to use nuclear weapons to retaliate against chemical or biological warfare.
- Massive retaliation- If any country attacks Indians with nuclear weapons retaliation will be very massive and terrible which may cause unacceptable and not easily recoverable damage.
- Command Control- Power lies with the political leadership to determine how to employ nuclear deterrents
  Nuclear Command Authority- consists of a political and executive council
- India supports multilateral disarmament to make the world free from nuclear weapons.
- Non-proliferation- India observes continuous and strict control over export of nuclear and missile related materials

Current Status

- Promoting nuclear disarmament- India's mission to United Nations actively advocates for reducing nuclear dangers.
  - Measures to minimize the risk of unintentional or accidental nuclear weapon use.
  - De-alerting and detargeting of nuclear weapons (reducing their readiness for immediate use.
  - It showcases a proactive role in promoting nuclear safety and reducing risk of nuclear war.
- Nuclear Non-Proliferation Treaty (NPT) (1970)-Not a member
  India views nuclear weapons as crucial for national security until global elimination is achieved
- Treaty on the Prohibition of Nuclear Weapons (TPNW) (2017)- India sees the TPNW as incomplete due to its lack of verification mechanisms.

- Conference on disarmament (CD)- India advocates for the CD as primary forum for multilateral disarmament negotiations.
- International Atomic Energy Agency (IAEA)- India maintains safeguard agreements with IAEA for specific facilities.
- Nuclear Suppliers Group (NSG)- India actively seeks NSG membership and has received support from several members however China remains opposed to India's membership
- Global Nuclear Security- India's proposal at UN showcase its proactive role in promoting nuclear safety and reducing risk of nuclear war

Significance of India's Nuclear Doctrine

Advantages of "No first Use"

- Credibility and clarity of India's intent to use nuclear weapons solely as deterrent, fostering regional stability.
- Non use against nuclear weapon states assure non-nuclear weapon states of their safety from an Indian nuclear attack + peaceful global environment
- Reinforces responsible images- The "No first use" policy and "Non-use against non-nuclear weapon states" project India as responsible nuclear power, enhancing its international standing.
  Despite having multiple wars with neighbouring states, India never opted for nuclear war
- Mitigates accidental war risk by eliminating the pressure for a hasty launch decision in a crisis, allowing for a more measured response.
- Reduced infrastructure costs- No first use policy avoids need for expensive, high-alert nuclear infrastructure.

INDIA'S NUCLEAR CAPABILITIES

- India's current **ballistic missiles** including the Prithvi, **the Agni-I and Agni-2, as well as the Agni-3** have the potential to deliver a nuclear warhead.
- India has a number of combat aircrafts which can be used as delivery vehicle, **including the Jaguar, the Mirage-2000 and the Su-30.**
- **The nuclear submarine INS Arihant** gives India the maritime strike capability.

These three launch mechanisms complete what is called the **Nuclear Triad.**

Supports Disarmament Goals- "Credible minimum deterrence" emphasizes maintaining a minimal nuclear arsenal, aligning with global disarmament efforts and reducing risk of an arms race.

Shifting blame of escalation- The onus of initiating escalation falls on the adversary, allowing India to defend itself without being seen as the aggressor

»» Enhanced international image- Adherence to the doctrine strengthens India's bid for a permanent UN Security Council seat and membership in Nuclear Suppliers Group(NSG)

Need to Review India's Nuclear Doctrine

01 **Arguments for Review**

- **Evolving Geopolitics-** Unlike US/Russia, India's doctrine lacks periodic review. China- Pakistan ties and Russian connections necessitate reevaluation.
- **Emerging Technologies-** Miniaturized nukes and hypersonic glide vehicles raise concern about potential tactical use.
- **Non-strategic nuclear weapons-** The concept of non-strategic nuclear weapons like artillery shells is gaining traction.
- India's nuclear doctrine does not explicitly mention a counter force strategy, focussing on enemy military assets.
- **India's 'Minimum Credible Deterrence'-** Whether India has enough nukes to deter China, considering China's fast military modernization and growing nuclear arsenal

02 **Debate on "No first Use"(NFU)-** High initial casualities for India in a first strike scenario. Costly missile defense system needed.

- May be ineffective against Pakistan's tactical nukes.
- In 2019, the Indian Defense Minister implied that India's "No first Use" policy would not be continued indefinitely.

03 **New Threats**

- Cyber security and nuclear terrorism- Doctrine lacks strategy to address these issues
- Chemical and Biological Weapons (CBW)- Option of nuclear retaliation for CBW attacks seen as aggressive and undermining NFU's credibility.

PYQs Corner
(Write the Answer and Get Free Evaluation)

1. Analyse the multidimensional challenges posed by external state and non-state actors, to the internal security of India. Also discuss measures required to take to be taken to combat the threat. [250 Words] [15 Marks] **[2021]**
2. How illegal transborder migration does pose a threat to India's security? Discuss the strategies to curb this, bring out the factors which give impetus to such migration. [200 Words] [12.5 Marks] **[2014]**

Border Management and Coastal Security

CHAPTER 02

Border is defined as nation's territory acting as barrier to restrict unwanted elements that could harm the country and its people.

India has 15,106.7 km of land border sharing with 7 countries (Bangladesh, China, Pakistan, Nepal, Myanmar, Bhutan, Afghanistan) and a coastline of 7516.6 km including island territories.

Border Management

- **About-** Border management is a comprehensive set of actions taken by a country to control and regulate the movement of people, goods and sometimes even animals across its international borders.
  It requires close collaboration between various government agencies.

- **Objective-** To secure borders and safeguards nation from potential threats associated with movement of goods and people across its international boundaries
- **Security-** Preventing cross border terrorism, illegal migration, trafficking of drugs and narcotics and smuggling.

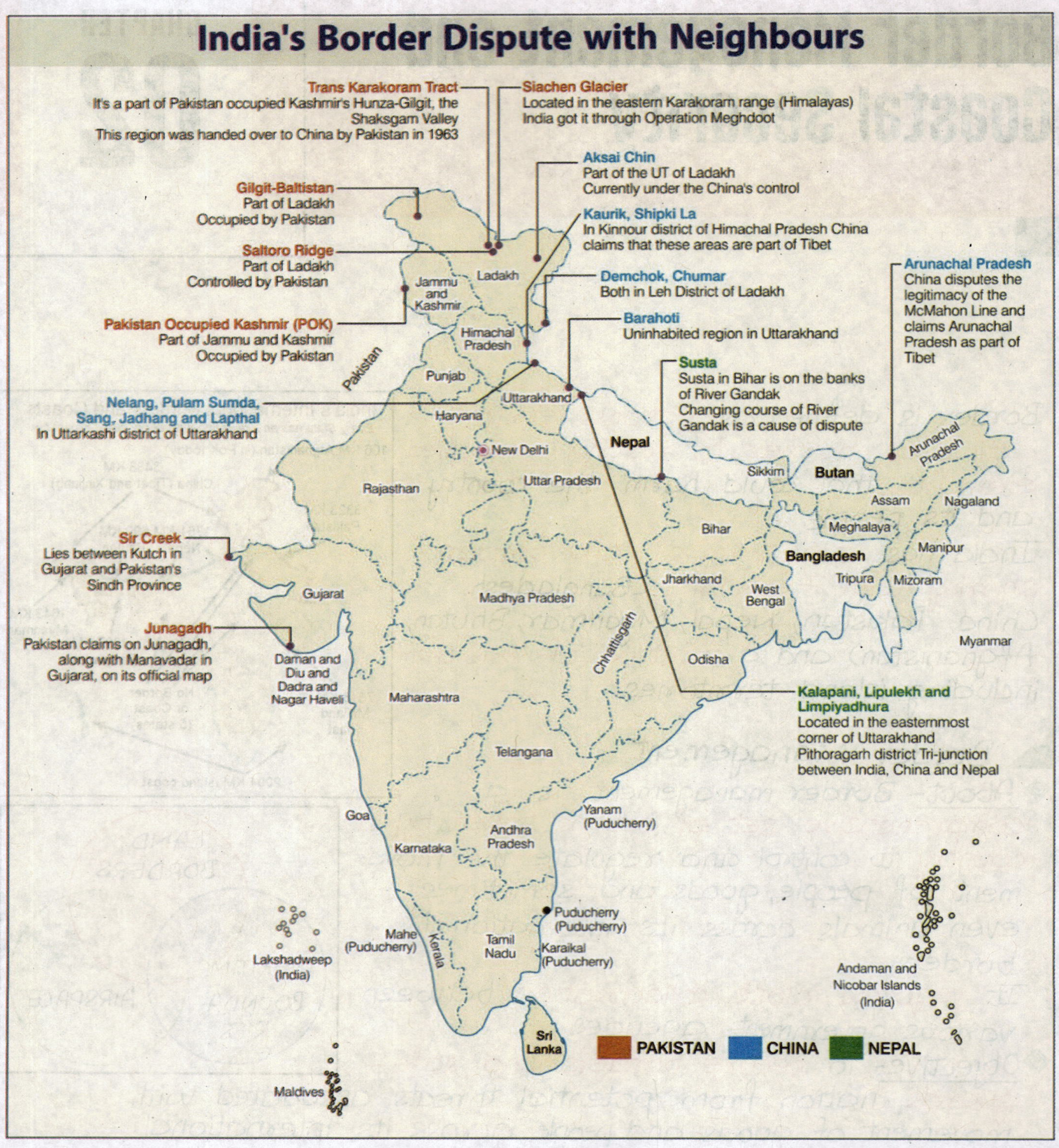

Apart from above border disputes, there are few other issues of India with neighbouring countries. These are

INDIA-CHINA
1. Large scale smuggling of Chinese electronic and other consumer goods
2. Inadequate infrastructure due to difficult terrain
3. Multiple forces(for eg- ITBP, Assam Rifles, Special Frontier Force) creating coordination issues
4. Water sharing issues

INDIA-NEPAL
1. Increasing extremism and anti-India activities
2. Fear of spread of Maoist insurgency due to links of Nepal's Maoists in India
3. Easy escape and illegal activities like smuggling, fake Indian currency,etc.
4. Land grabbing on each side of the border
5. Chinese investment in core sector of Nepal

INDIA- PAKISTAN
1. River water sharing issue of Indus river
2. Infiltration and cross border terrorism
3. Diverse terrain including desert, marshes, snowcapped mountains and plains
4. Time and cost overruns in infrastructure projects
5. Other issues include drug smuggling,arms trafficking,etc.

INDIA-BHUTAN
1. Insurgency
2. Smuggling of goods such as Bhutanese cannabis
3. Free movement of people and vehicle

INDIA-SRI LANKA
1. Fishing rights in Palk Strait and Gulf of Mannar
2. Border security and smuggling of goods(Narcotics and illegal immigrants)
3. Tamil ethnic issue
4. Increasing Chinese influence (Hambantota port leased to China)
5. Katchatheevu islands dispute concerns ownership and usage rights

INDIA-MYANMAR
1. Free movement regime
2. Drug trafficking due to proximity to golden traiangle
3. No physical barrier along the border
4. Poor infrastructural facilities

INDIA-BANGLADESH
1. Water disputes with regard to Teesta river, Barak river
2. Illegal migration
3. Inadequate border fencing
4. Smuggling of goods like jamdani sarees

INDIA-MALDIVES
1. China Influence: Current Political leadership tilt towards China
2. Ongoing Lakshadweep Issue, affecting Maldives Tourism
3. India Out Campaign in Maldives
4. Sovereignty and Security Dilemma: Indian military presence

BORDER ISSUES WITH NEIGHBOURING STATES

India's Security Apparatus

→ Cabinet Committee on Security (CCS) - Chaired by Prime Minister, it provides overall direction and guidance for India's security apparatus, including border security.

→ Ministry of Home Affairs (MHA) - Serves as central ministry responsible for most operational aspects of both border security and internal security It oversees various paramilitary forces deployed along India's borders

→ Department of Border Management (MHA) plays a central role in this effort

- Management of land and coastal borders
- Strengthening border security - Patrolling, infrastructure and enhanced border policing.
- Border infrastructure development like roads, fencing and flood lighting along the borders.

↳ Border Area Development Program (BADP) - to address specific needs and challenges faced by communities residing near border

→ Deployment of forces is based on principle of "One Border, One Force - Guarding force" (BGF). It ensures a dedicated force for each specific border area.

Indo-Pakistan Border	Border Security force (BSF)
Indo-Bangladesh Border	Border Security force (BSF)
Indo-China border and Indo-Tibetan Border	Indo-Tibetan Border force (ITBP)
Indo-Nepal Border	Sashatra Seema Bal (SSB)
Indo-Bhutan Border	Sashatra Seema Bal (SSB)
Indo-Myanmar Border	Assam Rifles (AR)
Coastal Security	Indian Coast Guard (ICG)

→ Cabinet Secretariat - Coordination between different ministries and agencies involved in border security → Seamless information flow and facilitates joint operations.

→ Prime Minister's Office (PMO) - Provides direct oversight and guidance to MHA and other security agencies on critical border security issues

Challenges in Securing India's Borders

01 Border Vulnerabilities

- Accessibility - Hostile elements exploit advancements in technology (drones), financial resources and organizational capabilities to launch surprise attacks in unexpected locations (eg- Pathankot, 2016)
- Porous borders - India's land borders with Pakistan (3323 km) and Bangladesh (4097 km) traverse diverse terrains (deserts, mountains, rivers) making them difficult to patrol and control.
- Undefined Boundaries - Uncertain maritime and land demarcations in some areas, like Line of Actual Control (LAC) between India and China, leads to confusion and potential conflicts.
- Contested Borders - A long history of mistrust with Pakistan along the Line of Control (LoC) fuels cross-border terrorism threats (over 200 infiltration attempts thrawted in 2023)
- Lack of infrastructure - Inadequate infrastructure like observation towers, bunkers and border lighting hinders border security and restricts deployment of advanced technology like thermal imaging cameras (CAG, 2019 highlighted deficiencies in border fencinc)

02 Resource Contraints

- Limited intelligence gathering capabilities make it difficult for security forces to ancipate and counter threats effectively (eg- Pulwama Attack, 2019)
- Resource deficiencies- Shortage of personnel and equipment weakens the ability of security forces to manage the borders efficiently (eg- gaps in manpower along the India- China border due to harsh weather conditions)

03 Socio- Political Issues

- Ethnic Tensions- Demographic shifts and ethnic conflicts in border states like Assam due to illegal migration can exacerbate social tensions and create security risks
- Overpopulation- High population density in some border areas, like West Bengal (1102/km²) compared to the national average (382/km²) strains resources and creates logistical challenges for border management
- Regional Instability- Political instability and conflicts in neighbouring countries like Afghanistan can have direct or indirect impact on India's security (spillover of extremism)

04 Systemic Issues

- Unclear borders- Undefined maritime borders and undemarcated land borders like parts of China- India border, create tension and complicate border policing efforts.
- Neglected Borders- Past neglect of border areas and a focus on national development over border management has left these regions vulnerable (limited road connectivity hinders troops movement)
- Artificial Borders- Many man-made borders, lacking natural demarcations like rivers (eg- Indo- Bangladesh border) and inherently more porous and difficult to control.
- Multiple forces, Divided Command- The deployment of multiple security forces (eg- BSF, ITBP, SSB) on the same borders can lead to issue of accountability and hamper effective command and control.
- Under equipped forces- Often lack adequate manpower and equipment to perform their duties optimally (eg- outdated night vision devices)
- Intelligence sharing gaps- Insufficient institutionalized arrangements for sharing and coordinating intelligence, particularly at field level, weakens overall border security. eg- lack of real time information sharing

- **Internal Deployment Strain**- frequent redevelopment of paramilitary forces from border duties (BSF deployed for anti-Naxalite operations) to address internal security concerns neglect border areas

05 **Migration and Transnational Crime**

- **Uncontrolled Migration**- Unchecked illegal migration poses a threat to national security, social harmony and economic well-being (eg- Rohingya refugees)
- **Demographic Shifts**- Large scale illegal migration has led to demographic changes in border regions with potential social, economic and political consequences (Assam NRC controversy)
- **Smuggling and Trafficking**- The porous nature of some borders facilitates smuggling of goods (fake currency) and narcotics (drugs trafficking route along Golden Triangle), posing a security risk.

INDIA-PAKISTAN BORDER

India shares a 3323 km long boundary with Pakistan which is majorly divided into three different parts.

01 **Radcliff Line (2308 km)**-Extendind from Gujarat to parts of Jammu district in Jammu and Kashmir

02 **Line of Control (LOC)**-Running along the district of Jammu and some portions of Leh

03 **Actual Ground Position line (AGPL)**- It divides current positions of Indian and Pakistani military troops across the entire 110 km long front line in disputed region of Siachen glacier. AGPL runs along the Saltoro mountains range.

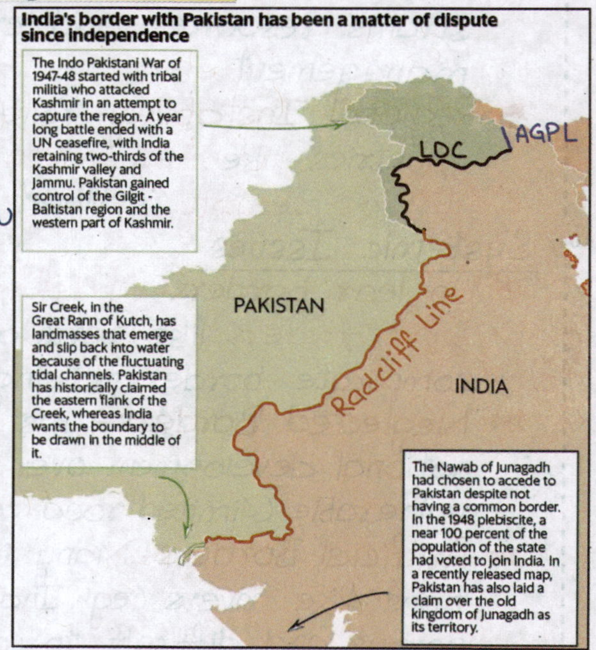

INDIA-PAKISTAN WARS

War of 1947(First Kashmir War)
Outcome- Jammu and Kashmir acceded to India, and the Line of Control (LOC) was established

War of 1965
Outcome: Ceasefire after 17 days; India had an upper hand due to Pakistan's insurgency.

War of 1971(Bangladesh liberation War)
Outcome: Bangladesh gained independence, leading to the establishment of present-day Bangladesh.

Kargil War(1999)
Outcome: India reclaimed territories; fragile ceasefire since 2003

Disputed regions between India- Pakistan

01 **Pakistan occupied Kashmir and Gilgit-Baltistan**

- Pakistan is in illegal and forcible occupation of approximately 78,000 sq. km of Indian territory
- Sino-Pakistan Border agreement (1963): Pakistan illegally ceded 5,180 sq. km of Pakistan occupied Kashmir to China.

02 Siachen Glacier

- Located in eastern Karakoram range in Himalayan Mountains, where Line of Control between India and Pakistan ends.
- India launched Operation Meghdoot (1984) to capture the 76.4 km long glacier on Saltoro ridge.
- Reason of Dispute- Ambiguous wording that exists in Karachi cease-fire Agreement (1949) following the 1947-48 war.
- Significance of Siachen- Strategic location with Pakistan on left and China on right.

  The entire Siachen Glacier with all major passes is currently under administration of India since 1984 (Operation Meghdoot)

03 Saltoro ridge

- Saltoro mountains is subrange of Karakoram heights or Saltoro ridge
- Located on southwest side of Siachen glacier
- Claimed as part of Jammu and Kashmir by India and as part of Gilgit-Baltistan by Pakistan
- 1984- India assumed military control of main peaks and passes of range with Pakistani forces into glacial valley just to the west.

04 Sir Creek Dispute

- Sir Creek is 96 km tidal estuary opening into Arabian Sea and dividing Gujarat (India) from Sindh province (Pakistan)
- **India's Position**– Boundary is defined by "mid channel" of the Creek as shown on map dated 1925
- **Pakistan's position**- Pakistan claims entire Sir Creek with eastern bank defined by a "green line" and represented on 1914 map. It also claims Junagarh (a part of coastal Gujarat)

05 River Disputes

- Indus Water Treaty (IWT)- It is a water distribution treaty between India and Pakistan, brokered by World Bank to use water available in the Indus river and its tributaries.
- Distribution - It gives control of three eastern rivers - Beas, Ravi and Sutlej to India and control of three western rivers- Indus, Chenab and Jhelum to Pakistan.
- India in 2023 notified Pakistan of its intent to modify IWT

  Reason- Pakistan's intransigence over objections to two Indian hydropower projects in Jammu and Kashmir:

  i) 330 MW Kishanganga hydroelectric project (Jhelum)

  ii) 850 MW Ratle hydroelectric project (Chenab)

Security Apparatus along India-Pakistan Border

Indian Army	• Role- Responsible for overall defense including border security • Deployment- Troops stationed along Line of Control and international borders.
Border Security force (BSF)	• Role- To guard Indo-Pakistan and Indo-Bangladesh border • functions- Ensure security during war and peace times • Responsibilities- Prevent illegal crossings, maintains peace and responds to threat.
Central Reserve Police force (CRPF)	• Role- Assist in maintaining law and order in conflict prone area • Deployment- Support BSF and local police in border regions.
State Police forces	• Role- Collaborate with central forces for border management • functions- Maintain law and order, assist in intelligence gathering.
Intelligence Agencies	• Role- Gather and analyze information related to border security • Coordination- Collaborate with other forces to prevent infiltration and terrorist activities.

Measures taken by Indian Government to safeguard its border

01 Physical infrastructure

- fencing- India has constructed fences along vulnerable stretches of India-Pakistan border to prevent illegal crossings.
- floodlighting- Illumination enhances surveillance and deters infiltration
- Roads- Well maintained roads enable rapid response and patrolling
- Border Out Posts (BOPs)- These manned posts monitor the border and respond to any threats.

02 Surveillance Systems- Deploying cameras, sensors, drones and radars for real time monitoring.

03 Diplomacy and confidence building measures-

- Agreements- Simla Agreement (1972) and Lahore Declaration (1999) signify diplomatic efforts to manage disputes
- Bilateral talks- Regular dialogues to address border issues
- Track two diplomacy- Engaging non-governmental organisations to foster understanding
- People to people exchanges- Cultural interactions to promote goodwill
- SAARC- Strengthening regional cooperation to address common challenges
- Trade and connectivity- Enhancing economic ties to reduce tensions

INDIA- CHINA BORDER

- India and China share 3500 km long boundary. The line which delianates the boundary between two countries is called McMahon Line.
- Line of Actual control (LAC) serves as boundary separating Indian controlled territory from Chinese-controlled territory. However, it is not clearly demarcated throughout and there is no mutually agreed LAC along certain stretches.
- States sharing boundary with China- Himanchal Pradesh, Uttarakhand, Sikkim, Arunachal Pradesh and union territory of Ladakh.
- Chategorisation of India-China border- 3 sectors - western, middle, eastern

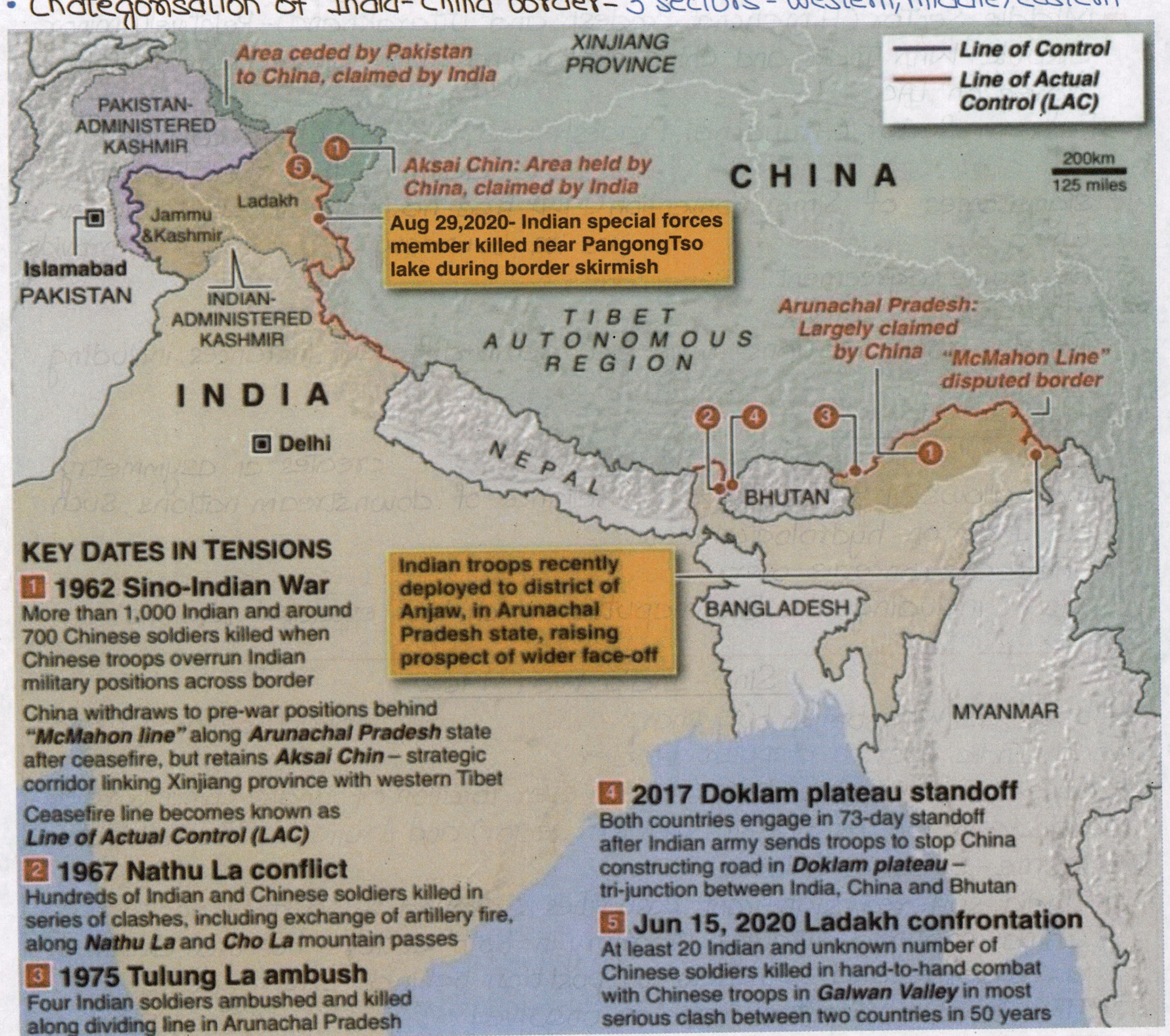

Disputes between India and China

01 Border Disputes

- Western Sector(Ladakh)- Johnson line proposed by British placed Aksai Chin in princely state of Jammu and Kashmir.
  - China rejected Johnson line and favoured McDonald line, asserting control over Aksai Chin
  - After the 1962 war, it is administered by China
  - While India claims entire Aksai Chin as well as Sakshgam valley (Indian territory gifted to China by Pakistan), China contests Indian control over Daulat Beg Oldi
- Middle Sector (Himanchal Pradesh and Uttarakhand)- Relatively minor dispute. With India and China exchanging maps where they broadly agree on LAC.
- Eastern Sector (Arunachal Pradesh and Sikkim)- China considers the McMahon line illegal and unacceptable claiming that the Tibetan signatories of Simla Convention (1914) had no right to do so. However, China accepts McMahon line as its boundary with Myanmar provided by same agreement.

02 Border incursions

Border confrontations have occured in different instances, including Demchok in 2014, Depsang in 2015, Doklam in 2017, Galwan in 2020

03 Water Sharing

- China's advantageous geographical positioning creates an asymmetry that allows it to capitalize on reliance of downstream nations, such as India on hydrological data
- There are concerns over China's dam building activities on transboundary rivers, including the Brahmaputra which had escalated tensions

Sino-India War 1962

- About- It was brief but sharp military conflict fought between China and India over a disputed border
- Cause- Long standing disagreement over location of India-China border particularly in Aksai Chin (western sector) and Arunachal Pradesh (eastern)
- Outcome- Decisive Chinese victory
  - India suffered significant casualities (around 3,100 to 4,000)
  - China captured strategic territory in both sectors but then declared a ceasefire and withdrew to position behind LAC
  - The border disputes remains unsolved

Security Apparatus along India - China Border

- **Indian Army** - Specialized units deployed in different sectors based on terrain and strategic needs.
  - Eastern Sector - Eastern Command leads here. High altitude specialists like the Tibetan frontier force and Mountain divisions are deployed for patrolling and border posts.
  - Central Sector - Central Command is responsible. Infantry divisions and mountain brigades with cold weather training handle border security
  - Western Sector - Mountain Strike Corps with rapid deployment capabilities and Infantry Divisions ensure border protection.
- **Paramilitary forces** - Vital role in supporting Army and managing border areas.
  - Indo-Tibetan Border Police (ITBP) - Specifically trained for border patrolling, guarding remote areas and assisting army during conflict

Initiatives for Border Management between India-Pakistan

1993 Agreement on Maintenance of Peace and Tranquility in border areas (includes establishing Working Mechanism for consultation and coordination on Border Affairs)

1996 Agreement on Confidence Building Measures in the military field along the LAC (measures to prevent military buildup and avoid misunderstandings

2003 Special Representatives Dialogue Mechanism established (aimed at resolving the boundary dispute)

2005 Agreement on Political Parameters and guiding principles for the settlement of India-China Boundary Question (sets framework for negotiations)

2012 Border Defense Cooperation Agreement (includes establishing hotline communication)

2013 Agreement on Cooperation in Border Management (includes patrolling cooperation and information sharing

2018 Wuhan informal Summit - Leaders agreed on strategic guidance for military to build trust and manage border affairs.

Wuhan spirit is in line with 5 principles of peaceful co-existence (Panchsheel) jointly advocated by China and India in the 1950s.

2019 India-China second informal summit - Mamallapuram Summit

Measures taken by Indian Government to safeguard its border

01 **High Altitude Border Infrastructure** - Roads, bridges and tunnels in the Himalayan region to improve connectivity and troop mobility

- Darbuk-Shyok-Daulat Beg Oldie (DSDBO) Road is strategic lifeline connecting Leh to Daulat Beg Oldie (DBO) airstrip near LAC
- Atal Tunnel (Himanchal Pradesh) facilitates year round access to Ladakh reducing dependence on vulnerable mountain passes

02 **Forward Airfields and Infrastructure** - India has upgraded several airfields near LAC, including Leh, Thoise and Nyoma.

- Significance - Rapid deployment of fighter jets, transport aircrafts, etc.
- The Advanced Landing Grounds (ALGs) in Arunachal Pradesh enhance air support in eastern sector.

03 **Integrated Surveillance System** - India is deploying advanced surveillance technologies along the border.

- Radar Stations - Enhance early warning capabilities
- Unmanned Aerial Vehicles (UAVs) - Monitor movement and provide real time intelligence
- Satellite Imagery - Tracks border activities
- Spy-cam Project - Putting up cameras with 20-25 km range at 50 locations in Himanchal Pradesh, Jammu and Kashmir, Sikkim and Tawang in Arunachal Pradesh.

04 **Strategic Partnerships** to counter China's assertiveness eg- QUAD (India, USA, Japan, Australia)

05 **Diplomatic Channels** - India engages in dialogues with China through mechanisms like Working Mechanism for Consultation and coordination on India-China Border Affairs (WMCC), SCO, BRICS, etc.

INDIA- BANGLADESH BORDER

- India shares longest border measuring 4096.7km with Bangladesh which touches five Indian states.
- The entire border consists of varied geographical features like plains, hills, riverine stretches, etc. with hardly any natural obstacles.

Challenges

- Illegal Migration from Bangladesh to India- It encompasses both refugees and economic migrants, impacting resources and security. eg- Rohingya refugees entering India through Bangladesh
- Terrorism and insurgency- Difficult terrain and porous borders have provided congenial environment for insurgency in North-eastern states. eg- Mizoram and Assam have seen a four fold rise in intruder apprehension- from 41 in 2018 to 721 in 2022 (data given by BSF)
- Trans border smuggling- Many incidences of cross border drug smuggling and traficking. Humans (especially women and children) are trafficked and various animals and birds are poached.

Initiatives for Border Management between India-Bangladesh

- Coordinated Border Management Plan (CBMP), 2011

  Aim- Reduced cross border crimes by curbing illegal activities like smuggling of goods (drugs, cattle), human trafficking and infiltration Smoother border crossings to facilitate legitimate trade and travel through efficient procedures.

- Land Boundary Agreement (2015)- Implements unresolved issues stemming from the undemarcated land boundary approximately 6.1km long in three sectors.

  India and Bangladesh swapped disputed islands and allowed inhabitants to choose their country of residence.

- Defense Cooperation- India and Bangladesh conduct joint exercises like Sampriti (Army) and exercise Bongo Sagar (navy).

STEPS TAKEN BY INDIA FOR STRENGTHENING BORDER MANAGEMENT

BOLD-QIT (Border Electronically Dominated QRT Interception Technique): By BSF to equip Indo-Bangladesh borders with different kind of sensors in unfenced riverine area of Brahmaputra.

Border Area Development Programme (BADP): Implemented through state governments and focuses on areas within 0-10 kilometers of the border in 16 states and 2 UTs.

Border Infrastructure and Management (BIM) Scheme: To strengthen border infrastructure to improve border management, policing, and guarding.

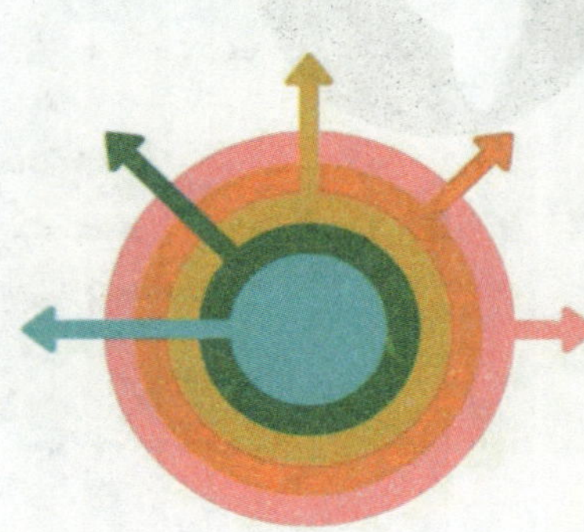

Border Protection Grid(BPG): The grid will comprise of various elements namely physical barriers, non-physical barriers, surveillance system, Intelligence agencies,etc for foolproof mechanism to secure our border

Enhanced budgetary allocation for BRO: Increases funding for the Border Roads Organisation (BRO), which is responsible for infrastructure development in border areas.

Pathways for Effective Border Management

01 Enhance Border Guarding

- Strengthen Physical infrastructure
  - Focus on fencing- Complete fencing projects along porous borders. eg- 90% of India- Bangladesh border remains unfenced (2017), making infiltration easy
- Improve Border Outposts (BOPs)
  - Modernize recruitment- Implement a system for attracting qualified personnel with competitive pay and benefits.
  - Specialized training- Provide regular training in counter- insurgency tactics, advanced weaponary and use of technology. eg- High altitude training for ITBP.

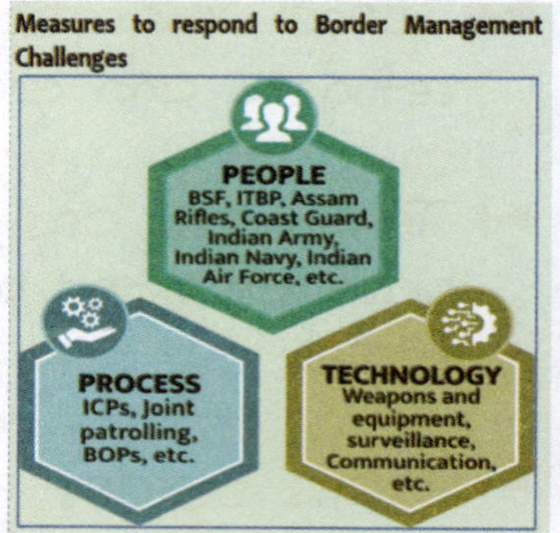

02 Streamline Border Management Administration

- Centralized Border Management Agency- Consider establishing a dedicated Ministry or agency solely focused on border management for better coordination and resource allocation.
- Inter agency collaboration with representation from all relevant agencies (BSF, ITBP, Army, Intelligence Bureau) for better coordination.

03 Strengthen International Cooperation

- Joint Border Patrols- Establish joint patrols with neighbouring countries to deter cross border crimes.
  eg- India- Bhutan joint patrolling initiatives

- Border Management Agreements- Negotiate and implement agreements on border management protocols and dispute resolution mechanisms. eg- Land Boundary Agreement with Bangladesh, 2015
- Fast Track Border Dispute Resolution- Pursue diplomatic channels and explore arbitration mechanisms to resolve out-standing border disputes with neighbouring countries.
- Facilitate Communication Channels- Create dedicated hotlines and communication channels for border communities to report suspicious activities anonymously

04 Focus on Border Area Development (BADP)

- Improve infrastructure- Invest in roads, bridges, healthcare facilities and educational institutions in border areas. eg- 73 strategic roads along Indo-China border.
- Promote Livelihood opportunities for border communities, reducing dependence on illegal activities. eg- BADP initiatives- Decrease in opium cultivation in border areas of Himanchal Pradesh.
- Bridge the Gap with mainland- Improve connectivity between border areas and major cities to integrate them better into national economy.

Intiatives taken by India

China

1. **Creating infrastructure** to cut down time for troop movement
2. Army infrastructure projects within 100km of LAC have been exempted from forest clearance
3. **Empowering Border Roads Organisation** to develop border road on priority
4. **Vibrant Village Programme** for border village development

Pakistan

1. Implementation of **Comprehensive Integrated Border Management System(CIBMS)** to establish an integrated security system
2. Deploying **National Security Guard(NSG) commandos in J&K**
3. Demand of amendment of **Indus Water Treaty (1960)**

Bangladesh

1. India-Bangladesh **Land Boundary Agreement,2015**
2. Establishment of **Border Protection Grid(BPG)**
3. Installation of **Border surveillance devices** such as drones
4. Raising awareness among the locals regarding crime prevention
5. **Joint River Commission** for solving river water dispute
6. **Comprehensive Integrated Border Management System (CIBMS)** for border

05 Cyber Security Measures

- Robust IT infrastructure- Invest in secure communication networks and data storage facilities for border management agencies. Implement robust cyber security measures to prevent hacking attempts and data breaches.

06 Leverage Technology for Surveillance- Madhukar Gupta Committee on border protection led to implementation of CIBMS in 2015.

- Integrated Border Management System (IBMS)- Implement nationwide IBMS for real-time data sharing and coordinated response between agencies (India- Bangladesh Border)
- Drone and Sensor Network- Deploy a network of drones for aerial surveillance and install advanced sensors for intrution detection. eg- India uses thermal imaging cameras at Indo-Pak border.
- Biometric Identification- Utilise fingerprint and iris scanners at entry points for faster and more secure identification at open borders.

07 Address Environmental Concerns

- Sustainable Border Infrastructure- Develop and implement eco-friendly border infrastructure projects to minimise environmental damage. eg-use of solar power and rainwater harvesting systems in BOPs.
- Border Area Conservation- Introduce programs to protect biodiversity and prevent illegal wildlife trafficking across borders
- Community Based Environmental Management- Involve border communities in conservation efforts to encourage sustainable practices.

08 Community Engagement and Outreach

- Building Trust- Organise regular interactions between security personnel and border communities to foster trust and understanding.
- Countering Radicalization- Implement programs to educate border youth about the dangers of extremism. Partner with local NGOs and community leaders to promote social harmony.

MARITIME SECURITY

Maritime Security involves protecting the nation's sovereignty from threats arising from oceans and seas. It includes protecting coastal seas, safeguarding available ocean resources such as fishes, offshore oil and gas wells, port facilities, etc.

ELEMENTS OF MARITIME SECURITY

- International and National peace and security
- Protection of sea lanes of communication
- Safeguarding sovereignty, territorial integrity & political independence
- Protection from crime at sea
- Access and security to the resources at sea
- Security of seafarers and fisherman
- Environmental Protection

Maritime Security in India

- India with its vast coastline of 7515 km and large Exclusive Economic Zone (EEZ) occupies a geostrategic location that necessitates robust coastal security measures.
- Coastal states of India- Gujarat, Maharashtra, Goa, Karnataka, Kerala, Tamil Nadu, Andhra Pradesh, Orissa, West Bengal and UTs of Andaman and Nicobar and Lakshadweep

- The 26/11 Mumbai attacks highlighted the vulnerability of India's shallow coastal areas, prompting a renewed focus on patrolling and surveillance

India's Maritime Boundary

Significance of Maritime Security in India

1. International Trade- Securing sea lanes of communication is essential for India's economic growth as majority of imports and exports are conducted via maritime routes.
   - 90% of India's trade by volume and 70% by value takes places through maritime transport (Ministry of shipping)
2. Coastal Security- India's 7,000 km coastline increases its vulnerability to maritime threats, as evidenced in 2008 Mumbai attacks
3. Chinese Assertiveness- China's growing influence in Indian Ocean region poses potential threats to India's regional interests (String of Pearl)
4. Harnessing the Blue Economy- The marine sector holds immense future potentials, but its development relies on secure maritime environment.
   - Economic activities dependent on marine resources constitute 4.1% of India's economy.
5. Protecting India's Coastal Infrastructure
   - Defense- Naval bases- Vishakhapatnam, Mumbai, Kochi, Port Blair
   - Power- Nuclear Power Plants (Tarapur, Kudankulam, Kalpakkam)
   - Space- Satellite launch and missile testing facilities (Satish Dhawan Space Centre, Wheeler islands)
   - Trade- 12 major ports (Kandla, JNPT, Mangalore, Haldia, etc.) handling 90% of maritime trade.
6. Technological Developments- The rapidly evolving nature of maritime threats necessitates a heightened focus on securing the marine environment.
   - eg- An Israeli ship was recently attacked by a drone in the North Arabian Sea, resulting in the death of two crew members.

Challenges faced by India in Ensuring Maritime Security

WEAK RULE OF LAW & POOR COASTAL WELFARE
Coastal poverty and political & economic disenfranchisement
Corruption, political exclusion, & statelessness
enables
RANGE OF ILLICIT MARITIME ACTIVITIES
VICIOUS CYCLE OF MARITIME INSECURITY
Trafficking of wildlife, drugs, & weapons
Piracy & armed robbery & kidnapping for ransom
IUU fishing & overfishing
Irregular migration & human trafficking
further weakens

01 Geopolitical Concerns- Perceived rivalry and zero sum game between USA and China could divert resources away from addressing broader security issues for smaller nations.

02 Emerging Threats

- **Asymmetrical Tactics-** Unconventional methods employed by state and non-state actors, like China's use of maritime militias, challenge traditional responses.
- **Grey Zone Warfare-** Actions blurring line between war and peace, such as violating Exclusive Economic Zones (EEZs), exploit legal ambiguities and make response difficult
- **New Technologies**
  - Combat drones- Used for reconnaissance, surveillance and attacks adding new dimension to maritime operations
  - Land Attack Missiles- launched from ship, they can target coastal facilities

03 Unconventional Security Threats

- **Illegal Fishing-** Depletion of marine resources and disruption of coastal communities' livelihoods by unauthorized fishing activities.
  eg- Sri Lankan fishermen in Indian waters
- **Illegal Migration-** UN estimates that over 73,000 Rohingya refugees fled from Myanmar to Bangladesh due to persecution, many using unsafe sea routes in Bay of Bengal.
- **Human Trafficking-** 2016 report by Justice & Care estimated that over 5,00,000 Bangladeshi women and children were trafficked to India in last decade using sea routes
- **Maritime Terrorism-** Presence of terror groups in some Bay littorals and use of maritime routes for financing terrorism.
- **Coastal Armed Robberies-** International Maritime Bureau (IMB) in 2019 reported 161 incidents of piracy and armed robbery at sea in Asia with a few concentrated in Bay of Bengal, particularly near Sunderbans mangroves

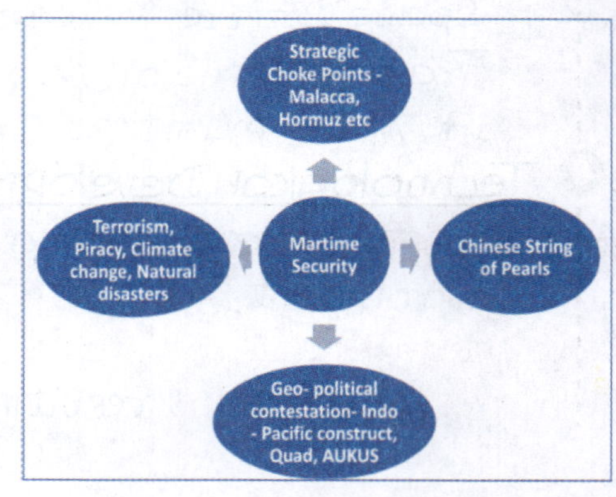

- **Climate Change Impact-** Rising sea levels, extreme weather events and other climate related issues disproportionately affect developing nations, making them more vulnerable.
- **Natural Disasters-** Increasing frequency and intensity of cyclones, tsunamis and other natural disasters challenge emergency response and maritime security.

Institutional Setup for Maritime Security in India

- **National Maritime Security Coordinator (NMSC)-** functions under National Security Advisor and is apex body for management of maritime affairs
- **Indian Navy (IN)-** Overall responsibility for maritime security including coastal and offshore security. It patrols International Maritime Boundary Line (IMBL)
- **Indian Coast Guard (ICG)-** Responsible for coastal security in territorial waters.
  - Patrols and surveillance upto 200 nautical miles (Exclusive Economic Zone- EEZ).
  - Overall coordination between state and central agencies 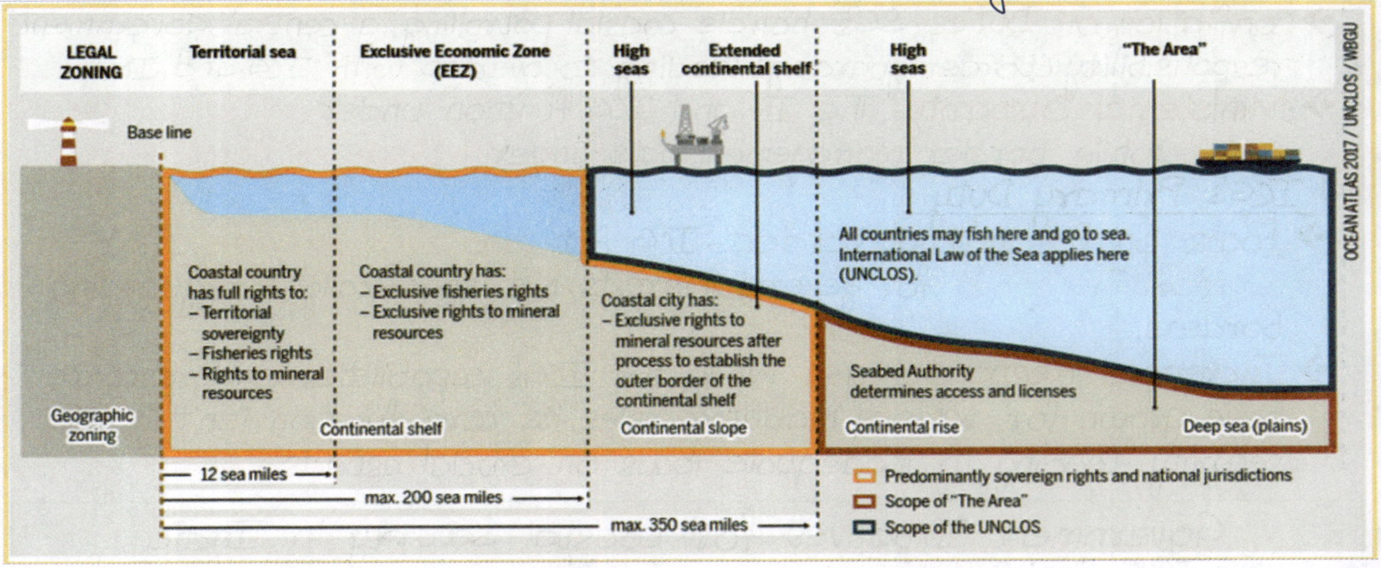
- **Ministry of Home Affairs (MHA)** implements Coastal Security Scheme.
  - Strengthens security infrastructure and capabilities of coastal police
  - Border Security Force (BSF)- Deployed in several creek areas of Gujarat and Sunderbans in West Bengal.
  - Central Industrial Security Force (CISF)- Security in major ports, select non-major ports and Indian Customs Port.

- National Committee for Strengthening Maritime and Coastal Security (NCSMCS)- Chaired by Cabinet Secretary, it periodically reviews coastal security with all stakeholders.
- State Coastal/Marine Police (SC/MP)-Boat patrolling in shallow coastal areas
  - Jurisdiction upto 12 nautical miles from the coast
  - Works in conjunction with ICG and IN in territorial waters

Challenges in Maritime Governance

01 Fragmented Approach

- Land vs. Maritime Borders- Land borders have well defined perimeters, while maritime borders encompass zones with varying degrees of jurisdiction (territorial sea, EEZ, continental shelf)
- One Border One force Principle- Maritime borders lack a unified command due to involvement of multiple agencies:
  - Indian Navy for overall maritime security.
  - Indian Coast Guard (ICG) for coordination between state and central agencies
  - State Coastal Police (SCP) for patrolling limited areas (5 nautical miles)
- Conflation of Duties- SCPs handle coastal patrolling, a central government responsibility (border guarding), leading to overlap with ICG and IN.
- Ministerial Disparity- The IN and ICG function under Ministry of Defense (MoD), while border management falls under Ministry of Home Affairs

02 ICG's Primary Duty

- Focus on Policing, not borders- ICG Act prioritises ensuring security of maritime zones for general interests, not specifically for guarding borders.
- Increased Responsibilities- While the ICG's capabilities and resource have grown for various maritime roles, its core function isn't border security leading to inadequate focus on crucial aspects

Government Initiatives for Coastal Security in India

- Indian Maritime Security Strategy (IMSS) 2015- Enhances coordination between maritime agencies, secures sea lanes and promotes regional cooperation
- Coastal Security Scheme (CSS)-Strengthens infrastructure for state marine police forces
- Coastal Surveillance Network- Provides electronic surveillance and is being expanded to cover gaps.

- Central Marine Police Force (CMPF) - Proposed force to protect coasts, ports and investigate coastal crimes.
- Fishermen Engagement - Trained fishermen assist with surveillance and intelligence gathering.
- Enhance Maritime Domain Awareness - Achieved through National Command Control Communication and Intelligence Network (NC3I)
- Capacity Building - Navy and coast guard train state marine police
- Indian Ocean Naval Symposium - Promotes discussion on regional maritime issues
- Sagar Prahari Bal - Specialised force for protecting naval bases and vulnerable areas.

Pathways for Strengthening Maritime Security

01 Leveraging Strategic Location of Andaman and Nicobar Islands (ANI)

- **Proximity to key trade routes** - Situated near East-West Shipping lane and Malacca Strait, ANI serves India's eastern naval command and hosts tri-service Andaman and Nicobar Command (ANC)
- **Bolstering Eastern Naval Defenses** - India is strengthening its Eastern Naval Command with more submarines and anti-submarine warfare vessels for enhanced underwater surveillance.
- **Deterrence through Infrastructure Development** - In 2019, $ 682 million military infrastructure development plan was initiated for ANI's naval and air force bases.

02 Balancing Militarisation with Regional Cooperation

- **Concerns about militarisation** - While India seeks to enhance its presence as a deterrent, some regional countries remain wary of excessive militarisation.
- **Engagement with Eastern neighbours and major powers** for collaborative development of islands
  - eg- exploring improved connectivity between Port Blair (India) and Port of Sabang (Indonesia)

03 Enhancing Maritime Domain Awareness (MDA)

- **Importance of MDA** - Effective maritime security strategies require a thorough understanding of activities in Bay of Bengal
- **India's MDA initiatives**
  - National Maritime Domain Awareness Centre - Links maritime agencies, coastal states and union territories for information sharing
  - Coastal Surveillance Network - Chain of coastal radars for surveillance

- National Automatic Identification System
- Information fusion Centre-Indian Ocean Region (IOR)-Tracks shipping traffic and other developments, collaborating with regional countries
- White Shipping Agreements with Bangladesh, Myanmar, Sri Lanka and Thailand. It allows for exchange of commercial shipping information
- BIMSTEC Information Sharing Centre- first step towards regional MDA cooperation.

04 Domestic Legislation and Cross-Border Cooperation

→ Anti-Maritime Piracy Bill- Criminalises maritime piracy and strengthens regional partnerships to combat it (awaiting Presidential assent)

→ Marine fisheries (Regulation and Management Bill)- Aims to prohibit illegal fishing in India's EEZ (to be passed)

→ Memorandum of Understanding with Bangladesh- On blue economy and combating illegal activities at sea (awaiting formalisation)

05 Joint Naval Exercises and Multilateral Platforms

→ SAGAR initiative (The Security and Growth for All in the Region) – India conducts patrols and naval exercises with Bay Littoral States and major powers (eg-Malabar exercise)

→ BIMSTEC– As a lead country for BIMSTEC's security sector, India has urged the grouping to address Bay security concerns. Existing legal instruments include:

- BIMSTEC Convention on cooperation in combating international terrorism, transnational organised crime, illicit drug trafficking.
- BIMSTEC Convention on Mutual Legal Assistance in criminal matters.
- Negotiations are underway for further conventions on trafficking in persons, transfer of sentenced person and extradiction

06 Addressing Environmental Concerns

→ Disaster Management- India has developed a robust disaster management system with a National Disaster Management Authority and state level bodies.

→ Humanitarian Assistance and Disaster Relief (HADR)–The Indian Navy plays a key role in HADR missions. eg- 2004 tsunami relief

→ BIMSTEC Cooperation- BIMSTEC is conducting HADR exercises and has finalized a concept paper on maritime cooperation in the Bay of Bengal, focussing on areas like HADR and disaster preparedness.

PYQs Corner

(Write the Answer and Get Free Evaluation)

1. What are the maritime security challenges in India? Discuss the organisational, technical and procedural initiatives taken to improve the maritime security. [150 Words] [10 Marks] **[2022]**

2. For effective border area management, discuss the steps required to be taken to deny local support to militants and also suggest ways to manage favourable perception among locals. [150 Words] [10 Marks] **[2020]**

3. Analyze internal security threats and transborder crimes along Myanmar, Bangladesh and Pakistan borders including Line of Control (LoC). Also, discuss the role played by various security forces in this regard. [250 Words] [15 Marks] **[2020]**

4. Cross-border movement of insurgents is only one of the several security challenges facing the policing of the border in North-East India. Examine the various challenges currently emanating across the India-Myanmar border. Also, discuss the steps to counter the challenges. [250 Words] [15 Marks] **[2019]**

5. Border management is a complex task due to difficult terrain and hostile relations with some countries. Elucidate the challenges and strategies for effective border management. [200 Words] [12.5 Marks] **[2016]**

6. How far are India's internal security challenges linked with border management particularly in view of the long porous borders with most countries of South Asia and Myanmar? [200 Words] [10 Marks] **[2013]**

Extremism

CHAPTER 03

EXTREMISM

- About- It refers to the advocacy of radical measures or views often involving the use of violence or other forms of use of coercion, to achieve political, religious or ideological objectives
- It rejects or undermines the status quo and undermines contemporary ideas and expressions of freedom.
- Extremism is an ideology that may or may not lead to violence

Factors Promoting Extremism in India

INTERNAL	• Unequal Wealth- Widening economic gaps fuels frustration among disadvantaged groups (eg- report on inequality in India) • Political Manipulation- Politicians exploit social divisions for votes, escalating tensions. • Diversity and competition- Large population with diverse identities creates competition for resources and marginalisation (eg- 64% of Indians see high religious tensions- Pew Research Center) • Justice System Issues- Weak institutions or slow judicial processes lead to a sense of impunity for violence.
EXTERNAL	• Hostile Neighbours- Support from neighbouring countries like Pakistan can provide resources and safe havens for extremists • Subversive Propaganda- External forces can exploit existing tensions through propanga, inflaming grievances • State and Non-State Actors- Both state actors (like Pakistan) and non-state actors (terrorist groups) can pose threats

EXTREMISM ⟶ UNDERDEVELOPMENT

- Infrastructure Crumbles- Roads, bridges and communication towers fall victim to extremist attacks, choking development
- Social fabric tears- Fear and violence erode trust within communities, hindering progress
- Economy bleeds- Businesses flee, tourism suffers and jobs disappear due to extremist activities
- Human rights trampled- Civilians caught in crossfire as both side commit abuses
- Development Stalls- fear discourages essential workers, keeping these regions isolated and poor
- Resources diverted- funds shift from social programs to fight extremist, hindering progress further
- Cycle of violence- Security operations can cause civilian casualities fueling resentment and perpetuating violence

Types of Extremism Witnessed in India

Left Wing Extremism (Naxalism)

Primarily anti-capitalist, advocating for radical change to systems causing social inequality, sometimes through violence.

eg- Red corridor in India

Ethnic insurgency

It involves militant and fundamentalist groups advocating a separation from India on the basis of ethnicity or any other factor. eg- North-east insurgency, Khalistan Movement in Punjab, militancy in Jammu & Kashmir

(Ethnic insurgency and ethnic conflicts explained in detail in Mains Pulse- Indian Society and Social Justice)

LEFT WING EXTREMISM (LWE)

→ Ideology- Naxalism is a form of armed rebellion against rebellion against Indian government, fueled by Maoist communist ideology. It is also known as Left Wing Extremism (LWE)

→ Inspiration- Political philosophy of Mao Zedong (former leader of China)

→ Origin in India- 1967 peasant uprising in Naxalbari (West Bengal) led by a radical faction of the Communist Party of India (Marxist)

→ Affected Area- Concentrated in eastern India, particularly within region called "Red Corridor" → Chattisgarh, Bihar, Jharkhand, Odisha, West Bengal and parts of Andhra Pradesh, Madhya Pradesh, Maharashtra and Kerala.

Goals and Strategies

- Overthrowing the government through "people's war"
- Disrupting Governance and create situations where government struggles to function, aiming to weaken its control.
- Instilling fear among law-abiding citizen
- Seizing power and establish state called "The Indian People's Democratic federal Republic"

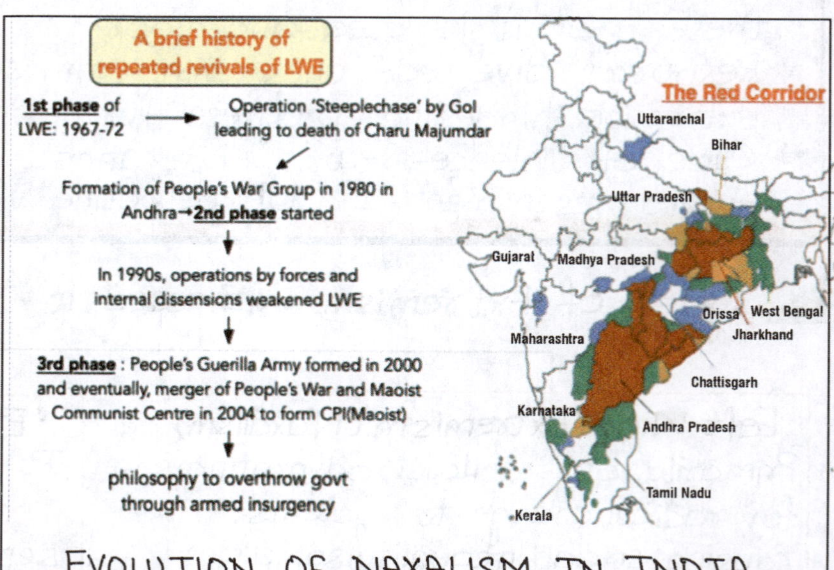

EVOLUTION OF NAXALISM IN INDIA

Naxalism in India

- **Decline in incidents**- Declined by 77%, from all time high of 2258 incidents in 2009 to 250 incidents in 2023.
- **Reduction in Deaths** by 89% from 1005 (in 2010) to 69 (in 2023)
- **Decrease in Affected areas**- 38 districts across 10 states are categorised as LWE affected with effect from April 1, 2024 compared to 75 in 2015. Chattisgarh (15 districts) > Odisha (7) > Jharkhand (5) > Madhya Pradesh (3) > Kerala, Maharashtra, Telangana (2 each) > West Bengal, Andhra Pradesh (1 each)
- **Surrender of Naxalites**- An estimated 16,780 Naxalites surrendered between March 6, 2000 and April 7, 2024

Factors Responsible for Rise of Naxalism

01 Land Issues

- Failed Land Reforms (eg- loopholes in land ceiling laws) left millions landless and frustrated
- Unequal access- Powerful groups control vast tracts of land (27% lack titles)
- Tribal Dispossession- Weak tribal land rights and inadequate compensation for development laws (as low as 15% market value) displaced millions

02 Governance Related factors

- Failure to implement welfare schemes effectively and efficiently
- Malfunctioning of government machinery in terms of inefficiency, corruption and exploitation.
- Weak governance allow Maoists to gain legitimacy in deprived areas
- Corruption and brutality- Allegations of police brutality (1000+ cases against Adivasis-National Human Rights Commission) eroded trust.
- Political Marginalisation of marginalised communities especially tribal population.

03 Environmental Degradation- Mining and industries destroyed tribal livelihoods (eg- Hasdeo Arand coal mining project threatens displacement)

04 Socio-economic and Cultural factors

- Poverty, inequality fuel LWE support, especially in rural areas
- Land acquisition displaces farmers/ tribes, fuels LWE violence in tribes
- Cultural alienation of tribal communities
- Lack of basic infrastructure, such as roads, schools, etc.
- Violence and abuse- violence by both security forces and Naxalites created fear
- Social Disconnect- Lack of integration with mainstream society fueled isolation
- Development Deficit- Naxalite areas have some of the Lowest Human Development Index Scores (NITI Aayog Report 2022)

Challenges Posed by Left-Wing Extremism (LWE)

- Security Crisis- LWE results in violent clashes, leading to numerous casualities among security forces and civilians (over 8800 killed since 2004- MHA)
- Strangled Growth- Maoist attacks cripple infrastructure projects like roads and bridges, hindering development in affected regions (eg- 2021 bridge destruction in Chattisgarh)

- **Forced Recruitment**- LWE groups exploit vulnerable children, forcing them into their ranks as soldiers (UNICEF-Hundreds of child soldiers in 2023).
- **Extortion**- Businesses are forced to pay "protection money" to Maoists, stifling economic activity.
- **Erosion of Trust**- LWE weakens governance in affected areas as trust in institution crumbles (eg- low voter turnout in LWE districts)
- **Human Right Abuses**- Both security forces and Maoists are accused of violating human rights, harming innocent civilians
- **Tribal Discontent**- Neglect by government creates fertile ground for LWE to exploit tribal grievances

Government Policies to Naxalism in India

National Policy and Action Plan to address LWE (2015)

- Aim- To enhance the capabilities of security forces to combat LWE
- Ensure that rights and entitlements of local communities are safe-guarded and focuses on socio-economic development in affected regions.

SAMADHAN Doctrine

- It is strategy of MHA to frame short term and long term policies to tackle LWE. 8 pillars of doctrine are-

S-Smart leadership
A-Aggressive Strategy
M-Motivation & Training
A-Actionable intelligence
D-Dashboard based KPIs
H-Harness Technology
A-Action Plan for each theatre
N-No access to financing

Offensive Strategy

- In 2022, security forces have achieved unprecedented success in Operation Octopus, Operation Double Bull and Operation Chakrabandha in fight against LWE

Centre-State Cooperation

- Government has made funds available for capacity building of states under various schemes such as security related expenditure (SRE) scheme and Special Infrastructure Scheme (SIS)
- Road Connectivity Project for LWE affected areas- 8124 km roads and 306 bridge works have been completed under this scheme.

Socio-Political Schemes for LWE

Panchayat Extension to Scheduled Areas (PESA) Act, 1996

Strengthen local governance in LWE affected areas by promoting democratic participation and empowering local institutions

Civic Action Programme (CAP)

Aim- To bridge the gaps between Security forces and local people through personal interaction and bring the human face of Security forces before the local population.

Limitation in Effectively Tackling Left Wing Extremism (LWE)

- **Neglecting Safety Protocols-** Lax adherence to standard operating Procedures (SOPs) puts security personnels at risk (eg- 2021 Sukma-Bijapur attack → 22 personnel died)
- **Vulnerable Security forces-** Security forces face limitations due to:
  - Poor planning and inadequate personnel
  - Insufficient intelligence gathering
- **Structural Deficiencies**
  - Over-reliance on IPS officers in senior CRPF positions, neglecting experienced CRPF personnel
  - Slow capacity building. eg- thousands of vacancies in Chattisgarh police and unestablished police stations
- **Money laundering-** Naxal leaders launder extorted funds through property acquisition
- **Technological Limitations-** Inaffective landmine detection technology leading to casualities
- **Operational Challenges-**
  - Difficult terrain- Dense forest, hilly areas impede operations
  - Lack of local knowledge- Central Police forces struggle due to unfamiliarity with local terrain and language

Pathways for Addressing Left Wing Extremism (LWE)

01 Role of Government

- **Financial Empowerment**
  - Encourage formation of 'Self Help Groups' (SHGs)
  - Improve access to credit and marketing

  Political empowerment- FRA Act, 2006
- **Infrastructure Development-** Road networks, Mobile towers network, irrigation canal, electricity feeder, etc.

02 Governance Reform

- Bridging Trust Deficit- Employ more local people in administrative process as a bridge to curtail trust deficit
- Centre State Coordination- Synchronised efforts in eliminating radicalisation and clear delineation of roles and responsibilities
- Counter Ideological Appeal- Cherish and nurture democratic way of life deeply enshrined in our constitution, as opposed to totalitarian and oppressive nature of Maoist ideology.

03 Security and Capacity Building

- Modernisation of local police forces and central forces should be used in small groups to maintain greater efficiency.
- Disrupting financial flow- Establish a dedicated anti-extortion and anti-money laundering cell within state police.

04 Use of Technology

- Tech Offensive- Enhanced surveillance with UAVs
  - focus on timely intelligence to strengthen counterinsurgency efforts
  - Geographic Information System (GIS) and Global Positioning System (GPS) can help in identifying camp locations

05 Adopting Best Practices

- Saranda Model (Jharkhand)- Infrastructure development (roads, offices) and social programs (subsidized food, employment) to address root causes.
- Sandesh Model (Bihar)- Panchayat elections weakened Naxalite control and empowered locals
- Greyhound Model (Andhra Pradesh)- Effective surrender and rehabilitation policy, specialized police unit (greyhound), strong leadership, local knowledge, intelligence based operations led to success

06 Global Collaboration

- UN Plan of Action to Prevent Violent Extremism (2016)- Comprehensive strategy addressing root causes of radicalization alongside critical counterterrorism measures
- Christchurch Call for Action- Eliminate violent extremist violent content online through improved cooperation among governments, civil society and online service providers.

INSURGENCY

Insurgency is an armed rebellion against established authority where those taking part in the rebellion are not recognised as aggressors.

Method → Mostly guerilla warfare tactics (surprise attacks, ambushes and sabotage) to slowly wear down the government's forces and win over local population.

Types of Insurgencies

1) Separatist insurgencies- fought by groups who want to break away from a country and want to form their own independent state (eg- in Nagaland)
2) Ideological insurgencies- fought by groups who want to overthrow a government and replace it with a new system, such as communist or religious state (Jammu & Kashmir insurgency)
3) Resource Wars- fought by groups who are trying to control access to valuable resources, such as oil, diamonds or timber

CHARACTERISTICS OF INSURGENCIES

- Asymmetric warfare against government forces
- Fight for political goals ➡ independence, autonomy or a change in government
- Control of and collaboration with local population

NORTH EAST INSURGENCY

North-east India is easternmost region of the country. It shares 5500 km borders with 5 countries

- Bhutan, Nepal and China on its North
- Myanmar on its east
- Bangladesh on its south and west

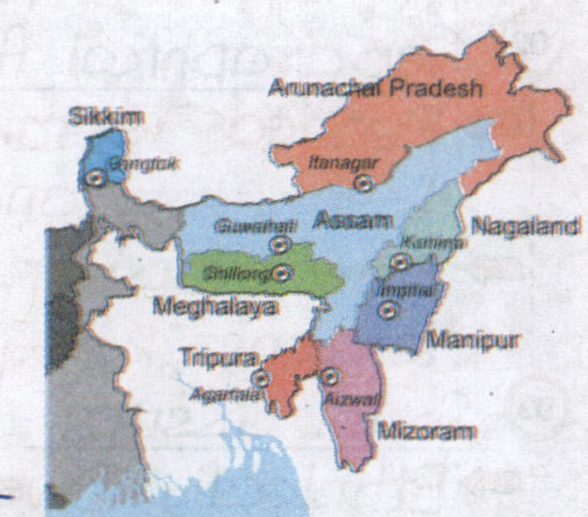

It covers 8% of India's geographical area and about 4% of national population.

Linked to mainland India by narrow Siliguri Corridor. The region comprise of 8 states-

- Seven Sister States- Arunachal Pradesh, Assam, Manipur, Meghalaya, Mizoram, Nagaland and Tripura.
- Sikkim- The Himalayan state, geographically distinct but culturally connected

SIGNIFICANCE OF NORTH-EAST

1. **Strategic Location:** Land bridge connecting India to South-east Asia
2. **Buffer Zone**
3. **Rich Natural Resources** like oil, gas, coal, hydropower potential etc.
4. **Regional Stability:** Cooperation and integration with regional organisation (BIMSTEC)
5. **Tourism Potential:** Kaziranga National Park
6. **Cultural Signi cance:** Hornbill festival

Insurgency in North-East India

2nd Administrative Reforms Commission- Northeast represents a state of stable anarchy where the rule of law and other institutions of governance are subverted directly or through collusive arrangements to serve personal or partisan ends of militants.

factors Responsible for Insurgency in North-East India

01 Historical factors

➡ Pre independence era
- British administered hills as a loose frontier area → region never fully experienced a centralised administration
- British isolated it from its traditional partners → Bhutan, Myanmar
- Religious conversion (by Christian missionaries) in present day Mizoram, Nagaland and Meghalaya were done.

➡ Post independence era
- Resistance to integration process- Distinct cultures of North-east into "mainstream" of India was often met with resistance + fear of losing identity
- Migration from neighbouring countries (eg- Bangladesh)

02 Geographical factors

➡ Rugged Terrain- Mountains and dense forests provide cover for insurgents and hinder security forces

➡ Demographic Shifts- Influx of refugees strains resources and fuels tensions (Refugees from Bangladesh into Assam)

03 Social Issues

➡ Ethnically Diverse Region- It is home to around 40 million people including 213 of the 635 tribal groups

➡ Ethnic Clashes due to competition for resources and cultural differences

➡ Displacement- Inter-ethnic violence displaces thousands, fostering instability (eg- over 8,00,000 displaced since 1990s)

04 Economic Disparity

➡ External Influence- Potential foreign support for insurgent groups (eg- China and Pakistan)

➡ Underdevelopment- Lack of infrastructure and industry limits job opportunities

05 Political Tensions

➡ Ideological Differences- Clashing goals between insurgents and government hinder progress

- ➡ Autonomy Aspirations- Unmet desire for self-governance fuels resentment
- ➡ Internal Divisions- Infighting within insurgent groups weakens peace efforts (eg- ongoing Naga faction disagreements)
- ➡ Feeling of Marginalisation- Distance from central government and limited representation breeds alienation

06 Governance Issues

- ➡ AFSPA controversy- Armed forces (Special Powers) Act is seen as oppressive by some.
- ➡ Inadequate Administration- Central government's policy is seen as ineffective.

Insurgency in North-Eastern States in India

ASSAM

- ➡ Major Insurgent Groups- United Liberation Front of Asom (ULFA), Bodoland Liberation Tiger Force (BLTF)
- ➡ Key Issues- Secessionist aspirations for an independent "Greater Asom", ethnic tensions between Assamese and Bengali communities, demands for autonomy by Bodoland tribes
- ➡ Status-
  - ULFA insurgency peaked in 1990s → Bombings and kidnappings.
  - Bodoland conflict resulted in displacement of thousands
  - Peace Accords with both ULFA factions and BLTF (Third Bodo Accord, 2020) have brought significant reduction in violence in recent years

NAGALAND

- ➡ Major Insurgent Groups- National Socialist Council of Nagaland (NSCN) (various factions)
- ➡ Key Issues- Secessionist aspirations for a sovereign "Nagaland" encompassing Naga inhabited areas of neighbouring states
- ➡ Status-
  - NSCN insurgency is one of longest running in region, dating back to 1950s
  - Ceasefire agreements have been signed, but final peace accord remains elusive

Current Status of insurgency in North-east

Significant downward trend seen in violence in past 9 years (2014-2023) compared to previous decade

- Violent incidents
  - 2004-2014 → 11,121 incidents
  - 2014-2023 → 3,033 (73% ↓)
- Security personnel casualities
  - 2004-2014 → 458 deaths
  - 2014-2023 → 130 (72% ↓)
- Civilian casualities
  - 2004-2014 → 2,652 deaths
  - 2014-2023 → 356 (86% ↓)
- Surrenders- Atleast 8,000

MANIPUR

- **Major Insurgent Groups**- United National Liberation front (UNLF), People's Revolutionary Party of Kanglepak (PREPAK)
- **Key Issues**- Secessionist aspirations for independent "Manipur", demands for greater autonomy, recent Manipur Crisis
- **Status**- Peace Accord with the UNLF in 2020 offers hope for a more peaceful time.

TRIPURA

- **Major Insurgent Groups**- National Liberation front of Tripura (NLFT)
- **Key Issues**-Secessionist aspirations for separate Tripura state for indigenous communities, displacement due to ethnic violence
- **Status**
  - NLFT insurgency primarily targeted Bengali settlers and government forces.
  - Tripura Accord in 2019 marked a significant step towards peace

MIZORAM

- **Major Insurgent Groups**-Mizo National front (MNF)- outlawed in 1967
- **Key Issues**-Secessionist aspirations for independent "Mizoram" fueled by cultural and ethnic identity.
- **Status**- MNF insurgency achieved a peace accord in 1986, leading to a peaceful Mizoram today.

MEGHALAYA

- **Major Insurgent Groups**- Hynniewtrep National Liberation Council (HNLC)
- **Key Issues**- Demands for greater autonomy for indigenous Khasi tribes
- **Status**- Insurgency in Meghalaya has been less prominent as compared to other states

Steps taken for promoting Peace in North-east India

01 Administrative Arrangements

- Ministry of North Eastern Region (DONER) - Responsible for planning, execution and monitoring of development schemes and projects
  - Aim - To accelerate socio-economic development
- Inner Line Permit (ILP) - Restrictions on entry of outsiders to maintain indigenous identity.

  Required for entry in Mizoram, Nagaland, Manipur and Arunachal Pradesh

Two of Assam's three Autonomous Districts Councils (Karbi Anglong and Dima Hasdeo)

Bodoland Territorial Areas District

Arunachal Pradesh

Assam

Nagaland

Dimapur

Meghalaya

Shillong

Manipur

Tripura

Mizoram

Under ILP regime

Areas under sixth schedule

Not exempted from CAB

MIZORAM Entire state under ILP Additionally three Autonomous District Councils also under sixth schedule

ARUNACHAL PRADESH: Entire state under ILP regime

NAGALAND: Entire state under ILP regime

TRIPURA: Sixth Schedule covers 70% of geographical area

MEGHALAYA: Almost entire state covered under Sixth Schedule, except a part of Shillong

ASSAM: 3 Autonomous District Councils under Sixth Schedule

MANIPUR: Entire state under ILP regime

- Constitutional Provisions
  - Article 244(1) - 5th schedule provisions for administration of scheduled areas and tribes
  - Article 244(2) - 6th schedule provisions for administration of scheduled areas in Assam, Meghalaya, Tripura, Mizoram.

    Creation of Autonomous District Councils (eg - Karbi Anglong, Khasi Hill district, Chakma District)
  - Article 371(A) - Special status of Nagaland

02 Act East Policy

- Mandatory embarking of atleast 10% of Gross Budgetary Support of Central Ministries/Departments for North-east Region.
- Initiatives like Swadesh Darshan Scheme, Comprehensive Telecom Development Project, Agri Export Zones, National Bamboo Mission

03 Infrastructure Development

- Road Networks - Schemes like Bharatmala Pariyojna (BMP) prioritize road infrastructure development (4,000 km of new roads.
- Affordable Air Travel - RCS-UDAN aims to make air travel more accessible (15 air connectivity projects)
- National Waterways on major rivers - Ganges, Brahmaputra and Barak rivers (NW-1, NW-2, NW-16) + Guwahati Multimodal Hub + Eastern Waterways Connectivity Transport Grid.
- Connectivity Projects
  - Indo-Bangladesh Protocol Routes - Increased from 8 to 10, facilitating trade and movement
  - Kaladan Multi-Modal Transit Project (Myanmar) facilitates water connectivity

- Bangladesh- China- India-Myanmar (BCIM) corridor promotes trade
- India- Myanmar- Thailand Trilateral Highway strengthens regional connections.

04 Peace Accords

Dialogues With Dissidents

MANIPUR

- **August 22, 2008:** GoI signs ceasefire agreement with 25 Kuki rebel groups.
- **Hurdles:** Kuki groups now demand an autonomous council in the hills region.

Nagas are opposed to the demand.

- **Status:** The ceasefire agreement is being renewed periodically.

No progress in talks.

- **Active Groups:** Meitei groups, like UNLF, PLA, PREPAK, KCP, KYKL
- **Demand:** Independent Manipur

MEGHALAYA

Talks underway with HNLC.

NAGALAND

- **1997:** Ceasefire signed between GoI and NSCN-IM.
- **August 3, 2015:** A "framework agreement" signed between GoI and NSCN (IM).
- **November 18, 2017:** A separate pact signed between GoI and Naga National Political Groups (NNPGs), a forum of seven other rebel groups.
- **Hurdles:** NSCN-IM's demand for a separate flag and a separate Constitution for the Nagas.

NSCN-IM's demand for Greater Nagalim, which, it says, should include Naga-inhabited areas of Manipur

Meiteis, other communities of Manipur opposed to NSCN-IM's Greater Nagalim demand

- **Status:** Peace-process with NSCN-IM stalled, further talks likely

Talks concluded with NNPGs.

MIZORAM

- **June 30, 1986:** Mizo Accord signed between GoI and MNF.
- **Status:** Implemented

ASSAM

- **February 10, 2003:** Agreement singed between GoI and BLT.
- **Status:** BLT disbanded, leaders joined politics.
- **January 27, 2020:** Agreement signed with all four factions of NDFB.
- **Status:** Leaders joined politics.

- **Pitfalls of Peace:** The deals triggered apprehensions among other tribal communities living in Bodo-majority areas about their rights.

The demands for **Bodoland for Bodos** and for **Kamtapur for Koch Rajbongshis** clash with each other.

- **September 3, 2011:** GoI signed ceasefire agreement with a faction of ULFA
- **Hurdles:** Another ULFA faction led by Paresh Baruah has not joined dialogue and has not given up demand for 'sovereign Assam'.
- **Status:** Talks underway.
- **2012:** Govt signs agreement with DHD-J in Dima Hasao. Leaders joined politics.
- **September 5, 2021:** Govt signs agreement with five rebel groups in Karbi-dominated districts of Assam

Hurdles: The demand for a separate autonomous Karbi State still active.

Karbis and Dimasas have mutually conflicting homeland demands.

- **February, 2012:** Five Adivasi militant groups surrender.
- **Hurdles:** The demand for Scheduled Tribe status for the Adivasis.
- **Status:** Talks on hold.

TRIPURA

- **August 2019:** Govt. signs agreement with NLFT-SD.
- **Status:** Some other factions of NLFT are still active.

What's on offer?

Scheme for surrender and rehabilitation of militants

 Fixed deposit of Rs. 4 lakh against each cadre.

 Montly stipend of Rs. 6,000 for each surrendered militants for three years.

 Incentives for weapons/ ammunition surrender.

 Vocational training for self-employment

 Funds for construction of the rehabilitation camps.

05 Policy Measure

- Tribal Panchsheel (five Principles) - Introduced by Jawaharlal Nehru, this foundational policy lays framework for guiding the development of tribal areas.
- North Eastern Region Power System Improvement Project (NERPSIP) - Strengthens intra-state power transmission and distribution for economic development
- Prime Minister's Development Initiative for North east (PM-DevINE) funds infrastructure and social development projects based on regional needs, aligned with PM Gati Shakti
- Tourism Promotion - Swadesh Darshan Scheme
- North East Industrial Development Scheme (NEIDS) - Encourages Micro, Small & Medium Enterprises (MSMEs) for job creation.
- Border Area Development Programme (BADP) - Improving the socio-economic conditions of remote areas along international borders

06 Proportionate Use of force

- While emphasizing dialogue and development, the government has also maintained a security presence-
  - Joint Operations - Coordinated efforts with neighbouring states and security forces
  - Balancing Act - Ensuring security without alienating local communities
  - AFSPA - Reducing the disturbed areas under AFSPA in Nagaland, Assam and Manipur.

Armed Forces Special Powers Act, 1958 (AFSPA)

- It grants special powers to armed forces in "disturbed 'areas" to maintain public order.
- Disturbed area is declared by central government or state governor where situation necessitates military intervention.

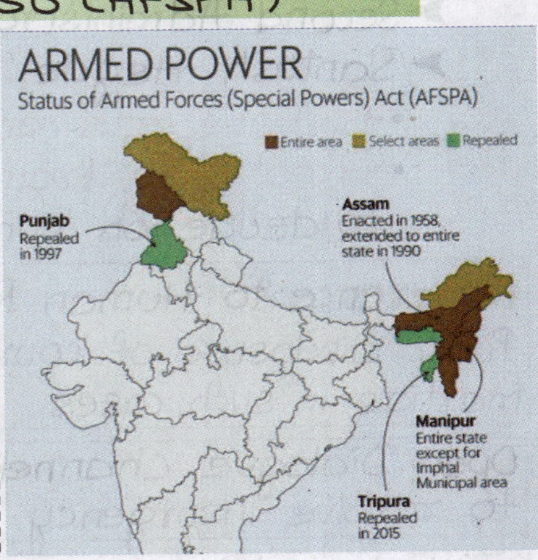

Need of AFSPA	Concern with AFSPA
• To protect the border • Address ongoing security threats posed by armed groups and insurgency in the region. • Empowering forces- legal authority for operations, arrests and maintaining law and order in disturbed areas • Legal Protections for personnel operating in these areas • Boosting morale and confidence of security forces in challenging environments • Provides organisational flexibility and effective utilisation of security capacity of state	• Violations of rights- Right to life + Right to legal remedy + freedom from arbitrary arrest and detention • Centre-state conflict- Law and order is a state subject, but AFSPA undermines state autonomy, especially during peaceful periods • Misuse of powers by armed forces under the act • Alienation- AFSPA furthered the sense of alienation among people • It fuels resentment towards Indian state • Lack of accountability- Section 7 of AFSPA makes prosecuting security forces difficult

Supreme Court and Committee on AFSPA

- **Naga People's Movement of Human Rights v Union of India (1997)**
  - Upheld constitutionality of AFSPA
    Procedures- State government's opinion required when declaring a "disturbed area." Act to be reviewed by state every six months
- **Committees**
  - B.P. Jeevan Reddy Committee (2005) - Repeal AFSPA and incorporate AFSPA into Unlawful Activities (Prevention) Act, 1967
  - Second Administrative Reforms Commission (2007) - Repeal AFSPA
  - Santosh Hegde Committee (2013)-
    - Humane and accountability proposals
    - Fixed Time frame- 3 month deadline for central government to decide on punishing security personnel for extrajudicial actions

Way forward

- Adherence to Human Rights: Public disclosure of court-martials in such cases
- Open Dialogue Channel to resolve insurgency
- Independent inquiry in cases of death caused by armed forces
- Accelerate Development of North-east region
- Examine AFSPA applicability on case to case basis
- Abiding guidelines by NHRC, Jeevan Reddy Commission, courts

Challenges to Peace and Prosperity Initiatives

- Presence of un-demarcated borders
- Natural challenges to the economic development and connectivity initiatives from disaster risks
- Limited FDI inflows and predominance of informal economy in Northeast region
- Presence of organised crime syndicates manifesting in recent attacks on Indian connectivity projects in Myanmar by rebel groups creating challenge to Act East Policy.
- Prevailing stereotypes about people and region among people from other regions.
- Border Disputes between states (eg- Assam-Mizoram border dispute)
- Ethnic Conflicts like Manipur violence over Meiti community's addition in list of Scheduled Tribes
- Rivalry in militant groups complicates peace process (NAGA factionalism)
- Lack of efficient infrastructure- Infrastructure both physical (like roadways, waterways, energy) and social (educational institutions, health facilities) is lacking in NER

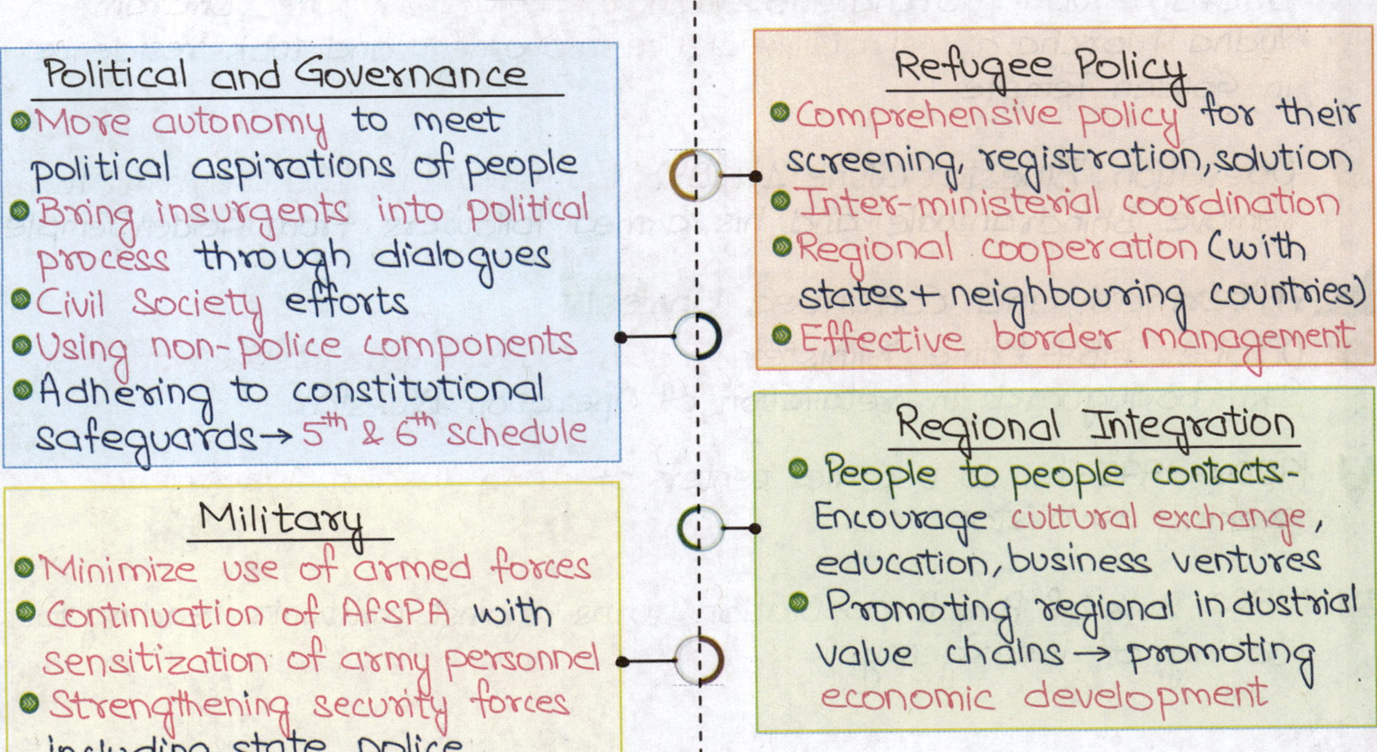

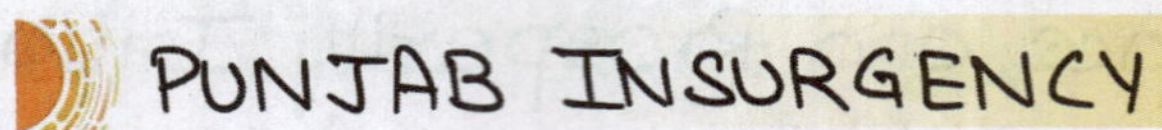

PUNJAB INSURGENCY

Emergence (Late 1970s)- Punjab saw an insurgency movement rise in the late 1970s. Also known as Khalistani movement, it advocated for creation of an independent Sikh state called "Khalistan"

Timeline of Khalistan Movement

1947 India's independence and partition along religious lines, divided Punjab province between India and Pakistan, leading to massive displacement and violence.

Formation of a Sikh-Majority State (1966) Punjab is reorganised to create Punjabi speaking, Sikh majority state.

Anandpur Sahib Resolution (1973) by Akali Dal demanding greater autonomy for Punjab, including right to a separate constitution

1980s Jarnail Singh Bhindranwale emerges as a vocal figure advocating for Sikh rights

Dharam Yudh Morcha (1982) Bhindranwale launches Dharam Yudha Morcha, a civil disobedience movement and took residence in Golden Temple.

Operation Bluestar (June 1, 1984) launched by Indian Army to remove Bhindranwale and his armed followers from Golden Temple

Aftermath and Continued Unrest

October 1984- Prime Minister Indira Gandhi was assasinated by Sikh bodyguards in retaliation of Operation Bluestar

1980s- 1995- Punjab becomes center of long lasting insurgency seeking Khalistan

1990s- Bulk of Punjab population turns against militants leading to waning of insurgency

Resurgence of Khalistan voices across the globe

Revival factors

- Political marginalisation of Sikhs
- Economic grievances in Punjab (eg- high unemployment)
- Perception of injustice (eg- 1984 anti Sikh riots)
- Concerns about cultural and religious identity erosion.
- International support from Sikh diaspora (financial and political)
- Suspected links between Khalistani groups and Pakistan's ISI (drug trafficking, social media)

Concerns

- Threat to national security and integrity
- Deterioration of law and order in Punjab
- Strained bilateral relations (eg- Canada, UK)

Role of Diaspora and Social Media

- Propaganda by parts of Sikh diaspora in Western countries using social media
- Misinformation Campaigns by Khalistani Organisations (eg- Referendum 2020)
- Increased identity consciousness among young Sikhs

Government Measures

- Counter-terrorism actions against Khalistan militants
- Legal actions (arrest, ban on Khalistani organisations)
- Dialogue with moderate Sikh leaders
- Development initiatives in Punjab (infrastructure, jobs and social programs)
- Diplomatic Pressure on foreign countries to counter Khalistan support

Way forward

- Foreign collaboration to monitor anti India Khalistani activities, restrict their funding source
- Diaspora engagement by fostering positive relations
- Diplomatically counter Khalistani misinformation
- Strengthen security measures (weapon, drones, intelligence, etc)
- Engage Pakistan- Pursue extradition of terrorists via diplomacy

INSURGENCY IN JAMMU AND KASHMIR

Kashmir insurgency is a complex and ongoing separatist militant conflict against the Indian administration. It has roots in local autonomy disputes and has seen various groups advocating for either complete independence or accession to Pakistan.

Evolution of Insurgency in Jammu and Kashmir

Pre insurgency (1947-1980s)

- Tensions post partition, Indo-Pakistani Wars
- Sheikh Abdullah's rule and growing discontent in 1980s

Early Insurgency (1980s-1990s)

- Emergence of militant groups (JKLF) seeking independence or joining Pakistan
- 1989- Rigged elections trigger open rebellion
- 1990s- Pakistan's support intensifies insurgency, Kashmiri Pandits exodus

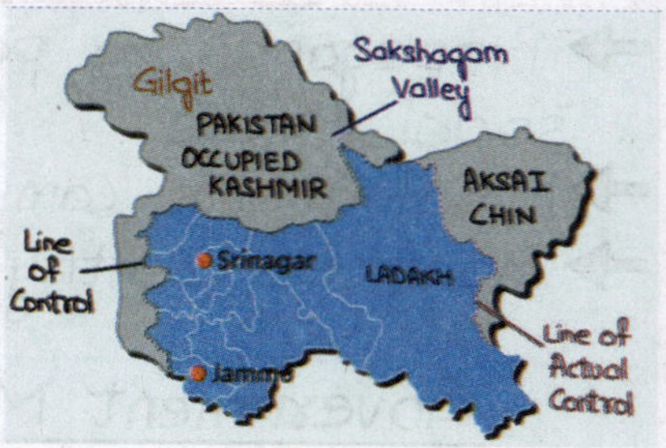

Protracted Conflict (1990s- 2000s)

- Peak violence in 1990s, decline in mid 1990s
- 2001- Indian Parliament attack strain relations

Recent Developments (2000s-Present)

- 2004- Improved security situation under Indian initiatives
- 2008 - Mumbai attack stall peace talks
- 2010s- Sporadic violence, major attacks (Uri, Pulwama)
- 2019- Abrogation of Article 370 reignites tensions

Present Insurgency waned but sporadic violence and online separatism remain a challenge

Factors Behind Jammu & Kashmir Militancy

01 Political

- **Disputed Sovereignty-** Both India and Pakistan claim Kashmir
  India's view- Points to UN Resolutions and Pakistan's failure to withdraw troops
  Pakistan's view- Emphasizes the Muslim majority in Kashmir and criticised instrument of accession.

02 Economic

- » Limited Opportunities- High unemployment, lack of job creation and decline of traditional crafts contribute to economic hardship
- » Poor Infrastructure- Inadequate industrial development fuels frustration among Kashmiri youth

03 Social

- » Limited services- Poor education and health care systems
- » Shifting Religious Landscape- The rise of radical Islam in a traditionally sufi region creates friction
- » Psychological scars- Unhealed wounds from 1980s insurgency and influence of extremist leaders fuel discontent
- » Pakistani Propaganda- ISI backed efforts spread anti-India sentiment and radical ideology

04 External factors

- » Pakistan's Role- Pakistan's alleged support for separatist groups through infiltration and terrorism aims to destabilize India.
- » International Support- Militant groups may attract fighters from other countries who view the conflict as a religious cause

Pakistan's objectives

- ➤ Avenge war losses
- ➤ Hurt India's economy by forcing expenditure on security.
- ➤ Keep anti-India sentiments on boil
- ➤ Internationalise India as an oppressive state

IMPACT OF MILITANCY

- → Economic Stagnation- Investment and tourism decline due to security concerns. Infrastructure development also suffers
- → Social and Political Disruption- Alienation from Indian state, radicalization of youth and hindered development
- → Displacement and Migration- Violence forces people to flee their homes. eg- exodus of Kashmiri Pandits
- → Governance Challenges- Disrupted daily life, eroded trust in institutions and weakened security

Security Strategies

- >>> Protecting Civilians- Prioritise safety of minorities and local populations, building positive relationships
- >>> Disrupting Support Networks- Legally address and investigate terrorist funding and infrastructure.
- >>> Real Time Intelligence- Ensure seamless information sharing among security forces

Jammu & Kashmir post Article 370 abrogation

- Less stone pelting: 76 incidents in Jan-Jul 2021 vs 618(2019)
- Decreased security force injuries and civilian casualties from stone pelting and security measures
- More militant arrests and OGW apprehensions (up from 82 in 2019 to 178 in 2021)
- 32% decline in terrorism acts (Aug 2019- June 2022)

- Enhanced Counter Terrorism- Improve coordination, intelligence gathering and operational tactics
- Community Engagement- Involves local through volunteer defense committees and initiatives promoting trust.
- Adaptability- Develop flexible tactics to counter evolving terrorist strategies
- Infrastructure Security- Protect critical infrastructure and identify vulnerable areas

Government Initiatives

01 Legislative Measures

- Repealing of Article 370
- Jammu and Kashmir reorganisation act 2019 (Recognizes J&K state into UT of J&K with a legislature and UT of Ladakh without legislature

02 Economic Development

- Udaan Skill Development Program- Equips unemployed youth with job ready skills
- PM's Development Package- Investment in infrastructure, healthcare, education and tourism
- Promoting Kashmiri saffron and Tourism- GI tagging and global marketing efforts

03 Social Development

- Preserving Art, Culture and IT infrastructure- focus on cultural heritage and improving online government services
- Educational institutions- Establishing institutes like AIIMS, IIT and IIM to boost education
- Infrastructure Development- Upgrading transportation networks and establishing hydro power projects

04 Investment and Industrial Growth

- New Industrial Policy- Aims to create more investor friendly environment
- Youth and Community Programs
  - Project Himayat (skill development)
  - Nai Manzil & USTAAD (education and skill training for minorities)
  - Project Sadbhavana (healthcare and empowerment)
  - Project Umeed (livelihood mission)
  - Parvaaz Scheme (competitive exam support)
  - Village Defence Groups (local security)

05 Human Rights and Rehabilitation

- Security force Guidelines- Upholding human rights and investigating alleged violations
- Surrender and Rehabilitation Policy- Encouraging former militants to reintegrate into society.

WAY FORWARD

- **Youth Engagement**- Actively involve youth in dialogue and peace building efforts
- **Media Campaign**- Expose Pakistan's support for terrorism
- **Kashmiri Pandit Return**- facilitate safe return and rehabilitation of displaced Kashmiri Pandits
- **Refined Rehabilitation Policy**- Effectively reintegrate former militants

Professor Amitabh Mattoo's 4D Approach to Peace in J&K

- Dialogue- Open communication between government and all stake-holders → confidence building measures → State Status to J&K and assembly election
- Demilitarisation- Reduce military presence to create a more peaceful environment
- Devolution- Empower regions with greater decision-making power
- Development- Collaborative economic and social development → tourism, education and infrastructure

OVERGROUND WORKERS

- About- Overground Workers (OGWs) are people who help militants or terrorists with logistical support, cash, shelter and other infrastructure with which armed groups and insurgency movements
- They are essentially "militants without weapons"
- Recruitment- They are systematically radicalized, starting with seemingly minor crimes and escalating to become OGWs. They can potentially become future militants
- eg- Hizb-ul-Mujahideen and Lashkar-e-Taiba rely heavily on OGW networks to sustain militancy in Kashmir.

ROLE PLAYED BY OGWs IN TERRORIST OPERATIONS

- Provide safe houses
- Collect and launder funds for sustaining terrorist activities
- Build false narratives to radicalise youth
- Instigate people to demonstrate on trivial grounds in order to demoralise and discredit the security forces
- Recruitment of local youths for joining terrorist attacks
- Logistics Network(supplies, weapons, shelter, movement)
- Infiltration aid (eg- Sunjuwan attack)
- Sleeper Cells (blurring lines between OGWs and militants
- Protect Orchestrators(destabilizing security force, create hindrance in search operations)

India's Approach to OGWs

- Operations (eg- Operation All Out)
- Legal measures- The Jammu and Kashmir Public Safety Act (PSA) detains anti-national elements and maintain peace
- Community Engagement- "Operation Sadbhavana" focuses on education, women's empowerment, healthcare and infrastructure development to address grievance and build trust.
- Youth Outreach- "Mission Pehal" involves face-to-face interactions with Kashmiri youth to address their concerns
- Education & Livelihood- Scholarship programs, skill development initiatives and employment opportinies
- Countering online Propaganda- Social media monitoring and positive messaging are used to counter extremist narratives

CHALLENGES IN HANDLING OGWs

Overreach can backfire- Aggressively targeting youth suspected of OGW activity can push them towards militancy

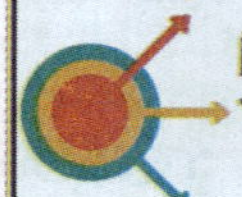

Alienation- Harsh tactics create "Us vs Them" mentality, isolating them from government

Difficult Detection as OGWs blend with population while carrying small scale operations/attacks

Measures to neutralize influence of OGWs

- Increasing intelligence
- Community leadership
- Control social interactions
- Development to counter alienation
- Academic Cleansing
- Breaking vicious cycle of alienation & support for separatists
- Choke funding (curbing black money, detection & tracking)

HYBRID WARFARE

- It generally refers to use of unconventional methods as a part of multi-domain warfighting approach. These methods aim to disrupt and disable an opponent's actions with or without engaging in open hostilities.
- Domains of hybrid warfare
  - Political Warfare- eg- alleged Russian interference in US elections.
  - Technological Warfare- Using technological capabilities to inflict harm
  - Military Warfare- Includes military actions (improvised explosives, guerrilla warfare, etc)
  - Economic warfare- To weaken economy by disrupting supply chains, introduction of counterfeit currency, etc.
  - Social Warfare- Exploiting already prevalent social issues and vulnerabilities via propaganda, provocative messaging, etc.
- Hybrid terrorists are individuals who are not classified as ultras but are radicalized enough to carry out a terror attack and return to normal life. They are also known as "sleeper cells/ Boys next door"

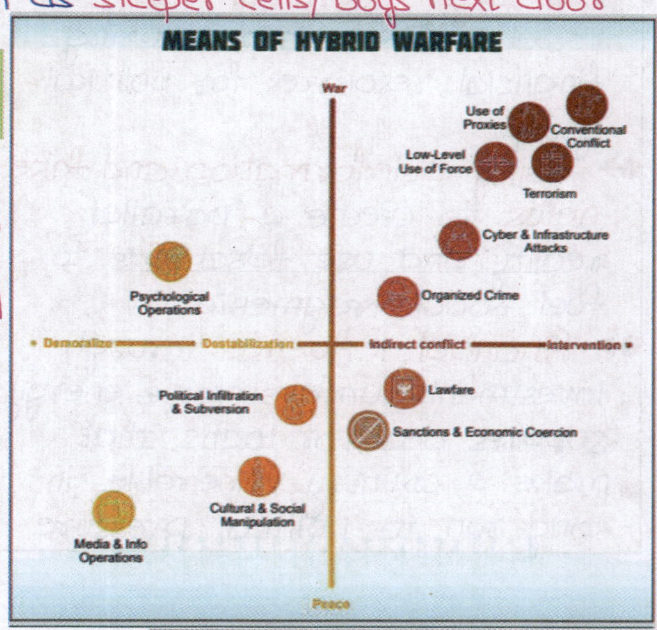

Reasons for Growing Adoption of Hybrid Warfare

- Hybrid warfare uses a wider set of military, political, economic, civilian and informational instruments which are usually overlooked in traditional threat assessments
- It targets highly vulnerable areas having high potential for damage
- It can involve state actors, non-state actors or both indulging in different roles but in a synchronised manner
- Scale and target of attack can be precisely controlled by staying below certain detection and response thresholds, including international legal thresholds
- A hybrid warfare campaign may not be discovered until it is already well underway

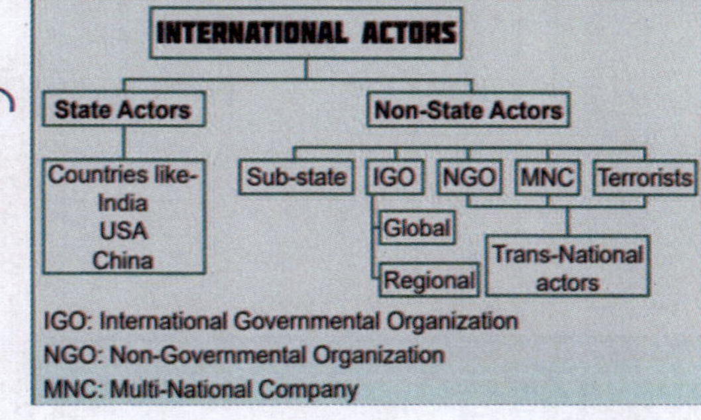

HYBRID WARFARE - A POTENTIAL ISSUE FOR INDIA	WAY FORWARD
New forms of terrorist attacks such as 'lone-wolf' attacks, creation of 'sleeper cells' and emergence of hybrid militants Cyber attacks • Privacy and personal theft • Insecure framework of mobile applications • Cyber espionage issues from Pakistan and China • Vulnerabilities to intellectual property Interference in electoral processes with techniques like campaigning through media and social networks and securing financial resources for political group. Using disinformation and fake news to create a parallel reality and use falsehoods to fuel social fragmentation Financial influence through investments, unfavourable energy supplies deals or loans that make a country vulnerable in long run to political pressure	Systematic and synchronised real time response • Institutional mechanism to ensure nimble response • Effective inter-domain coordination • Use of intelligence tools like Real Time Situational Awareness (RTSA) Institutional Measures • Conduct a self assessment of critical functions and vulnerabilities • Enhance traditional threat assessment activity Strengthening the safety of digital ecosystem to make it more secure and robust Strengthening our democracy from within- • Inclusion of civil society institutions • Raise media literacy by investing in journalism Developing international cooperation • Developing clear definitions, protocols • Institutionalising intervention stages and methods • Mainstreaming and integrating the issue of hybrid warfare in the prevalent security dialogues

PYQs Corner

(Write the Answer and Get Free Evaluation)

1. Winning of 'Hearts and Minds' in terrorism-affected areas is an essential step in restoring the trust of the population. Discuss the measures adopted by the Government in this respect as part of the conflict resolution in Jammu and Kashmir. [150 Words] [10 Marks] **[2023]**

2. Naxalism is a social, economic and developmental issue manifesting as a violent internal security threat. In this context, discuss the emerging issues gets a multilayered strategy to tackle the menace of Naxalism. [250 words] [15 Marks] **[2022]**

3. What are the sound determinants of left-wing extremism in Eastern part of India? What strategy should Government of India, civil administration and security forces adopt to counter the threat in the affected areas? [250 Words] [15 Marks] **[2020]**

4. The banning of 'Jammat-e-Islami' in Jammu and Kashmir brought into focus the role of over-ground workers (OGWs) in assisting terrorist organizations. Examine the role played by OGWs in assisting terrorist organizations in insurgency affected areas. Discuss measures to neutralize influence of OGWs. [150 Words] [10 Marks] **[2019]**

5. Left Wing Extremism (LWE) is showing a downward trend, but still affects many parts of the country. Briefly explain the Government of India's approach to counter the challenges posed by LWE. [150 Words] [10 Marks] **[2018]**

6. The north-eastern region of India has been infested with insurgency for a very long time. Analyze the major reasons for the survival of armed insurgency in this region. [150 Words] [10 Marks]**[2017]**

7. The persisting drives of the government for development of large industries in backward areas have resulted in isolating the tribal population and the farmers who face multiple displacements. With Malkangiri and Naxalbari foci, discuss the corrective strategies needed to win the Left-Wing Extremism (LWE) doctrine affected citizens back into mainstream of social and economic growth. [200 Words] [12.5 Marks] **[2015]**

8. "The diverse nature of India as a multi-religious and multi-ethnic society is not immune to the impact of radicalism which is seen in her neighborhood? Discuss along with strategies to be adopted to counter this environment. [200 Words] [12.5 Marks] **[2014]**

9. Article 244 of the Indian Constitution relates to administration of schedules area and tribal areas. Analyse the impact of non-implementation of the provisions of the Fifth schedule on the growth of Left-Wing extremism. [200 Words] [10 Marks] **[2013]**

CHAPTER 04

Terrorism

TERRORISM

- Terrorism is the use of violence and intimidation in the pursuit of political aims.
- It is a global phenomenon that affects people from all walks of life, regardless of their nationality, religion or ethnicity.
- India and terrorism
  - → India ranks 14th in Global Terrorism Index (GTI) 2024 report (published by Institute for Economics & Peace
  - → India is among top ten countries with largest decrease in deaths from terrorism
    49 deaths (2020-21) ⟶ 45 deaths (2021-22) ⟶ 18 deaths (2022-23)
  - → However South Asia remains most impacted region by terrorism

Timeline of Terrorist Activities in India

- Partition of India and Pakistan in 1947
- **1980s - 1990s** Rise of Sikh separatism in Punjab
  eg- Operation Bluestar in 1984 at Golden Temple launched to combat separatism
- **1990s onwards** Insurgency in Jammu and Kashmir by Pakistan backed militant groups.
  eg- Kashmiri Pandit exodus
- **1900s onwards** Naxalite movement (Maoist insurgency) in Central and Eastern India, targeting government and security forces.

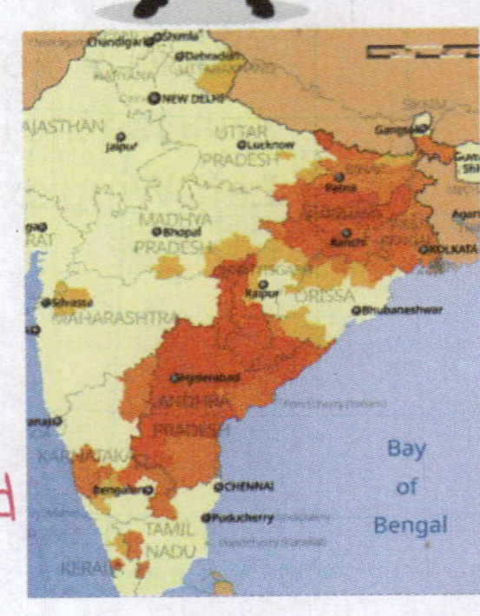

2000s Increased focus on attacks targeting civilian in major cities like 2008 Mumbai attacks by lashkar-e-Taiba

2010s- 2020s

- **Shifting tactics-** Rise in low intensity blasts and targeted killings. eg-Pathankot Air force Station attack in 2016.
- **Emerging Threats-** Rise of ISIS → homegrown radicalisation. eg- in 2021, a Kerala based ISIS module was busted

Recent attacks

June 2024- Reasi attack of Hindu pilgrims bus (Jammu district)

VARIANTS OF TERRORISM (2nd ARC)

Ethno-Nationalist Terrorism- Violence by a subnational ethnic group to achieve goals like separation or dominance (eg-Sri lankan Tamil nationalists, North East Indian insurgents)

Religious Terrorism- Violence motivated by religious beliefs, often seen as religious duty. (eg- The Afghan Taliban)

State sponsored Terrorism- It involves using of one country's soil to create terror in neighbouring countries (eg- proxy war in Kashmir)

Lone - Wolf Terrorism- Terrorist acts commited by single individual acting alone (eg- beheading of Tailor in Udaipur, 2022)

Narco-Terrorism- Drug traffickers using violence to influence governments (eg- golden crescent/triangle)

Ideology oriented Terrorism

- **Left wing extremism-** Violent opposition to ruling class, often inspired by Marxism (eg- Maoist groups)
- **Right wing terrorism-** Violence by groups seeking to maintain or restore a perceived ideal past, often involving ultranationalism or white supremacy. (eg- Malegaon Blasts, 2008)

Factors Facilitating Cross-Border Terrorism

Geography
- Porous Borders- Easy to cross (eg-Bangladesh, Pakistan, Myanmar)
- Complex Terrain- Mountains, desert hinder border security.

Administration
- Lack of strategy- Inefficient border management
- Internal Support- Locals aiding incursions (transport, hiding)
- Corruption- Bribed officials enabling illegal entry.

Foreign Support
- Non-State Actors- Militants receiving aid.
- ISI (Inter-Services Intelligence) sponsors and finances terrorism (sources- drugs, illicit operations, contributions)

Hawala Transactions
Indirect fundings for groups (JeM, LeT, HM); donations from Islamic countries + Drug trafficking + fake Indian currency notes

Modern Terror Landscape

- Bioterrorism- Covid-19 pandemic exposed devastating potential of biological agents as weapons
- Drone Warfare- Affordable, advanced drones pose a new threat for attacks, intelligence gathering and weapon delivery (eg- 2021 Jammu Air force station attack)
- Safe Havens- Unstable regions in Africa and Middle-east offer safe havens for terrorist to train, plan and launch attacks across borders
- Terror Crime Nexus between terrorists and organised crime is increasing - combining finances (cryptocurrency), networks (drug trafficking) and expertise (weapons, human trafficking) for greater impact. eg- drug supplies in Punjab.
- Tech Savvy Terror like encrypted communication and dark web for recruitment, radicalisation, planning and execution.
- CBRN Threats- Terror groups may acquire capability to use chemical, biological, radiological or nuclear (CBRN) materials

Reason for the Spread of Terrorism

01 Grievance and oppression- When people feel their government is unfair or oppressive, they may resort to violence to achieve change. (Naxalite movements in India)

02 Poverty- Limited economic options in border regions (eg-Jammu and Kashmir)

03 **Psychological Motivations**- Some terrorists act out of personal hatred, a desire for power or a troubled mental state. eg- revenge attacks - 2014 Bangalore blast

04 **Ideological fanatism**- Terrorist organisations like Indian Mujahideen, etc. are driven by strong ideologies that promotes violence for their cause.

05 **Accessibility of Terror**- Low cost attacks with easy to obtain explosives. eg- 2017 Jaipur blasts

06 **Post conflict Backlash**- After peace agreements, extremists may resist, compromise and incite violence to regain power. eg- North-east insurgency.

07 **Resource Control**- Terrorist violence can be used to influence resource allocation and decision making. eg- pipeline attacks in Northeast India.

ROLE OF TECHNOLOGY IN AMPLIFYING TERRORISM

Social Media: Estimates suggests that in 2016, social media platforms played a role in 90% of radicalisation cases

3D Printing: Use of online manuals and a 3D printer to print parts of gun

Autonomous vehicles: Turning vehicles into a remote controlled weapon

Drones: Using drones for intelligence, surveillance and reconnaissance missions and conducting attacks with drones carrying explosives

Artificial Intelligence(AI): Will enhance cyberattacks and digital disinformation campaigns and can target vulnerable youth in many new ways

The Metaverse: Extremists will be able to do preemptive reconnaissance missions in virtual world before engaging in physical attacks

Terrorism Emerging as a Competitive Industry

- **Terror groups fight for funding** (extortion, smuggling), recruits (online propaganda, exploiting grievances) and territory (control of training, planning)
  - This competition can lead to infighting between groups and brutal attacks to grab headlines and intimidate the public.
- **Resource Wars**- Groups like Lashkar-e-Taiba fight for funding (drugs, counterfeiting) and recruits (unemployed youth in Kashmir) to survive
- **Ideological Clashes**- Sectarian tensions and rivalries between groups fuel violence, with each vying of dominance.
- **Media Spectacle**- 26/11 Mumbai or Pulwama aim to grab headlines, attract recruits and intimidate the public.
- **Territorial Control**- Group struggle for strategic expansion

India's Doctrine to Tackle Terrorism

- Malayan Doctrine
- Good Grievance Doctrine
- Counter Proxy War

01 Malayan Doctrine (Adapted for India)

- **Agencies Involved**- Army, Military Intelligence (MI), National Security Guard (NSG), Research and Analysis Wing (RAW), Intelligence Bureau (IB)
- **Process**
  - Identify and Map- MI locates the terrorist-affected area and identifies front organisations creating "terrorism map"
  - Neutralise- Army and NSG conduct counter terrorism operations to neutralise threats.
  - Governance and Rehabilitation- Once the area is free of Over Ground Workers (OGW) supporting terrorists, it's handed over to civilian authorities to promote participatory democracy.
  - Monitoring- IB monitors to ensure no OGWs re-emerge.

02 Good Grievance Doctrine

- **Infiltration and Information Gathering**- IB agents infiltrate sensitive communal areas to gather information about potential riots arising from grievances.
- **Grievance Resolution**- IB identifies grievances and reports them to political executive for resolution, aiming to prevent riots.

03 Counter Proxy War

- **Identify Proxy**- RAW identifies foreign states attempting to create proxy wars within India.
- **Counter Strategy**- India may try to influence existing proxy groups within the adversary state by sympathising with their ideology or offering financial support.

Institutional framework to deal with Terrorism

Legislative Measures

01 **Unlawful Activities (Prevention) Act (UAPA), 1967**- To provide for more effective prevention of certain unlawful activities of individuals and associations, for dealing with terrorist activities and for dealing with activities directed against integrity and sovereignty of India.

Key Provisions of UAPA

- Cognizable offences- Arrests can be made without a warrant
- Penalty- Death or life imprisonment and liable to a fine if the act results in death

- Unlawful Association
  - Declaration by Centre through official gazette notification
  - Investigation conducted by State Police and NIA
  - Other Powers → Prohibit use of funds of unlawful association
    → Notify places used for the purposes of an unlawful association
- Terrorist Act - Act intended to threaten India's unity, integrity, security or sovereignty or to strike terror among people in India or any foreign country.
  - Forfeiture of Proceeds - Investigating officers can forfeit proceeds of terrorism with prior approval of the designated authority

Advantages of UAPA Amendment Act, 2019

- Individual Designation as Terrorists - Previously, only organisations could be labelled 'terrorists'. Now, it empowers government to designate individuals involved in terrorism.
- Seizure of Property with oversight - Prior approval of Director-General of Police for seizing terrorism linked properties.
- Definition of Terrorist Acts - It encompass acts covered by nine international treaties on terrorism, broadening the scope to include international terrorist activities

Concerns Associated with UAPA Amendment

- Low convictions (3% in 2018-2020) raise question about effectiveness of UAPA
- UAPA use in tribal and social media activism cases
- Strict UAPA bail burdens the accused to prove innocence, reversing the presumption of innocence.
- Broad government discretion (secret witnesses, closed hearings) raises transparency and due process concerns.
- UAPA allows detention without charges (up to 180 days), potentially violating fundamental rights.
- Restricts freedom - Parliament can restrict rights and freedoms of citizens to protect 'the sovereignty and integrity of India.'

Way forward

- Safeguards against misuse - Ensure due process during investigations
- Central Evidence Collection Agency - Establish a central agency to oversee evidence collection for UAPA cases, especially those with cross-border connections.
- Protect Political Dissent - Enact legislation to safeguard political dissent

- Police Reforms- Prioritize police reforms including sensitization training and reducing arbitrary powers
- Compensation for wrongly detained- Provide compensation to individuals proven innocent after UAPA detention.

02 National Investigation Agency (NIA) Act, 2008

It establishes National Investigation Agency (NIA) to address various aspects related to terrorism and security

➤ Role of NIA in Anti-Terrorism Efforts

- Cooperation with states- Assist all states and other investigating agencies in terrorist case investigations.
- Effective and Speedy Trials- Achieved an overall conviction rate of 94% in 2022.
- Data Collection- Tasked with creating a national database in seven areas → narcotics, hawala transactions, arms struggling, counterfeit currencies, bomb blast, terror funding, terrorism.
- In-depth Professional Investigation- Conducts thorough investigations in cases where gathering evidence is challenging
- Alert and Responsive Measures- NIA has registered multiple cases against overground workers in Jammu and Kashmir, effectively dismantling their sleeper cells.

Institutions

→ National Security Council (NSC)- Role in coordinating counterterrorism efforts across various ministries and agencies

→ National Security Guard (NSG)/Black cats- Elite force specialising in counter-terrorism and anti-hijacking operations (2008 Mumbai attacks)

→ Anti-Terrorism Squad (ATS)- focus on preventing terrorism, investigating cases and dismantling terror networks. eg- ATS units exists in several police agencies → Maharashtra, Gujarat, Kerala, Tamil Nadu, etc.

→ Multi Agency Centre (MAC)- It is common counter terrorism grid under the Intelligence Bureau (IB) that was made operational in 2001- post Kargil War.

Aim- Sharing intelligence inputs among various agencies.

→ National Intelligence Grid (NATGRID)- Counter terrorism program using Big Data and analytics to analyse vast amount of data from various intelligence and enforcement agencies.

Aim- To track suspected terrorists and prevent attacks

→ Ministry of Home Affairs (MHA)- Counterterrorism and counter-radicalisation division and Cyber and Security division in MHA → Issues relating to terrorism, counter radicalisation, cyber security, etc.

Global Initiatives to Counter Terrorism

- Comprehensive Convention on International Terrorism (CCIT)- Intends to criminalise a number of terrorism related activities. India proposed this convention
- United Nations Global Counter Terrorism Strategy (GCTS)- To improve international cooperation on terrorism.
- Global Counterterrorism forum (GCTF)- Informal group to discuss counterterrorism
- United Nations Countering Terrorist Travel Programme- Helps countries improve their ability to detect and stop terrorists from traveling.

Reasons for Non-Adoption of CCIT by UN

- **Definitional Clash:** India pushes for a broad definition of terrorism (including state actors) while some oppose (e.g., excluding "legitimate" military actions).
- **Exclusion Woes:** Some countries (OIC) seek exemptions for national liberation movements (double standard concerns for India).
- **Geopolitical Baggage:** Regional tensions (e.g., India-Pakistan) and historical mistrust complicate negotiations.
- **Evolving Threats:** Lone wolf attacks and online radicalization weren't major considerations when the CCIT was drafted.
- **Limited Leverage:** India may lack the political clout to overcome opposition from larger power blocs.
- **Shifting Priorities:** Global crises and emerging threats like climate change.

- Financial Action Task force (FATF)- Sets international standards for fighting money laundering and terrorist financing
- SCO Regional Anti-Terrorist Structure (RATS)- To improve cooperation on counterterrorism among member states
- Christchurch Call to Action- To eliminate terrorist and violent extremist content online.

Indian Approach of Countering Terrorism

- Intelligence Gathering and analysis- Disrupt plots, identify threats eg- IB preventing 2012 Delhi bombings
- Law Enforcement and investigations- Ensure prosecution, deter future attacks. eg- NIA investigating Pulwama attacks
- Border and Transportation Security- Prevent infiltration, movement of weapons. eg- BSF patrolling borders, coastal radars
- Counter-Radicalisation and Community Engagement- Ministry of Minority Affairs promoting interfaith dialogue
- Military Actions and Operations- Neutralise terror groups, dismantle infrastructure. eg- surgical strikes across LOC
- Financial and Economic Measures- Cripple terrorist financing. eg- UAPA freezing assets, FATF membership

- Diplomacy and Internation Cooperation- Share intelligence, dismantle global networks. eg- SCO, RATS, etc
- Legal frameworks and Judicial Cooperation- Effective prosecution, uphold human rights. eg-NSA for preventive detention, judicial oversight
- Hot Pursuits and Surgical Strikes- Decisive action against terrorists eg- Balakot air strikes across LOC in 2019

Challenges in India's Counter-Terrorism Response

01 Political and Policy level Constraints

- Legal Constraints- Schedule 7 of constitution restricts central government intervention in state police matters related to terrorism.
- Hierarchical Confusion- Involvement of multiple entities (PMO, Ministries, NSA) leads to communication breakdowns and delays.
- Coordination Issues- Lack of coordination between military, state police and paramilitary forces creates confusion and hinders effectiveness
- Limited Accountability- Lack of transparency in intelligence agencies operations and parliamentary oversight reduces accountability.
- Overlapping Mandates- Duplication of efforts and inter agency competition occur due to overlapping mandates. eg- RAW and IB in organised crime.

02 Intelligence failures

- Substandard Surveillance- Defecient infrastructure and expertise lead to inadequate border surveillance, enabling terrorist activity.
- Incomplete Intelligence- Information gathering is often delayed or incomplete hindering accurate threat assessment. eg- Mumbai attacks
- Data Credibility- Delays in acting on intelligence due to doubts about its credibility (eg- Pathankot airbase attacks) hampers effectiveness
- Database Gaps- The absence of a comprehensive national database of suspected individuals hinders investigations (eg- NATGRID initiative stalled)

03 Other Challenges

- Internal Conflicts- India's ongoing internal conflicts (Naga insurgency, Kashmir militancy) expose weakness
- Limited International Collaboration hinders information and evidence sharing and extraction of suspects.
- Workforce Issues- A chronic shortage of specialised personnel and inefficient use of existing plagued intelligence agencies
- Legal Delays- Delays and complexities in legal and judicial system can hamper effective prosecution

- **Skilled Personnel Shortage**- Poor recruitment practices and an under-developed education system hinder the hiring of qualified language specialists and technical experts.

Pathways for India's Counter Terrorism Response

Domestic Measures

- **Strengthen Existing Institutions**- Invest in training, resources and technology for police, intelligence agencies and border security forces
- Identify Capacity Gaps in each state's counterterrorism infrastructure
- Anticipation of Threats in advance to prevent and mitigate possible security breaches
- Multi-agency Cooperation for greater sharing of intelligence among agencies
- **Madhukar Gupta Committee (2016)**- Strengthening of borders through construction of border protection grids.
- Border Management Reform to improve detection and prevention of terrorist infiltration.

  Including gender perspective in counter terrorism
- Protect human rights and fundamental freedoms in the context of counter terrorism measures
- Raising public awareness about the threat of terrorism and about universal counterterrorism instruments.

Global Efforts

- Push for Universal Definition of Terrorism and establishment of a permanent sectariat to combat terrorism at international level.
- **No Money for Terror**- Curbing terror financing by bringing together banks and governments globally, utilises routes such as FATF, UNCAC and UNODC.
- **Safe Internet Use**- Actions for deradicalisation and ensure safe usage of internet and social media by flagging extremist content
- **Indian Ocean Region Security**- Adopt a collaborative approach with member countries for security, exploring an arc of surveillance involving Sri Lanka, Maldives and India.
- **UN Coordination**- Enhance collaboration within UN system for a unified global approach to countering terrorism.

TERROR FUNDING/TERROR FINANCING

Terrorism financing is act of providing financial support to terrorists or terrorist organisations to enable them to carry out terrorist acts or to benefit any terrorist or terrorist organisation.

NEED OF TERROR FUNDING

- **Spreading propaganda:** Social media, magazines (ISIS magazine Dabiq), websites
- **Planning attacks:** Surveillance, fake IDs(26/11 Mumbai attackers), weapons, bombs(IEDs used in Pulwama)
- **Training fighters:** weapon training, ideology indoctrination (Al Shabaad training camps)
- **Paying members:** Salaries for fighters and operatives, family support (Al-Qaeda Network)
- **Social services** like healthcare, education and food assistance (Hamas in Gaza)

Aim- To conceal both financing and nature of financed activity.

Sources of Terror financing

SOURCES: Drugs and smuggling; Donations; State sponsored terrorism; Misused charities (Fake NGOs); Extortion; Crowd funding

- Donations- Al Qaeda received funding from wealthy individuals like Osama Bin Laden
- Misused Charities (fake NGOs)- FATF identified cases where fake NGOs were created to funnel donations to terrorists.
- Drugs and smuggling- Taliban benefits from drug trafficking in Afghanistan
- Extortion- Hamas extorts businesses in Gaza to fund its activities
- Self--funding- Small scale attacks might be funded by robberies or credit card fraud.
- State Sponsors- Iran is accused of supporting Hezbollah
- Social Media- ISIS used social media to spread propaganda and solicit donations
- Crowdfunding- fake online fundraising campaigns can be used to mask terror funding
- Virtual Currencies- Anonymity of Bitcoin makes it attractive for financing
- Natural Resources- ISIS profited from oil smuggling in Iran, Syria.
- Counterfeiting of Indian Currency to spread terrorism and hurt India's economy.

Challenges in Countering Terror financing in India

01 Internal Challenges

- Rapid evolution (online fundraising)- Terror groups like ISIS use online platforms to raise funds and radicalize recruits, demanding constant adaptation.

- Legislation Delays can slow down the passage and implementation of effective anti-terror financing legislation
- Crime Terror Link (Northeast India)- The link between organised crime, local politics and terror financing in some regions.
- Resource Constraints- Limited manpower and potential corruption within enforcement agencies can hinder effective action
- Domestic Implementation (Remote Areas)- India's vast landscape makes enforcing financial regulations challenging, especially in remote areas.

02 External Threats

- Cross Border Financing- India faces a significant threat from Pakistan, accused of financing terror groups in Kashmir (eg- Pulwama attack)
- Money Laundering- Weak regulations in neighbouring countries can make laundering terror funds easier (eg- drug trafficking or extortion money)

03 Negligence at Global level

- Political Tensions- Sharing information with Pakistan on terror financing is limited due to ongoing political disputes
- Suspicious Activity- Massive volume of daily cash-based transactions in border areas makes identifying suspicious activity difficult

International Efforts to Curb Terror financing

01 Financial Action Task force (FATF)- Sets international standards (FATF recommendations) for countries to prevent money laundering and terrorist financing.

02 Financial Intelligence Units (FIUs)- National agencies analyse suspicious financial transactions and share information with domestic and international partners (Egmont Group facilitates co-operation)

03 UN Counter Terrorism Committee (CTC)- Monitors compliance with UN Resolution 1373 (2001) which requires countries to combat terror financing.

04 UN Office of Counter Terrorism (UNOCT)- Coordinates global counter-terrorism efforts (leadership, collaboration, capacity building for member states)

05 International Convention (1999)- Criminalizes financing of terrorism and facilitates international cooperation in investigations and prosecutions (188 states signed)

06 No Money for Terror (NMFT)- focusses on:

- Criminalizing terror financing (even without specific attack link)
- Improve traceability of financial flows (cash, anonymous payments)
- Implementing FATF standards for non-profit organisations (prevent misuse, safeguard legitimate activities)

India's fight Against Terror financing

- **Strengthened Laws (2019 UAPA Amendment)**- To criminalise activities like counterfeiting Indian currency (Tactic for terror funding)
- **Centralised Monitoring**- Financial Intelligence Unit-India (FIU-IND) is central agency responsible for analysing financial transactions reported by banks and other financial institutions
- **Combating financing of Terrorism (CFT)** under MHA to collaborate with Central Intelligence/Enforcement Agencies and State Law Enforcement Agencies to combat terror funding.
- **Specialised investigation**- NIA established dedicated Terror Funding and Fake Currency (TFFC) Cell in 2018
- **Police Training (Maharashtra Initiative)**- focussed on identifying and combating terror financing. This program has been adopted by other states as well
- **FICN Coordination Group (FCORD) under MHA** facilitates the sharing of intelligence and information on terror financing activities between central agencies.
- In 2016, Operation fake note was launched as a nationwide crackdown on counterfeit currency.
- **International Cooperation (Nepal Police Training)**- focus on identifying and combating smuggling and counterfeiting of Indian currency.
- **Border Security (increased patrolling)** along international borders to disrupt smuggling activities that could be linked to terror financing.

6 Pillars of India's strategy against the financing of terrorism

1. Strengthening the Legislative and Technological Framework
2. Creation of a Comprehensive Monitoring Framework
3. Actionable intelligence sharing mechanism and strengthening of the investigation and police operations
4. Provision for confiscation of property
5. Prevent misuse of legal entities and new technologies
6. Establishing international cooperation and coordination

Pathways to Curb Terror financing in India

- Cross Border Sharing of Data - Enhance information sharing with Pakistan and Bangladesh to disrupt cross-border smuggling and fake currency.
- Virtual Currency Monitoring - Increase monitoring of online fundraising platforms and track transactions involving Bitcoin used for terror financing
- Regulated NGOs (Targeted Audits) - Conduct risk based audits of NGOs, especially in sensitive areas, to prevent misuse for terror financing.
- Hawala Networks Regulation - Develop a framework to monitor and disrupt informal money transfer systems (Hawala) exploited by terror groups.
- Invest in advanced technology (thermal imaging, drones) to strengthen border security and prevent smuggling of goods financing terror
- De-radicalization - Develops program to counter extremist narratives that attracts potential terror recruits.
- Inter-agency Coordination for information sharing on terror financing activities between agencies for real time response.

LONE WOLF TERRORISM

Lone wolf terrorism refers to violent terror attacks carried out by extremist individuals acting on their radicalized beliefs. The unpredictable nature of lone wolf attacks makes them a serious threat to security.

Motive
- Inspired by - specific terrorist organisation or ideology
- Influenced by - particular social atmosphere that fosters extremist views.

India's Vulnerability to Lone Wolf Attacks

01. Possibility of Pakistan using it as tool to advance its state-sponsored terrorism against India.
02. Group like ISIS visualise India's secular, democratic and open social fabric as threat to their Islamic Caliphate
03. Heavy concentration of people in public areas offer a large number of potential targets.

Lone wolf attacks activity range
- Threatening and intimidating people
- Indiscriminate shootings
- Vehicle ramming
- Stabbing
- Suicide Bombings

04 A fast growing population, especially youth with access to mass media and social media, opens limitless avenues of unrestrained radical propaganda.

05 Level of intolerance- While the popular discourse seem to suggest an increasing level of intolerance, the reality is quite different.

06 Increasing Propaganda especially among minorities and weaker groups who run the risk of falling prey to fear-mongering.

Challenges to Lone Wolf Terrorism

- **Unpredictability-** Lone wolves operate independently, making it difficult for counter-terrorism agencies to detect and prevent attacks. (eg- 2022 Udaipur killings)
- **Online Radicalization-** The internet provides anonymity for communication and access to extremist propoganda, facilitating radicalization. eg- Jamia Millia Islamia shooting in 2019.
- **Low Barrier to Entry-** Lone wolf attacks often require minimal resources and planning, making them easier to carry out compared to complex coordinated attacks. eg- Pulwama attack, 2019.
- **Copycat Effect-** Successful lone wolf attacks can inspire copycat attacks, creating a ripple effect of violence. eg- Kerala Blast 2021 inspired from Sri lanka attack.
- **Role Models-** Lone wolves can become role models for vulnerable individuals, further propogating extremist ideologies. eg- Burhan Wani

Therats associated with Lone Wolf Attacks

- **Hard to distinguis from internet** banter between those extremists who intend to commit attacks and those who simply express radical beliefs
- **Hurdle in Profiling** As lone wolf terrorists comprise a wide variety of violent extremists.
- **Providing a template** to violence-prone misfits who might otherwise not have octed.
- **Hard to detect and prevent** As individual is not communicating his plans and intentions to others.

Steps Taken by India to Combat Lone Wolves

- Limited Weapon Access- Unlike the US, India's stricter gun laws make obtaining firearms a hurdle.
- Countering Online Radicalization to identify individuals susceptible to extremist content.
- De-radicalization Programs- State run initiatives like Kerala's Operation Pigeon offer counselling to potentially vulnerable individuals.
- Improved intelligence- Enhanced information sharing between agencies aims to detect suspicious activities before attacks
- Community Outreach- Programs promote social inclusion and interfaith dialogue to address alienation (Operation Sadbhavana (goodwill) by Indian Army in Jammu and Kashmir)

Future Pathways

- **Diverse Policy Measures**
  - Local Law Enforcement Training to handle potential lone wolf attacks
  - Establish National Counterterrorism Doctrine for combating terrorism
  - Welfare Policies to address different motivations and methods used by lone wolves. eg- programs to address poverty and marginalisation
- **Capacity Building**
  - Enhance technical intelligence capabilities, eg-social media monitoring
  - Develop contingency plans for rapid response to lone wolf attacks.
  - Utilize human intelligence and build strong ties with communities and leaders.
- **De-radicalization and counter-radicalization**
  - Sensitive policing (eg- friend officers in Maharashtra)
  - Foster community engagement to counter extremist narratives Provide access to professional counselors and psychologists for vulnerable individuals.
- **Strengthening International Cooperation** to disrupt terror financing networks
- **Big Data Analytics**- Utilize big data to identify potential recruits, their networks and sources of funding and leadership disrupting the roots of radicalization.

PYQs Corner

(Write the Answer and Get Free Evaluation)

1. Give out the major sources of terror funding in India and the efforts being made to curtail these sources. In the light of this, also discuss the aim and objective of the No Money for Terror (NMFT Conference recently held at New Delhi in November 2022. [250 Words] [15 Marks] **[2023]**

2. Analyse the complexity and intensity of terrorism, its causes, linkages and obnoxious nexus. Also suggest measures required to be taken to eradicate the menace of terrorism. [250 Words] [15 Marks] **[2021]**

3. The scourge of terrorism is a grave challenge to national security. What solutions do you suggest to curb the growing menace? What are the major sources of terrorist funding? [250 Words] [15 Marks] **[2017]**

4. Terrorism is emerging as a competitive industry over the last few decades. Analyse the above statement [200 Words] [12.5 Marks] **[2016]**

CHAPTER 05

Organised Crime

- Organised crime refers to illegal activities carried out by groups or networks working together.
- Organised Crime Group- Organised criminals that work together for the duration of a particular criminal activity or activities.
- These activities often include- violence, corruption and related actions to gain financial or material benefits
- Transnational Organized Crime (TOC) occurs when these activities or groups operate in multiple countries. United Nations Convention against Transnational Organised Crime (UNTOC) define it as:

01 **Multiple States Involved**- Crime is committed in more than one country. (eg- D-Company of Mumbai)

02 **Planning Across Borders**- A substantial part of planning, preparation or control of crime occurs in a different country than where it is committed (eg- Jaish-e-Mohammed)

03 **Organised Crime Groups**- The crime is committed by criminal organisation that operates in different countries (eg- Al-Qaeda)

04 **Significant Cross Border Impacts**- Crime is committed in one country but has substantial negative effects on other countries.

CHARACTERISTICS

- **Built to Last**- Survive leadership changes and survive on long term
- **Hierarchical Structure**- Clear division of power and responsibility
- **Selective Membership**- Based on shared traits and strict loyalty requirements
- **Profit Driven Crime**- Reliant on continuous illegal activities
- **Violence and Intimidation**- Used for control and protection
- **Power and Profit**- Seek both wealth and political influence through corruption

DIFFERENT FORMS OF ORGANISED CRIME

Drug Trafficking- Most lucrative form. Estimated annual value ~ USD 650 billion

Money Laundering- Disguising financial gains from illegal activities to make them appear legal. Estimated annual value ~ USD 800 billion to 2 trillion

Human Trafficking- Exploiting people for forced labor or sex. Estimated annual profits ~ USD 150 billion with 25 million victims worldwide

Illicit firearms trafficking- Estimated annual value- USD 170 million to USD 320 million

Smuggling- India's vast coastline and open borders make it susceptible to large scale smuggling. In 2009, generated estimate is USD 6.6 billion

Trafficking in natural resources like mineral, wildlife, timber. Sale of elephant ivory, rhino horn and tiger parts alone was worth USD 75 million in 2010

Fraudulent Medicines- Selling fake or diverted medicines that can harm people.

Cybercrime and identity theft- Stealing personal data online for financial gain.

Framework for Combating Organised Crime in India

- IPC- Criminal Conspiracy provisions (Section 120A) penalize planning or conspiring for illegal acts.
- State Specific Laws- Maharashtra Control of Organised Crime Act (MCOCA)
- National Security Act allows preventive detention for threats to national security.
- Specific Crimes
  - UAPA (1967)- Empowers authorities to address threats like terrorism potentially linked to organise crime.
  - NDPS Act (1988)- Target drug trafficking
  - FEMA (2000)- Targets illegal financial activities
  - PMLA (2002)- Targets money laundering as key funding source for organised crime.
- International Cooperation
  - UNSC Resolution 2482- To address links between terrorism and organised crime
  - UNTOC (2000)- Global agreement against transnational organised crime

Reason for India's vulnerability to Organised Crime

01 Socio-economic and Political factors

- **Socioeconomic Disparity**- Poverty and wealth inequality create breeding ground for recruitment (eg- red sandalwood smuggling)
- **Social and Ethnic Divisions**- Existing divisions are exploited for recruitment and violence (eg- Kuki-Meitei conflict)
- **High Demand for Illegal Goods**- Drug abuse and unregulated markets creates lucrative market (eg- ivory demand)
- **Government Policy and Unmet Demands**- Restrictive policies create black markets. (eg- IPL betting scandal)
- **Politicisation of Crime**- Gangs influence politics and politicians seek power through funding. (eg- Atiq Ahmed in UP)

02 Law Enforcement Challenges

- **No Specific Law**- India lacks a comprehensive law to tackle organised crime, relying on scattered provisions across IPC and other laws.
- **Anonymity of Leadership**- Hierarchical structures and frequent leadership changes make it difficult to identify and target key figures
- **Limited Resources**- Many states struggle to invest sufficient resources in law enforcement, hindering their ability to combat organised crime effectively (eg- limitations of CBI)
- **Silos in Law Enforcement**- Limited cooperation between agencies hinders information sharing and coordinated action (eg- 2008 Mumbai attacks)
- **Challenges in Gathering Evidence**- Hierarchical structures make evidence collection difficult.
- **Poor Criminal Justice System**- A backlog of millions of pending cases, coupled with delays and potentially weak investigations allow organised crime to exploit the system.

03 Technological Advancements- Organised crime utilises technology for illicit activities (eg- cybercrime)

04 Corruption- Officials are bribed to turn a blind eye, allowing crime to flourish (eg- mining mafia)

05 Cross-Border Challenges-

- **No Central Agency**- The absence of a central agency to coordinate with state agencies creates gaps in national efforts against organise crimes.
- **Transnational Presence**- Crimes planned outside India and safe havens from criminals in neighbouring countries with challenging terrain further complicate law enforcement efforts.

Relationship Between Organised Crime and Terrorism

DIFFERENCES

Basis	Organised Crime	Terrorism
About	• Goal- Profit through illegal activities. No ideology or political agenda. • Violence- Minimised, used mainly for expansion of influence	• Goal- Create violence to achieve a political or ideological aim
Nexus Building	• Purpose- Avoid law enforcement • Method- Build networks with corrupt officials for protection	• Avoids- Nexus building to maintain surprise. • Risk- Exposure of plans with connections
Popularity	Stay out of media to operate secretly	Crave media attention and sensationalize their acts to spread fear
Economic Regimes	Flourishing economies for more illicit profit (eg- Russia, South Africa, India)	• Weak or unstable regimes with lawlessness (eg- Syria) • Dislike- Strong, stable regimes • Exploitation- Take advantage of power vacuums to launch attacks (eg- potential for Taliban controlled Afghanistan to become a greeding ground for terrorism)

INTERDEPENDENCE

Financial Inter-dependence	• Organised Crime provides crucial financial resources to terrorist organisations through activities like ↳ Money Laundering- Converting illicit funds into seemingly legitimate income. (eg- Lashkar-e-Taiba (LeT) rely on Hawala to fund its operation) ↳ Drug Trafficking- UN estimates the global drug trade to be worth hundreds of billions of dollar annually. Organised Crime → Illegal Money → Money Laundering → Terror financing → Terrorism → Organised Crime
Operational Collabora-tion	• Description- Criminal networks offer logistical support to terrorist activities, such as:

	↳ Transnational facilitation- Smuggling weapons, explosives and fighters across borders (eg- Kurdistan Workers' Party (PKK) has been accused to smuggle weapons into Turkey) ↳ Arms and logistics- Criminal networks provide weapons, explosives and logistical support for terrorist operations. ↳ Counterfeit currency- Terrorists exchange counterfeit money for supplies and weapons through criminal collaboration.
Mutual Amplification (each group benefits from other's actions)	• Destabilisation- Terrorist attacks can weaken governments and create a power vacuum, which organised crime can exploit for their own gain. eg- Syrian civil war- ISIS flourished alongside criminal groups trafficking oil and antiquities. • Targeting Security forces to create distractions or weaken law enforcement, benefitting organised crime operations. eg- 2008 Mumbai attacks diverted Indian security forces, allowing criminals to exploit the situation.
Enabling Environment	• Weak Governance- Corruption and a lack of enforcement capacity create a safe haven for illicit activities (eg- countries with weak rule of law often see a rise in both criminal gangs and terrorist organisations) • Socio-economic Disparity- Limited opportunities and poverty can make individuals vulnerable to recruitment by both groups • Uncontrolled Borders- Open borders facilitate movement of arms, drugs and people for illicit activities • Technological Advancements- Growing IT environment allows easier communication and coordination between them.

Pathways for Countering Organised Crime

01 Law Enforcement

- Boost Capacity- Address police vacancy rates (20-25%) through recruitment and training.
- Specialisation- Create units for drug trafficking, human trafficking and financial crimes (eg- strengthen Narcotics Control Bureau)
- Strengthen Legal framework- Update laws to address evolving crimes and increase penalties for organised crime offenses (eg- enact specific organised crime legislation)
- Witness Protection to encourage information sharing
- Rehabilitation- Consider programs for low-level offenders to prevent recidivism (eg- skill development initiatives in prisons)

- Inter Agency Coordination- Improve collaboration between central, state and international law enforcement (eg- India-Bangladesh border cooperation)

02 Financial Disruption

- Target Money laundering- Address vulnerabilities in anti-money laundering framework (as identified as FATF)
- Promote Transparency- Implement e-governance to reduce corruption opportunities.

03 Addressing Root Cause

- Socioeconomic Development- focus on job creation in crime prone areas (link between unemployment and crime rates)
- Education and De-radicalization- Promote education (eg- Padhega India) and counter extremist ideologies
- Community Engagement- Build trust and collaboration for intelligence gathering (eg- community policing initiatives)

04 Leveraging Technology

- Cybersecurity- Invest in robust infrastructure to counter online crimes
- Data Analytics- Use data to identify patterns and predict threats (eg- crime mapping software)
- Technological Solutions- Invest in advanced technologies like Artificial Intelligence (AI) based analytics, blockchain tracing for financial transactions and surveillance tools to monitor and track suspicious activities online and offline.

MONEY LAUNDERING

- **About-** Money laundering is the process of disguising the illegal origin of money, making it appear legitimate.
- Criminals obtain funds through illegal activities like drug trafficking, corruption or embezzlement
- **Extent-** 2 to 5% of global GDP, or upto $2 trillion in one year (FATF)

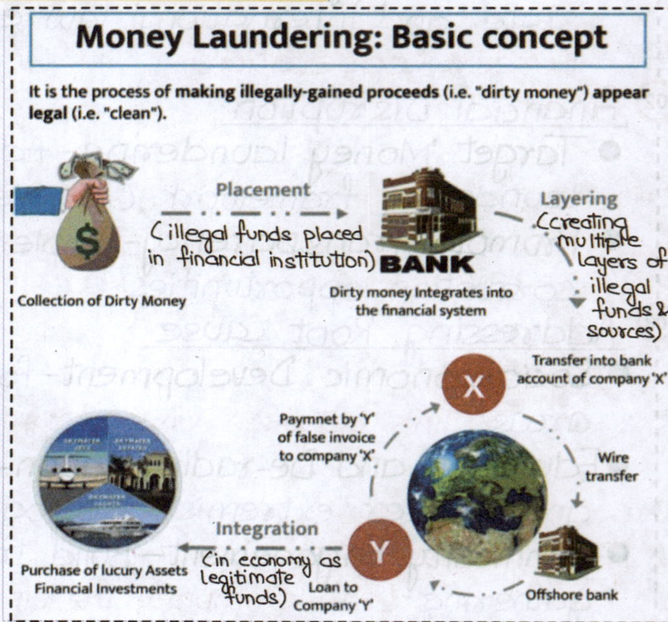

Money Laundering Aims

→ Conceal the Source- Hide the origin of the illegal funds

→ Move the money- Transfer the funds through various financial transactions

→ Integrate the money- Reinvest the laundered funds into legitimate businesses or assets.

Challenges in Curbing Money Laundering in India

01 Regulatory and Enforcement

- **Complex framework-** Multiple agencies create coordination issues (FATF Report 2019)
- **Enforcement Gaps-** Low prosecution rate (19% for PMLA cases since 2005)

  Pending Asset Confirmations- Just 62% of attached assets by the ED have been confirmed by authorities, leaving a large portion in legal limbo.
- **Capacity Building-** Limited resources hinder investigations
- **Cultural and Social Barriers-** Norm of acceptance of cash based transactions
- **Ineffective KYC-** Lax implementation of KYC norms create vulnerabilities.
- **Fragmented Enforcement-** Separate agencies for digital crimes, money laundering, etc. hinder collaboration.
- **Lack of Will-** Investigations exposing powerful figures is stalled

MONEY LAUNDERING TECHNIQUES

1. **Smurfing:** Breaking down large sums into smaller deposits below reporting thresholds
2. **Trade-based Laundering:** Disguising illegal funds through inflated or deflated invoices in international trade
3. **Shell Companies:** Funnelling illicit funds through fictitious companies with fake business activities
4. **Real Estate:** Converting illegal cash into seemingly legitimate assets by buying and selling property

02 Technology and Cyber Threats

- Digital vulnerabilities- Criminal exploit loopholes in cybersecurity (RBI report 2022)
- Cryptocurrency Challenges- Anonymity hinders tracking and regulation (Indian government report 2023)

03 Corporate Vulnerabilities

- Shell Companies- Rise in registrations (MCA report 2022)
- Trade Misinvoicing- Stricter trade finance regulations needed
- Weak Governance- Promoting transparency is crucial.

04 Awareness and Reporting Culture

- Financial Literacy- Low rates in rural areas (RBI Survey 2023)
- Whistleblower Protection- Limited implementation discourages reporting (Whistleblower Act 2014)

EFFECTS OF MONEY LAUNDERING

	Short Term	Long Term
Real Economy	• Disruption of consumption and saving • Disruption of investments • Corruption of Professionals • Changes in prices (eg-housing) • Changes in output, income and employment • Changes in imports-exports	• Illegal business contaminates legal business • Changes in direct foreign investment • Higher or lower growth rates
Financial Sector	• Changes for demand for money, interest rates, exchange rates • Increased volatility in interest rates and exchange rates • Increased availability of credit • Increased inflation due to increased capital flows	• Erosion of public trust in banks (FICCI 2023 Survey) • Billions of tax loss due to black money (Assocham estimate) • Suspicious cross-border transactions linked to currency fluctuations (RBI report 2022)
Political and Civil Society	• Higher or lower income tax • Distorted economic statistics	• Corruption and bribery • Security threats (terrorism, cybercrime boom, etc)
Society	• Increase income inequality	• Widening inequality (Oxfam report) • Crime surge (NCRB report 2022)

India's Anti-Money Laundering Initiatives

→ **Prevention of Money Laundering Act (PMLA) 2002**

- About- Its accompanying rules (PML Rules) serves as primary legal framework for the prosecution, enables authorities to confiscate the property earned from illegally gained proceed.
- Three main objectives
  - i, To prevent and control money laundering
  - ii, To confiscate and seize property obtained from laundered money
  - iii, To deal with any other issue connected with money laundering in India

→ **Institutional framework**

- Enforcement Directorate (ED)- Primary investigating agency for PMLA offenses
- Financial Intelligence Unit- India (FIU-IND)- Analyses suspicious financial transactions and disseminates information to law enforcement.

→ **Empowered Regulations**

- Reserve Bank of India (RBI)-Sets AML (Anti-Money laundering) standards for banks and financial institutions
- Securities & Exchange Board of India (SEBI)- Oversees AML compliance in the securities market

→ **Other Supporting Agencies**

- Economic Offenses Wing, Central Bureau of Investigation (CBI)- Investigates economic offenses with potential money laundering links
- Income Tax Department- Identifies and investigates undisclosed foreign income, a potential source of money laundering

→ **Global Efforts Against Money laundering**

- Vienna Convention (1988)- first international treaty criminalising money laundering, linked specifically to drug trafficking
- Global Programme Against Money laundering (GPML)- A UN led initiative promoting national coordination and international cooperation against ML and terror financing.
- Financial Action Task force (FATF) Recommendations- To combat money laundering and terrorist financing
  - Customer Due Diligence (CDD)- knowing your customers
  - Reporting suspicious activity
  - International cooperation and information sharing
- INTERPOL- facilitates international law enforcement collaboration to combat transnational crime, including money laundering

- MLATs (Mutual Legal Assistance Treaties)- Enabling information and evidence exchange between countries for criminal investigations, aiding in tracking illicit funds across borders

HAWALA- A Concern for Money Laundering

- Hawala is an informal money transfer system which bypasses traditional banking system. Money is transferred through a network of brokers without physical movements of cash. This lack of oversight makes it susceptible to money laundering.
- Hawala used for
  - Black money circulation
  - Terror funding
  - Drug Trafficking
- India's Response
  FEMA (2000) and PMLA (2002)- These acts criminalise hawala transactions and empower Enforcement Directorate to investigate money laundering.
- Why people use Hawala?
  - Low fees as compared to banks
  - Minimal Documentation- No ID or income source verification required
  - Efficiency- It can be faster than traditional banking system
  - Better exchange rates as compared to banks
  - Convenience- Hawala avoids complex bank procedures
  - Unaccounted Income Transfers- Hawala allows transfer of undeclared funds

Pathways for Combating Money Laundering

- Leverage AI to streamline transaction monitoring and improve efficiency
- Public-Private Partnerships for information sharing and network identification
  Bringing Cryptocurrency under ambit of PMLA Act
- International Cooperation to prevent criminals from exploiting loopholes across borders
- FATF Recommendations
  - Risk Based Approach- Tailor AML measures to identify risks
  - National cooperation through dedicated authorities and clear policies
  - Criminalisation of money laundering with international standards.
  - Asset confisication by law enforcement agencies
  - Counter Terrorist financing
  - Targeted sanctions to freeze terrorist assets

BLACK MONEY

Black money refers to money that is not fully legitimate in the hands of the owner. It is mostly hidden from tax authorities. The source of black money can be legal or illegal.

Factors contributing to generation of black money- Tax evasion, corruption, unregulated cash transactions, illegal activities, offshore accounts and money laundering, parallel economy.

Impact of Black Money on India

Extent of Black Money in India

- Finance Ministry (2014)- About 90% of unaccounted wealth or black money, was lying within India, not outside
- Leaks like Panama Papers expose hidden wealth offshore (Rs 20,353 cr)

01 Economic Leech

- Lost Tax Revenue- Billions lost, crippling investment in infrastructure, education, etc.
- Unfair Competition- Fuels an underground economy, hurting legitimate business
- Market Distortion- Inflation in sectors like real estate.
- Discourages foreign investments seeking transparency.

02 Social Erosion

- Widening inequality- Black money concentrates wealth, exacerbating social divide
- Public loses faith in institutions due to perceived black money fueled corruption
- Crime funding- Black money finances organised crime, jeopardizing public safety.
- Human Exploitation- Black money facilitates human trafficking as criminal launders money.
- Policy Manipulation- Special interest groups fueled by black money can sway policies
- Cybercrime Motive- Black money can be a motive for cyberattacks

India's Efforts to Curb Black Money

01 Legislative Measures

- Voluntary Disclosure Schemes- Offer opportunities to declare black money (controversial)
- Prevention of Money Laundering Act (2002)- Crack down on money laundering methods (hawala, shell companies)
- Benami Transaction Prohibition Act (1988)- Ban anonymous property transaction

- Black Money (Undisclosed foreign Income and Assets) Act 2015- Encourage disclosure of foreign black money.
- Demonetisation (2016) of Rs. 500 and 1000 was carried with the primary view of making black money useless

02 Institutional Measures

- Central Board of Direct Taxes (CBDT)- Responsible for enforcing direct tax laws and tackling black money.
- Enforcement Directorate (ED)- Investigates and prosecutes money laundering cases.
- Financial Intelligence Unit (FIU)- Coordinates efforts against terrorism financing, a major use of black money
- Directorate of Revenue Intelligence (DRI)-India's chief anti-smuggling agency.

03 International Measures

- G-20 Initiatives- Proper automatic tax information exchange and combat tax base erosion and profit shifting.
- Double Taxation Avoidance Agreements- Ensure proper taxation of income.

Challenges in Combating Black Money	Pathways for combating Black Money
Political Patronage-Corrupt network shields criminals, hindering enforcement Uneven Regulations-State level variations create loopholes for exploitation. Financial Complexity- Loopholes and low capital gains taxes enable tax evasion Globalized hurdles- Anti-money laundering rules can impede legitimate cross-border transactions Cash Reliance-Difficulty in tracking cash movements weakens tax enforcement Resource Constraints-Under equipped agencies like CVC and CBI struggle to tackle the problem Real Estate Vulnerability-Real estate remains a haven for laundering illicit funds.	Legislative overhaul- Enact strong anti-bribery laws, improve citizen grievance redressal mechanisms and tighten regulations to curb black money transfer abroad Skilled Workforce- Train financial regulators in advanced financial investigation techniques to identify and track black money. Electoral Integrity- Empower the Election Commission to fight black money in elections and foster information sharing with financial enforcement agencies Tech powered Defense- Equip agencies with advanced technology to counter threats like cryptocurrency and shut down

- Outdated Laws- Existing legislation may be inadequate to address current black money tactics
- Lax Administration- Bureaucratic corruption create avenues to evade legal consequences
- Data Limitations- Lack of digitisation and reliance on non-quantifiable data hinder effective monitoring.

new black money avenues

- Digital Shift- Promote digital literacy and build trust in digital transactions to reduce cash dependence and enhance financial transparency

DRUG TRAFFICKING

Drug trafficking is the illegal trade involving the cultivation, manufacture, distribution and sale of illicit drugs.

Features

- Production of drugs like cocaine, heroin, methamphetamine and synthetic drugs
- Transportation and distribution of these substances
- Transnational in nature- Drug trafficking operations span across borders, regions and even continents

Reasons behind Drug Trafficking in India

- Geographical Vulnerability- India's position between major opium producing regions (Golden Crescent- Iran, Afghanistan, Pakistan and Golden Triangle- Thailand, Laos, Myanmar) makes it prime transit route
- Porous Borders- India shares border with countries known for drug production and these borders are often poorly guarded.
- High Demand- India's large population fuels a high demand for drugs, both recreational and medicinal.
  - eg- Marijuana and cocaine are in high demand in metropolitan areas
- Pharmaceutical Abuse- Abuse of prescription drugs like buprenophine and codeine based cough syrups

EXTENT OF DRUG TRAFFICKING IN INDIA

Major trafficking route: Sea routes(70%) from Pakistan and Afghanistan are key for drug smuggling

India's seizures: Despite large seizures (4th in opium, 3rd in morphine in 2020), the problem persists.

Online Drug Trafficking: Over 60% of the darknet is used for drugs, with crypto payments and delivery services making it more attractive

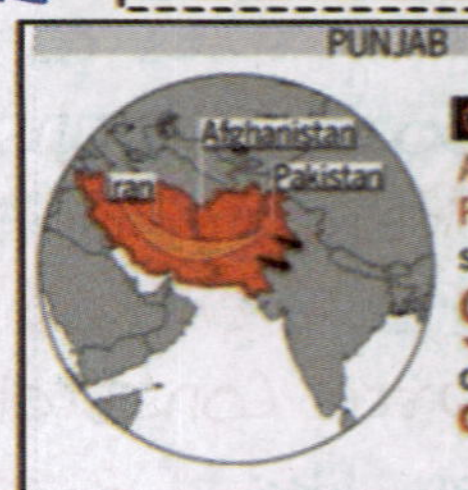

- Virtual currencies simplifies funding for smugglers
- Turf wars and corruption- Disagreements between agencies and corruption can hinder efforts
- Limited Resources- Lack of manpower, infrastructure and training for drug detection weakens enforcement.

Initiatives to curb drug menance

- Narcotics Control Bureau (NCB)- Nodal agency for drug law enforcement in India.
- Narcotics Drug and Psychotropic Substances (NDPS) Act, 1985 provides for identification, treatment, rehabilitation, etc.
- Nasha Mukt Bharat Abhiyaan- Launched in 272 most vulnerable districts for community outreach
- SIMS (Seizure Information Management System) portal for cases involving large seizures
- National Action Plan for Drug Demand Reduction (NAPDDR) for 2018-2025 provides for a multi-pronged strategy.
- UN Conventions (Convention on Narcotic Drugs, 1961; Convention on Psychotropic substances, 1971)

Impact of Drug Trafficking in India

- National Security
  - Weapons Smuggling- Porous borders used for drug trafficking can also facilitate weapons and terrorists entering India. (eg- Mumbai blasts 1993, Pathankot attack 2015)
  - Funding extremism- Drug profits finance insurgencies and terrorism (eg- Jammu and Kashmir, Northeast India)
- Social Breakdown
  - Crime and Violence- Drug addiction fuels a cycle of poverty, crime (theft, robbery) and social unrest (eg- Punjab, Manipur)
  - Youth Vulnerability- Approximately 13% of drug abusers in India are under 20 years of age. Addiction also creates vulnerability to radicalization.
- Anonymous marketplaces- Darknet markets (62% for drugs) facilitate arms, child trafficking and money laundering hindering law enforcement efforts.
- Violent conflicts- Rival gangs in Golden Crescent/ Triangle clash for control, causing violence spillover

- Institutional erosion- Drug traffickers collude with corrupt officials, weakening law enforcement and national security
- Environmental impact- Illicit drug markets can have impacts on environment such as carbon footprint, deforestation, waste generation, etc. for instance phenomenon of narco driven deforestation is taking place in Amazon basin

Challenges in Regulating Drug Trafficking	Pathways for Effective Regulation
Tech-Savvy Traffickers- Dark-net markets, crypto payments and drone deliveries make tracking and interception difficult Law Enforcement Lag- Poor inter agency coordination and resource limitations hinder effective action Social Stigma and Rehabilitation Gap- Stigma discourages prevention, while limited rehab facilities leaves addicts unsupported Political Hurdles and Global Connections- Alleged interference weakens enforcement, while NRI and terror links complicate control Local Gangs join the fray- Existing criminal networks readily exploit drug trafficking opportunities.	Empower Law Enforcement- Boost training, technology and resources for key agencies. fortify borders- Enhanced surveillance with advanced technology and bolster border security forces Address root cause- Tackle poverty, unemployment and limited education fight Addiction and Demand- Launch public awareness and expand rehab facilities Go Glocal- Collaborate with other nations to dismantle trafficking networks. Harden laws & Regulations- Increase penalties and strengthen drug-related legislation Reduce Demand- Implement community programs and education initiatives. Effective coordination and information sharing among agencies Develop accountability mechanisms and practices Control online drug supply chain by regulating crypto currency markets. Enhancement of punishment under NDPS and other drug laws Creating awareness among citizens through various programs

PYQs Corner

(Write the Answer and Get Free Evaluation)

1 Discuss the types of organized crimes. Describe the linkages between terrorists and organized crime that exist at the national and transnational levels.[150 Words] [10 Marks] **[2022]**

2 Discuss how emerging technologies and globalization contribute to money laundering. Elaborate measures to tackle the problem of money laundering both at national and international levels. [150 Words] [10 Marks] **[2021]**

3 Money laundering poses a serious security threat to a country's economic sovereignty. What is its significance for India and what steps are required to be taken to control this menace? [200 Words] [10 Marks] **[2013]**

4 India's proximity to the two of the world's biggest illicit opium growing states has enhanced her internal security concerns. Explain the linkages between drug trafficking and other illicit activities such as gunrunning, money laundering and human trafficking. What counter measures should be taken to prevent the same? [250 Words] [15 Marks]**[2018]**

5 Money laundering poses a serious threat to country's economic sovereignty. What is its significance for India and what steps are required to be taken to control this menace? [200 Words] [10 Marks]**[2013]**

Communication Networks, Social Media and Cyber Security

CHAPTER **06**

CYBER SECURITY

→ Cyber Security or information technology security are techniques of protecting computers, networks, programs and data from unauthorised access or attacks that are aimed for exploitation.

It includes prevention of, detection of and responses to attacks on networks, systems and data.

→ Defensive vs Offensive Security

- Offensive security is a proactive and adversarial approach to protecting computer systems, networks, individuals from attack
- Conventional Security or defensive security focuses on reactive measures, such as patching software and finding and fixing system vulnerabilities

→ Cyber Space- A global domain within the information environment consisting of interdependent network of information technology infrastructures, including internet, tele-communication networks, computer systems and embedded processors and controllers

- Cyberspace is global common, hence has shared sovereignty
- Hostile actions in cyberspace can impact the nation's economy, cohesion, political decision making and ability to defend itself.

→ Critical Information Infrastructure (CII)- According to Section 70(1) of Information Technology Act, CII is defined as a "computer resource, the incapacitation or destruction of which shall have debilitating impact on national security, economy, public health or safety"

→ Cyber Attack- It is a malicious or deliberate attempt by an individual or organisation to breach the information system of another individual or organisation

Cyber Security-Threats

01 **Cyber Warfare**- Virtual conflict initiated as a politically motivated attack on the enemy's computer and information systems waged via internet.
Aim- To disrupt the systems, destroy them partially or entirely.
eg- Stuxnet, a malicious computer worm to attack an Iranian nuclear programme

TYPES OF CYBER WARFARE

Cyber Terrorism- Misuse of cyberspace to cause harm or further social, ideological, religious, political or similar objectives

Cyber Spying- Aimed at gaining information for perpetrators

Cyber Fraud- Aimed at getting monetary or related gains for perpetrators

Cyber Bullying- Designed to frighten and intimidate individuals rather than government/ business

02 **Cyber Espionage**- Use of computer networks to gain illicit access to confidential information, typically held by government or other organisations.
eg- Operation Shady RAT, the hackers had access to seventy government and private agencies around the world.

03 **Cybercrime**

- **Hacking**- Illegal invasion into a computer system or network
  Nearly two in five (33%) of web users in India face it in 2023
- **Denial of Service (DoS)**- It is technology driven attack that occurs when an attacker prevents legitimate users from accessing specific computer systems and networks
  eg- DoS attacks strike Indian airports in 2023.

- **Malware**- It is a malicious software design to perform an unwanted illegal act via the computer network.
  eg- Wannacry ransonware
  Common Malwares → Viruses, worms, trojans, hoax, etc.
- **Phishing**- It is a cybercrime in which targets are lured by mails to provide sensitive information (personal information, bank details) by some posing as a legitimate website
  India recorded 79 million cyber attacks in 2023, ranks 3rd globally (ThreatLabz 2024 Phishing Report)
- **Botnet**- Botnets are number of internet-connected devices, with each running its own bots eg- Mirabai botnet

- **Child Pornography**- Creation, distribution or possession of sexually explicit material involving minors
  Section 67-B of the IT Act punishes it in India
- **Other Types**- Trojans, ransomware, wiper attacks, intellectual property theft, data manipulation, data destruction, spyware, network travelling worms, etc.

TYPES OF CYBER ATTACK

1. **Network**
   - Denial of service attack (Fake traffic)
   - Adware
2. **Devices**
   - Malware(virus,worms, etc)
   - System Vulnerabilities
   - Ransomware(eg-wannacry)
   - "Zero Day" Attacks
   - Botnets
3. **Website/Apps**
   - Cross site scripting
   - SQL injection attacks
   - Cyber espionage
   - Cyber sabotage
   - Tabnabbing
   - Pharming
   - ClickJacking
   - Spam
4. **Individual's Vulnerability**
   - Phishing
   - Man-in-middle attack
   - Spear Phishing
   - Whaling

Elements of Cyber Security

- Application security- Use of sofware or hardware to protect applications from external threats
- Information Security- Set of strategies for managing the processes, tools and policies for securing digital information
- Network Security against internal and external threats
- Disaster Recovery Plan- Response to unplanned incidents
- Operational Security- Classify information assets and determine controls required to protect these assets
- End-user Education- Policies to guide users for secure use of an organisation's systems

Importance of Cybersecurity

- Shields from attacks- Protects against malware, phishing, ransomware (data theft, device damage)
- Regulation Ready- Ensure compliance to avoid penalties and reputational harm
- Secures your data- Safeguards personal and business data
- Builds Trust- By preventing damaging breaches
- Keeps Business flowing- Prevents disruptions caused by cyberattacks
- Protects Innovation- Safeguards intellectual property (trade secrets, patents, etc)
- Strengthens National Security- Protects from cyberattacks

India's Vulnerability to Cyber Attacks

01 Critical Infrastructure Vulnerability- Power grids, transportation systems and communication networks are susceptible.
eg- Cyberattack on Kudankulam Nuclear Power Plant (Oct 2019)
- System compromise of AIIMS Delhi (2022)

02 Data breaches expose sensitive information, impacting individual and organisational privacy and security.
eg- Aadhaar Data Leak → 81.5 crore Indians on dark web

03 Financial Sector Threats- Attack on banks, financial institutions and online payment system
India is second largest online market globally, following China.

04 Cyber Espionage- Stealing confidential information and gaining a strategic edge through cyberattacks
eg- Operation SideCopy targeting Indian military and diplomatic personnel

05 Advanced Persistent Threats (APTs)- Designed to infiltrate and remain hidden within networks for extended periods.
Impact- Data theft, manipulation or sabotage
eg- China linked APT group targeting India's power sector (feb 2021)

06 Copyright Infringement- Done not just by people with ill intentions, but also people who are not even aware that they are committing a crime.

THE TRENDS

- Surat (15%) and Bengaluru (14%) report the highest number of malware attack detections
- The automobile industry experiences the highest number of detections, followed by the government and education sector
- 50% of detections are associated with removable media and network drives
- 25% of attacks result from clicking on malicious links in emails and websites

KEY FINDINGS

Total detections Over 400 mn

Rate of threat detection: Over 761 per minute

Cryptojacking (emerging as significant threat): over 5.28 million detections in a year

Android detections 39% malwares, 32% adwares, 29% potentially unwanted apps

TOP 3 HOTSPOTS (State-wise)

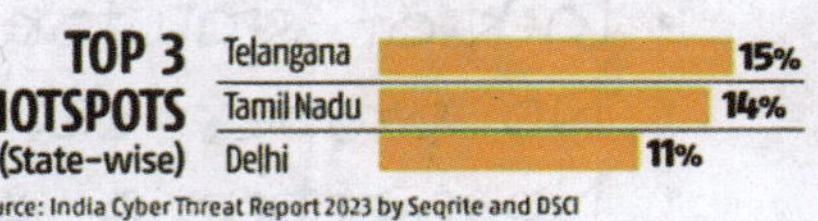

Source: India Cyber Threat Report 2023 by Seqrite and DSCI

DIFFERENT MODES OF FINANCIAL CYBER CRIMES

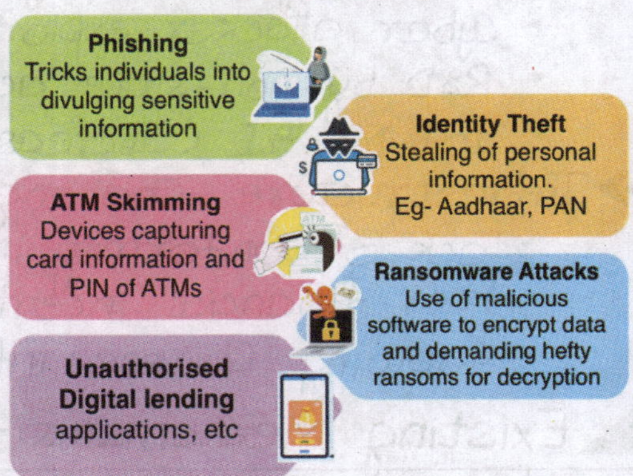

Challenges of Cyber security in India

- **Data Colonisation-** India exports information but data resides outside the country, raising privacy and manipulation concerns
- **Digital Illiteracy** makes citizen vulnerable to cybercrime
- **Substandard security in devices** makes them easy target for malware
- **Legacy Infrastructure-** Outdated banking infrastructure using magnetic strips are susceptible to fraud
- **Non uniform standards** hinders security protocols
- **Under Reporting** due to fear of reputational damage

- **Import dependence** creates vulnerabilities in critical infrastructure
- **Workforce Shortage** of skilled cybersecurity professionals far outstrips supply
- **Fragmented Coordination** between public and private sectors weakens security efforts
- **Anonymity of Threats**- Attribution of cyberattacks to specific actors, state or non-state is difficult
- **Rapidly evolving threats** makes it challenging to establish robust security framework
- **Administrative Challenges**
  - Lack of statutory backing, national level architecture
  - No proper security audit and poor enforcement of regulations
  - No mention in seventh schedule
  - Lack of coordination (NATGRID is opposed by states)
- **Fast evolving Technologies**
  - Cyber attacker exploiting vulnerability
  - R&D by non-state actors
  - IoT, ML, AI (Increased vulnerability of internet)
- **Infrastructure Challenges**
  - Lack of uniformity in devices
  - Poor financial incentives
  - Growing Chinese influence in Indian telecom sector

Existing Mechanisms for Cyber Security in India

LEGAL FRAMEWORK	
	→ National Cybersecurity Policy 2013 • Setting up 24x7 National Critical Infrastructure Protection Centre • Create task force of 5,00,000 cyber security professionals in next five years → Information Technology Act 2000 (As amended in 2008) Regulates use of computer systems, networks and their data → National Digital Communication Policy, 2018 provides for ensuring sovereignty, safety and security of digital communications → Digital Personal Data Protection Act, 2023 • Data Security- Mandates data protection to hinder unauthorised access to information that might threaten security • Data Localisation (potential)- To give government easier access to data for investigations, but privacy concerns exist • Incident Reporting- Data breaches involving internal security threats might be reported, triggering investigations

INSTITUTIONAL FRAMEWORK	➔ National Cybersecurity Coordination Centre (NCCC) It is India's cyberspace intelligence agency which will conduct security and electronic surveillance ➔ India's Computer Emergency Response Team (CERT-In) Mandated under IT Act 2008, it serves as national agency in charge of cyber security ➔ National Critical Information Infrastructure Protection Centre (NCIIPC) - Designated as national nodal agency in respect of Critical Information Infrastructure Protection ➔ Indian Cyber Crime Coordination Centre and Cyber Warrior Police force → to tackle internet crimes ➔ Cyber Swachchta Kendra (CSK) to enhance awareness among citizens for analysis of malware, botnets affecting network system
OTHERS	➔ Digital Army Programme- Dedicated cloud to digitise, automate processes, procedures and services for Indian Army, launched as a part of Digital India. ➔ Audit of government websites and applications ➔ Various state government initiatives- Telangana (established a cybersecurity centre of Excellence), Kerala (Cyberdome), Maharashtra ('Cyber Safe Women'), etc

Global Cooperation

- Budapest Convention- Promotes collaborations on cybercrime investigations and legal frameworks
- Tallinn Manual- Identifies international law principles applicable to cyber warfare and enumerates ninety-five "black letter rules" governing such conflicts.
- Paris Call for Trust and Security in Cyberspace- Agreement on nine fundamental cybersecurity principles and a commitment to work together to promote safe and secure cyberspace for all
- International Telecommunications Union (ITU) - UN specialized agency for information and communication technologies. (ICTs)
- Internet Governance Forum (IGF) - It brings together all stakeholders i.e, government, private sector and civil society on internet governance debate
- Christchurch Call to Action- It is series of voluntary commitments that bring governments, tech companies and civil society together, with common goal of eliminating terrorist, violent extremist content online

Pathways for Strengthening Cyber security in India

01 Deterrence

- Develop Comprehensive Cyber Deterrence Strategy including defensive and offensive capabilities (cyberweapons) if necessary
- Established clear norms for responsible behaviour in cyberspace to prevent a proliferation of offensive tools.
- India's Cybersecurity framework based on 4D principles- Deter, Detect, Destroy, Document.

02 Detection and Response

- Time bound implementation of recommendations from committees like Rao Inderjit Singh and Gulshan Rai committees
- Update Policy- Revise National Cyber Security Policy 2013 to provide a clear operational roadmap for detection and response
- Security Audits adhering to international standards for government websites and applications
- State Level Initiatives- Establish State level CERTs (Computer Emergency Response Teams) to collaborate with national CERT-In
- Continuous Monitoring- Regularly assess the cybersecurity landscape and identify potential risks from interconnectedness and third-party service providers

03 Workforce and Awareness

- Invest in Workforce- Build a skilled cybersecurity workforce through training and development programs
- Public Awareness Campaigns- Educate citizens on protecting sensitive data and preventing online threats

04 Policy and Coordination

Empower National Cybersecurity Coordinator (NCC) to foster collaboration among institutions for a unified approach

- Cyber Insurance Adoption- Encourage companies to adopt cyber insurance to mitigate financial losses from cyber incidents
- Data Localisation- Consider data localisation for critical sectors, mandating internet server hosting within India.
- Cybersecurity Management- Integrate cybersecurity into corporate governance with defined security roadmaps and regular simulated attack testing.

05 Adopting Smart Security Solutions

- Space Time Awareness- Location (GPS) and real time clocks
- Learning, Adaptation and Self Organisation- Real Time intelligence
- Massive Money and Storage- local and remote cloud storage
- Sustainability- Embedded Security- Everywhere in the Network
- Scalable Networked Architecture- Small architectures will need to scale in space and time from micro cells to macro solutions
- Decision focus- "Knowledge lens" for data mining and "Big Data" from Global Social Networks, search and online trade and commerce
- Systems Integration- Cyber and physical solutions and operations

GEO-SPATIAL DATA AND NATIONAL SECURITY

- **Geospatial Data**
  - Data about objects, events or phenomena that are located on earth's surface
  - Captured using photogrammetry, LIDAR, RADAR, satellite based remote sensing, etc.
  - Prominent technological application of geospatial data- Geospatial Information Systems (GIS), Navigation Systems, Digital Cartography and Geospatial analytics.
- It combines 3 types of information.
  - **Location information** (coordinates on earth)
  - **Attribute information** (characteristics of object-event, phenomena concerned)
  - **Temporal information** (time or life span at which attribute or location exists)

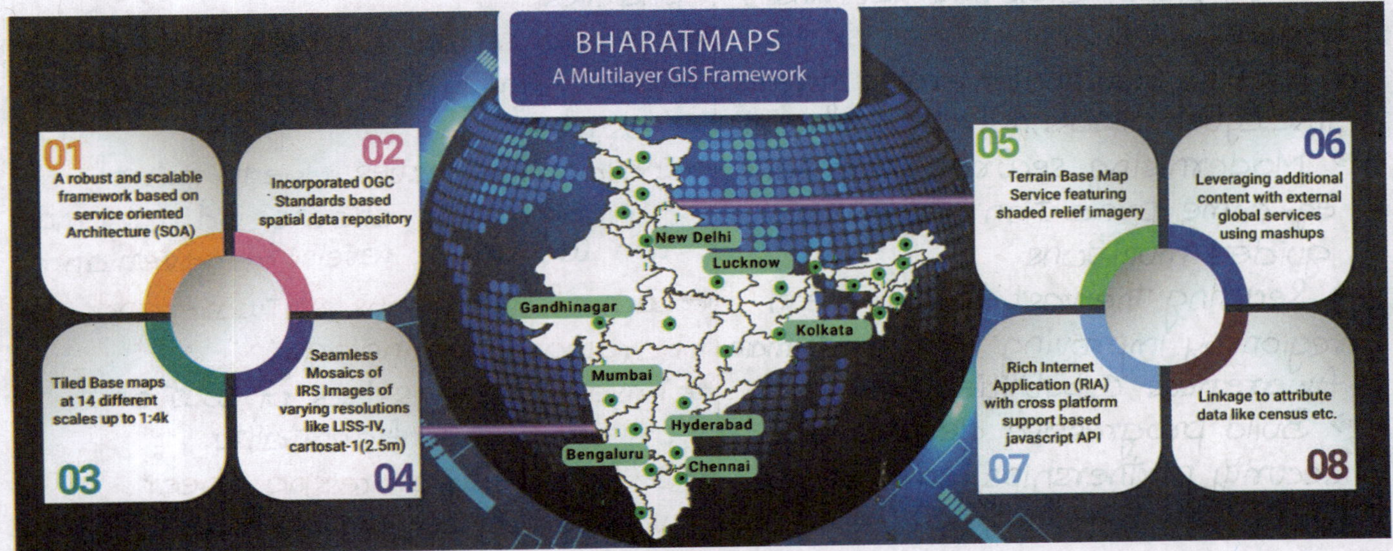

India's Step to develop its geospatial capabilities

- Buiding constellation of earth observation satellites
- Establishment of dedicated institutions → eg- Indian Institutes of Remote Sensing, National Centre of Geo-Informatics (NCG), etc.
- National Spatial Data Infrastructure, Bharatmaps platform, Bhuvan portal.
- India's indigenous navigation system "NaVIC" (Navigation with Indian Constellation) designed to provide accurate position information service to users in the region extending upto 1500 km from India's boundary
- Policy framework to regulate Geographic Information - National Map Policy, Remote sensing data policy, National Data sharing and Accessibility policy and recent Guidelines for acquiring and producing geospatial data and geospatial data services including maps.
- Geospatial data gathering as part of schemes in initiatives like PM Gati Shakti and SVAMITVA

Significance of geospatial data in National Security	Challenges in utilizing geospatial data for National Security
» Enhancing the precision and reliabi-lility of intelligence, surveillance and reconnaissance activities » Advancing situational awareness for quick and secure decision-making to handle critical insurgencies » Support military operations in logistics management, developing tactical plans, exploring terrains virtually, etc. » Tackling new and emerging threats like cyber attacks, hybrid warfare, etc. » Modernising security operations eg- crime prediction and precision guided munitions » Securing the vast Indian Ocean region by improving Maritime Domain Awareness Capabilities » Build progressive defence and security partnerships eg- BECA with USA.	➠ Access to comprehensive, accurate data ➠ Research outputs are usually stand alone and lack unanimity ➠ Shortage of trained human resource in government agencies ➠ Financial constraints in technological adoption and advancement in emerging and experimental fields like geospatial analytics ➠ Ensuring secure shortage of geospatial data, given India's vulnerable digital ecosystem ➠ Coordination issues due to lack of clarity on data sharing and collabora-tion with lower levels of governance ➠ Lack of indigenous software and hardware technology ➠ Privacy concerns - Lack of locational privacy and confidentiality ➠ Difficulties in processing sheer volume of geospatial data

Way forward

WAY FORWARD

- Strengthening the security of digital infrastructure
- Awareness and capacity building among decision makers and users
- Promote development of indigenous software and hardware
- Promoting education in specialised fields like geo-informatics, big-data analytics
- Ensuring privacy of citizens
- Enhancing coordination among agencies (state police, defense, intelligence bureau)
- Creation of dedicated department and enhancing financial allocation for better utilisation of geospatial data
- Bringing cohesiveness to geospatial sector by enhancing collaboration among stakeholders

SOCIAL MEDIA, COMMUNICATION AND INTERNAL SECURITY

Social media refers to internet platforms that allow users to create and share content or to participate in social networking.
eg- Facebook, Instagram, WhatsApp, etc.

Role of Social Media

01 Political
- Participation and feedback from citizens
- Tool of political campaigning and advertising
- Citizen journalism
- 5th pillar of Democracy
- Culture of Debate and Democracy

02 Governance
- Instrumental for behavioural change
- Participatory and Citizen-led governance
- People centric political communication

03 Ethical
- Means for free speech and expression
- Recognition to Right to Internet

04 Economy
- New source of employment
- Digital Marketing (eg- youtube ads)
- Tools for feedback for companies (concept of prosumer)

05 Security
- Influence and propaganda
- Improved intelligence capabilities
- Warning against various issues (social/political/economical)

06 Others
- Social media and communication between people living far away. eg- facebook calls
- Sharing of knowledge → eg- everyday hacks
- Expressing opinion related to major issues. eg-voicing concerns against religious discrimination
- Platform for small business. eg-facebook business
- Source of entertainment. eg- Travelling vlogs
- Source of knowledge. eg- India's geography

The use of social media for policing may be seen by many initiatives like:

- Delhi Traffic Police using platforms like Facebook and Twitter to ease handling of traffic related issues,
- Delhi police online FIR facility for lost articles,
- Indore police using the medium to track criminal activity
- Bengaluru police twitter handle selected for "Twitter Samvad".
- Social Media Labs Project by Maharashtra Police tracks activity on social media to anticipate and handle sudden flare ups.

Challenges Posed by Communication Networks and Social Media for Internal Security

- Foreign Interference - Malicious actors (eg- states) manipulate online information to sway public opinion, often using fake accounts and content (eg- Russia's 2016 US election activities)
- Echo Chambers - Algorithmic filtering and social connections create online spaces where users primarily encounter reinforcing viewpoints, hindering exposure to diverse perspectives (Polarization)

Correct content
False content i.e. source of misperception
can result in
spread deliberately
Rumour
Conspiracy theory
Disinformation
spread in journalistic format
Fake news genre
spread unintentionally
Misinformation
can be applied for purpose of propaganda

- Unequal Participation - Disparities in access and digital literacy can marginalise voices while amplifying fringe groups, distorting the perception of public opinion
- Supreme Court corners for uncharitable comments, trolls and aggressive reactions on social media platforms on almost every issue, including judges and judicial proceedings
- Illicit activities - Spreading child pornography + phishing scams + spreading virus and malware
- Criminal Activities - Drug Smuggling + human trafficking + money laundering
- Propaganda Platforms by their politically biased controllers instead of unbiased opinions. eg- UPSC Jihad by a media channel
- Irrelevant News that doesn't hold any value for citizens. eg- covering celebrity marriages when country is suffering from droughts
- Lack of Accountability for sharing fake or wrong news
- Radicalisation - 72% of terror recruits were radicalised online
- Insurgency Support - Online propaganda garnering over 1 lakh views
- Exam Paper Leakages - law and order challenge
- Deep fakes can lead to a law and order situation in the country.

Deepfake Threats	Way forward
Democracy at Risk - Deepfakes manipulate public opinion, weakening trust (eg- Capitol Hill violence) Truth Dies - Deepfakes fuel "Liar's Dividend" letting leaders dismiss facts (eg- Trump's Deepfakes)	Platform actions - Social media needs tools to detect deepfakes (eg- Microsoft's video authenticator) Track the truth - Blockchain can verify media origin and edits, reducing deepfakes

→ Cybercrime Boom- They fuel phishing, fraud and identity theft (230% increase) → Weaponised misinformation- They are used for espionage & manipulating conflicts (eg- China vs India) → Women Targeted- Primarily target women with harmful pornography (eg- Rashmika Mandanna's Deepfake) → Radicalisation machine- Incite violence and extremism (eg- ISIS propaganda)	» Law and Order- Include penalties for malicious deepfakes in Digital India Act » Think Before You Share- Promote public awareness and responsible sharing online » Global Rules- Lead efforts to create a global framework for responsible AI (Bletchley Declaration)

Social Media and Radicalisation

- About- Phenomenon where people embrace views that could lead to development of extremist ideas → social, political or religious
- Radicalisation often encourages the threat of lone wolf operations (Udaipur beheading 2022)

Factors Responsible for Online Radicalisation	
Push factor	**Pull factor**
→ Economic factor- eg-lack of employment opportunities → Socio- Religious factor- Lack of access to education (however educated are also becoming its prey), ethnic or religious marginalisation, ideological belief (considering one's religion as superior than other), etc. → Political factor- loss of trust in institutions such as judiciary → Psychological factors- Lack of personal identity, feelings of alienation, etc.	➤ Propaganda- Religious philosophies are distorted by the violent extremist group. Social media has emerged as key sphere of it. ➤ Capitalising Crisis- Crisis events create an environment of fear, anger and insecurity, driving individuals towards extremists ideologies. eg- recent Israel- Gaza conflict is used to radicalise youth worldwide ➤ Economic factor- Economic incentive provided by the group ➤ Other- Ideals of alternative outlet for political engagement, sense of adventure, etc.

Reasons for Increasing Trend of Social Media Misuse

- **Easy Access to Digital Devices**- Access to mobile phones have increased social media penetration (32.2% Indians use social media)
- **Cheaper Internet**- India has one of cheapest internet in the world at $0.17 per GB
- **Lack of Accountability**- Social media giants such as Meta and Twitter enjoy protection from prosecution due to safe harbour provisions
- **Lack of social media policy** in many countries, including India, to address social media specific challenges
- **Advanced encryption** such as end-to-end encryption have made it difficult to identify miscreants on social media.
- **Gamification Techniques**- Extremist ideology is transmitted to children using elements of gaming

Steps Taken to Prevent Misuse of Social Media

Global Level	India
EU Digital Services Act seeks to regulate intermediaries such as social media and other content sharing platforms	Information Technology Act, 2000- Section 69 allows government to ask social media platforms to block information for public access. Section 79- Requires intermediaries to advice users of its services not to post information which is harmful/ offensive and violates Indian law
US Social Media Privacy Protection and Consumer Rights Act, to increase transparency, strengthen consumer rights and make companies comply with privacy policies	Information Technology (Intermediary Guidelines and Digital Media Ethics Code) Rules 2023 Amendment- fact-checking unit to prevent spread of false information on social media
Australia Social Media Bill will apply to providers of internet, hosting or content services that do not comply with guidelines on individual privacy and rights	Digital Personal Data Protection Act- To prevent misuse of personal data of its citizens
New Zealand Harmful Digital Communications Act 2015 seeks to punish individuals who share private data of individuals on the internet, including social media	National Cyber Security Strategy 2020- It is being formulated to improve cyber awareness and cyber-security through more stringent audits

Way forward

- **National Cyber Security Policy** needs to be revised to include social media challenges, which are distinct from cyber security threats
- **Code of Practice on Disinformation**- In line with the code by the EU, it should allow platforms and agencies to take action in five areas
  - Disrupting Advertising Revenues- Target accounts and websites that spread disinformation
  - Transparency in Political and Issue Based Advertising- Make advertising more transparent
  - Addressing fake Accounts and Online Bots- Tackle the issue of fake accounts and bots
  - Empowering Consumers to report disinformation and access different news sources, while improving the visibility and findability of authoritative content
  - Support Research Community- Empower researchers to monitor online disinformation through privacy complaint access to platform data.
- **Centralised Monitoring Systems** to monitor social media activity
- **Judicial Oversight**- Necessary to balance the necessity of government's objectives with the rights of the impacted individual
- **Decentralised and Open-Source Tracking Systems**- Systems should be designed in such a way that data is shared without any privacy breach.
- **Strengthening Privacy Laws** for user data and privacy
- **Reform IT Act, 2000**- Increasing the financial penalties for violating the social media policy

  Protecting confidential business information
- **Data Localisation** will help law enforcement agencies get access to user data for investigation and prosecution

PYQs Corner

(Write the Answer and Get Free Evaluation)

1 What are they different elements of cyber security? Keeping in view the challenges in cyber security, examine the extent to which India has successfully developed a comprehensive National Cyber Security Strategy. [250 Words] [15 Marks] **[2022]**

2 Keeping in view India's internal security, analyse the impact of cross-border cyber attacks. Also discuss defensive measures against these sophisticated attacks. [150 Words] [10 Marks] **[2021]**

3 Discuss different types of cyber-crimes and measures required to be taken to fight the menace. [150 Words] [10 Marks] **[2020]**

4 What is Cyber Dome Project? Explain how it can be useful in controlling internet crimes in India. [150 Words] [10 Marks] **[2019]**

5 Data security bas assumed significant importance in the digitized world due to rising cyber-crimes. The Justice B. N. Sri Krishna Committee Report addresses issues related to data security. What, in your view, are the strengths and weaknesses of the report relating to the protection of personal data in cyber space? [250 Words] [15 marks] **[2018]**

6 Discuss the potential threats of cyber-attack and the security framework to prevent it. [150 Words] [10 Marks] **[2017]**

7 Use of internet and social media by non-state actors for subversive activities is a major security concern. How have these been misused in the recent past? Suggest effective guidelines to curb the above threat. [200 Words] [12.5 Marks] **[2016]**

8 Considering the threats cyberspace poses for the country, India needs a "Digital Armed Force" to prevent crimes. Critically evaluate the National Cyber Security Policy, 2013 outlining the challenges perceived in its effective implementation. [200 Words] [12.5 Marks] **[2015]**

9 Religious indoctrination via digital media has resulted in Indian youth joining the ISIS. What is ISIS and its mission? How can ISIS be dangerous to the internal security of our country. [200 Words][12.5 Marks] **[2015]**

10 Cyber warfare is considered by some defence analysts to be a larger threat than even Al Qaeda or terrorism. What do you understand by Cyber warfare? Outline the cyber threats which India is vulnerable to and bring out the state of the country's preparedness to deal with the same. [200 Words] [10 Marks] **[2013]**

11 What are social networking sites and what security implications do these sites present? [200 Words] [10 Marks] **[2013]**

Security Forces

CHAPTER 07

INDIAN SECURITY FORCES

India's security apparatus is a complex system with various forces working together to ensure national security and internal order

Security forces Governance

- Supreme Commander- The President of India holds the ultimate authority over the Indian Armed forces
- Ministry of Defence (MoD)- Manages the Indian Armed forces, responsible for external threats and national security.
- Ministry of Home Affairs (MHA)- Oversees federal law enforcement agencies, tackling internal threats

Types of Security forces

Dealing with External Threats	Dealing with Internal Threats
→ Indian Armed forces • focus- External threats and national security • Composition ↳ Army- The largest branch, responsible for land-based operations ↳ Navy- Protects India's maritime interests and borders	→ Central Armed Police forces (CAPF) (MHA)- • Focus- Internal Security and assisting state governments • Key forces ↳ Central Reserve Police force (CRPF)- Countering terrorism and internal disturbances ↳ Border Security forces (BSF)- Guards land borders ↳ Central Industrial Security force (CISF)- Secures critical infrastructure and government installations

↳ Air force- Maintains air superiority and conducts aerial warfare ↳ Indian Coast Guard- Conducting round the year real life operation at sea	↳ Others include- Assam Rifles, Indo-Tibetan Border Police (ITBP), Sashatra Seema Bal (SSB) & National Security Guard (NSG) ➜ State Police • Responsibility- Law and order within their respective states • Examples- Metropolitan Police forces (MPfs) in major cities

Indian Armed forces and Their Mandate

INDIAN ARMY	››› Defense of Nation- Primary mandate is to defend India's sovereignty and national interests. ››› Land Warfare- Conducts military operations on land, including conventional warfare, counterinsurgency and counterterrorism ››› Border Security- Secures country's borders, maintaining border posts and defending territorial integrity. ››› Internal Security- It assists civil authorities in maintaining law and order and dealing with internal security threats ››› Humanitarian Assistance and Disaster Relief- Provides aid during natural disasters and emergencies. eg- Operation Dost ››› Peacekeeping operations- It contributes to UN peacekeeping missions worldwide
INDIAN NAVY	➜ Maritime Security- Safeguards maritime interests and ensures security ➜ Naval Operations- Conducts surveillance, defense and patrols in EEZ and territorial waters ➜ Power Projection- Maintains capabilities for power projection and protecting national interests. ➜ Deterrence- Plays a crucial role in detering potential threats ➜ Humanitarian Assistance and Disaster Relief- Actively involve in providing aid during disasters ➜ Naval Diplomacy- Engages in cooperation, joint exercises and initiatives to strenghten relationships.
AIR FORCE	››› Air Defense- Defends airspace and deters aerial threats ››› Aerial Operations- Conducts offensive and defensive missions including airstrikes and reconnaisance ››› Strategic Reach- Maintains capabilities for rapid deployment and strategic airlift

AIR FORCE	»» Aerospace Dominance- focuses on maintaining superiority in air warfare capabilities »» Disaster Relief and Humanitarian Aid- Provides support during disasters and humanitarian crises »» Peacekeeping Operations- Participates in UN Peacekeeping missions, providing air support and logistics

Indian Armed forces - Challenges and Shortcomings

- Budget Squeeze- Shrinking defense budget (1.5-1.7% of GDP) hinders modernisation plans (eg- artillery gun procurement delays)
- Unclear Strategy- Lack of unified national security strategy creates hurdles in inter-service coordination and doctrine development. (eg- initial delays during Kargil Wars)
- Procurement Delays- Bureaucratic hurdles and corruption lead to lengthy delays in acquiring new equipment (eg- decade long wait for attack helicopters)
- Outdated Equipment- Reliance of aging weaponry (eg- T-72 tanks) compared to modern adversaries (eg- China's T-90 tanks)
- Ammunition Shortages- Concerns about quality and quantity of stockpiles, impacting operational readiness (eg- reliability issues with indigenous ammunition)
- Top Heavy Structure- High officer to soldier ratio (1:16) creates inefficiencies and high operational costs.
- Limited Domestic Technology- Reliance on foreign imports (60% of needs) (eg- delays in AMCA fighter jet development)
- Limitations of India's Defense Sector-
  - Bureaucratic Inertia leads to delay in reforms as well as delivery of projects
  - Lack of technological depth to design/ manufacture major systems and critical parts
  - Scalability issues- Present defense exports are mainly composed of spare parts and components
  - Budget issues and dependency on PSUs.
- PSU/ DRDO Inefficiencies- Delays, cost overruns and unmet requirements plague domestic defence production (eg- Arjun tank project)
- Inter-service Disconnects- Limited joint exercises and communication between Army, Navy and Air force (eg- need for improved coordination during Balakot strike)

Initiative for Strengthening Indian Armed forces

01 Establish Chief of Defence Staff (CDS)- Approved in 2019, CDS is four star military officer who serves as head of Army, Navy and Air force

→ Recommended by- Kargil Review Committee (2000) + Naresh Chandra Committee (2011) + Shekatkar Committee (2016)

→ Aim- To increase efficiency and coordination among armed forces + reducing duplication + better civilian-military coordination.

→ Significance

- Bypass interservice rivalry- Provides holistic advice on critical issues such as joint strategy, planning, weapons procurement, manpower allocation
- Collaboration and coordination by integrating armed forces to operate cohesively in a constantly evolving security landscape
- Prioritising military procurement to ensure operational capabilities + Resource efficiency
- Reflect global trend of jointness and integration in armed forces (Italy, France, China, UK and USA)

CHALLENGES FOR CDS

Other Pending Reforms
Without other structural reforms, including creation of unified theatre commands, questions are bound to be raised about the wisdom of appointing a CDS

Domination of Army
It is argued that CDS will establish the Army's domination and other services may be reduced to a supporting role.

Balancing Procurement Requirements
For example, while the Air Force is embarking on a programme for 114 new fighters, the Navy is running a parallel procurement programme.

02 Inter Services Organisations (ISOs), 2024 Act

It empowers the commander-in-chief or office-in-command of ISO to manage personnel from all branches of the military, streamlining operations and fostering collaboration.

→ Theaterisation of Armed forces- Integration of all manpower and assets of Indian Army, Navy and Air force under single operation control in a specific geographical region through Integrated or Joint Theatre Commands (JTCs)

→ Significance of Theaterisation for India.

- Unified Approach- Better coordination against security threats
- Improved efficiency- Streamlined processes, optimised resources, faster decision making.

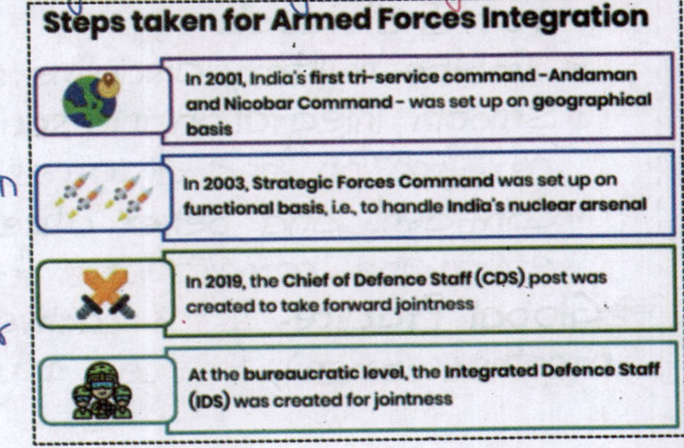

- Modernisation- Prioritised spending, readiness for future warfare
- Military Efficiency- Unified advice, tailored training for specific theaters
- Better training and acclimisation for specific operational environments and requirements
- Enables readiness for multi-dimensional battlefields (including economic, cyber and space domains) through unified command and control structures

03 Reforming Armed force Recruitment: Agnipath Scheme

→ About- It is short service manpower model under which around 45,000 to 50,000 soldiers will be recruited annually.

- Of these, 75% will leave the service in four years. 25% will be allowed to continue for another 15 years under permanent commission.

→ Significance

↳ For Nation

- National integration based on unity in diversity with equal opportunity to youth including women from all regions
- Nation building through empowered, disciplined and skilled youth with military ethos in civil society
- Potential Social transformation as any citizen can apply for Agniveer recruitment diluting caste and regional composition over time

↳ for Armed forces-

- Improved battle preparedness through transformative evolution with energetic, fitter, diverse more trainable and resilient youth, suited to changing dynamics
- Youth profile by optimal balance of youth and experience
- Harness benefits of SKILL INDIA by induction from tech institutes
- Addressing manpower cost of Ministry of Defence

↳ for Individuals

- Imbibe military discipline, motivation skill and physical fitness
- Smooth integration into society with Skill screening Assessment sets, certification and diplomas / higher education / credits
- Confident and better citizens by military training, team building, ethos and camaraderie forged over the years.

→ Global Practice- Israel (active duty for 32 months (men) and 24 months (women); France (1 year or 3-5 years renewable contracts)

→ Concerns

- Cohesion- 4 years might be insufficient to build strong unit bonds
- Candidate Pool- May not attract top talent who might prioritise permanent positions elsewhere
- Job security- Uncertainty after 4 years could demotivate recruits
- Implementation- No pilot project or independent study to access feasibility
- Societal Impact- Disgruntled, unemployed veterans might be susceptible to extremism.
- Regional Balance- All India recruitment could alter the regional composition of armed forces.

→ Way forward

- Link to Reforms- Integrate the scheme with reforms to optimise manpower and restructure the military
- Education and Selection- Raise the minimum qualification to 10+2 and implement a stricted all-India entrance exam with psychological evaluations for a tech-savvy force.
- Regimental Ethos- Ensures the scheme upholds traditional spirit of Indian Army
- Service Extension- Consider extending initial service period and offering re-enlistment options for a larger percentage of Agniveers
- Training Efficiency- Mitigate shorter training time with focused training methods and innovation.
- Reintegration- Implement effective programs to ensure succesful reintegration of Agniveers into civilian life.
- Incentivisation- Explore financial aid and educational opportunities for Agniveers, similar to programs in US.

04 Integrated Battle Groups (IBGs)- IBGs are brigade-sized agile and self sufficient combat formations designed to swiftly launch strikes against adversaries in case of hostilities.

→ Objectives

- Enhance lethality and effectiveness of forces in modern warfare scenarios
- Utilise advanced technology to support operations

Pathways for Empowering Indian Army

IMPORTANT FACTS

1	India ranks as **fourth largest military spender globally**
2	Budget allocation for defence sector has grown 2.75 times over the past decade
3	Defence exports have surged almost 14x in past 7 years
4	Ratio of imports to exports declined from 35.73 in FY14 to 3.9 in FY22
5	Defence production surpassed Rs. 1,00,000 crore mark in FY23
6	2513 intellectual property rights granted out of 5823 filed

- Modernize Equipment- fast track procurement of next-gen weapons, drones and armoured vehicles.
- Increase Defense Budget- Secure predictable funding for long term military planning.
- Optimise manpower- Ensure right people are in critical roles and streamline civilian staff (Agnipath scheme)
- Enhance jointness- Establish permanent CDS and create theater commands for unified operations
- Boost Indigenous Developments- Ministry of Defence (MoD) aims of reaching a turnover of USD 26 billion in aerospace and defence manufacturing by 2025 with USD 5 billion earmarked for exports.
- Defence Acquisition Procedure 2020 + Make-I + Technology Development fund (TDF) + Innovations for Defence Excellence (iDEX) projects.
- Improve logistics- Integrate and outsource non-core functions, build procurement expertise (Military logistic agreement with Vietnam, QUAD, etc)
- Political Support for Key Projects- High level political commitment to major defence projects such as Light Combat Aircraft (LCA)
- Focus on Essential Military Supplies- Greater emphasis on domestic production of critical items, highlighted by India's recent achievement of self sufficiency in 155 mm ammunition
- Develop National Security Strategy- Guide military planning and resource allocation.
- Ensure Transparency and Accountability- Mitigate corruption and build public trust.
- Strengthen International Cooperation with allies for technology sharing (Brahmos missile) and joint exercises (Malabar exercise)

Central Armed Police forces (CAPFs) and Internal Security Challenges

- CAPF is formerly referred to as paramilitary forces, seven main armed police forces are in existence.
- They function under Ministry of Home Affairs and each of the forces is led by an IPS officer (exception- Assam Rifles)

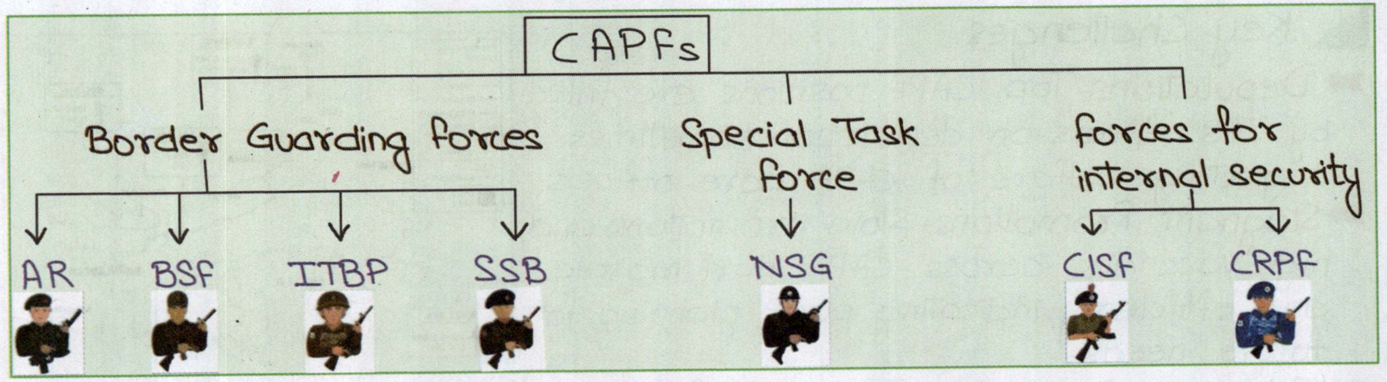

Name	Description
Assam Rifles (AR)	➜ Objectives • Conducting anti-terrorist operations in NER • Ensuring security at India- China and India-Myanmar borders ➜ Important role in • Sino-India War 1962 • Indian Peace Keeping force (IPKF) to Sri-Lanka (1987)
Border Security force (BSF)	➜ Objectives • Securing land borders with Pakistan and Bangladesh • Also performing Anti-infiltration in Kashmir Valley • Counter insurgency in NER • Anti-naxal operations in Odisha and Chattisgarh
Central Reserve Police force (CRPF)	➜ Objective- Crowd control, riot control, counter militancy/ insurgency operations, etc.
Indo-Tibetan Border Police (ITBP)	➜ Objectives • Deployed on border from Karakoram Pass (Ladakh) to Jachep La (Arunachal Pradesh) (~3488 km of Indo-China border) • Manning border outposts on altitudes 9000ft-18700ft in Western, middle and eastern sectors on Indo-China border
National Security Guard (NSG)	➜ Objective- Counter-terrorism unit/ federal contingency force
Sashastra Seema Bal (SSB)	➜ Objectives • Guarding Indo-Nepal and Indo-Bhutan borders Enhance border security, curb trans-border crimes, prevent unauthorised entry/ exit, etc.
Central Industrial Security force (CISF)	➜ Objective- Ensuring security of major critical infrastructure installations

Key Challenges

- **Deputations-** Top CAPF positions are filled by IPS officers on deputation, sometimes neglecting welfare of CAPF cadre officers
- **Stagnant Promotions-** Slow promotions and high vacancies across CAPFs hurt morale and efficiency, indicating poor planning for future needs
- **Grievance Bottlenecks-** The lack of strong internal grievance redressal system forces
- personnel to take extreme measures like social media protests (eg- BSF soldier in 2017)

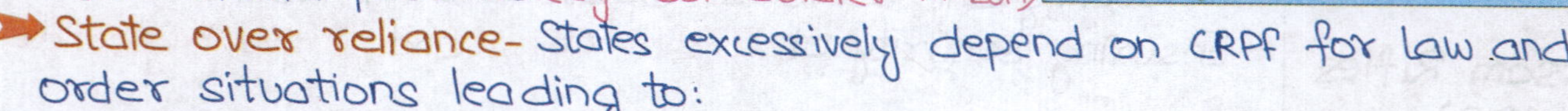

- **State over reliance-** States excessively depend on CRPF for law and order situations leading to:
  - Disruption of CRPF training and rest due to deployment of training companies
  - Reduced operational efficiency of CRPF
- **Poor infrastructure-** Deficiencies like
  - Lack of electricity in Border Out Posts (BOPs) impacting working conditions and operations
  - Cases like 2010 Dantewada incident highlighting inadequate facilities, security and living conditions.
  - These factors contribute to low morale, psychological vulnerability and incidents of suicide or fratricide.
- **Infrastructure Delays-** Slow execution of road projects due to clearances, terrain, seasonality and material availability hinders CAPF mobility
- **Equipment Shortages-** Delays in acquiring combat-ready equipment and inadequate medical facilities especially in hostile environments put personnel at risk.
- **Outdated Training-** CAPF training needs an overhaul to include modern technology like IT, Cybersecurity and counter terrorism tactics.
- **Procurement Delays-** Modernisation plans are hampered by a cumbersome procurement process for equipment and infrastructure
- **Intelligence Gaps-** Weak intelligence gathering
- **Stress and family separation-** CAPF personnel experience high stress and lack opportunities for regular interaction with families due to deployment locations

Recommendations

01 **Boosting Morale and Efficiency**

Promotion Reforms- filling top CAPF positions from within the CAPF cadres and addressing promotion bottlenecks

Internal Grievance Mechanism- Establishing a robust system for addressing CAPF personnel grievances

02 **Strengthening law and Order Response**

State Police Capacity Building- Investing in better training and equipment for state police forces to reduce reliance on CAPFs for routine tasks

Modernized CAPF Training- Updating training curriculum and infrastructure to combat contemporary threats.

03 **Improving Operational Effectiveness**

Infrastructure Upgrade- Prioritising infrastructure development in CAPF deployments, including reliable electricity, proper facilities and secure living conditions.

Modernisation and Equipping- Streamlining procurement processes to ensure timely acquisition of combat ready equipment and adequate medical facilities for CAPFs.

Mine Detection Technology- Collaborating with research agencies to develop technology for detecting landmines in LWE zones

04 **Enhancing Personnel Well-being**

Focus on Housing- Collaborating with states to ensure timely construction of housing for CAPF personnel

Family Support- Considering family needs during CAPF deployments to facilitate better work-life balance.

05 **Enhanced Intelligence Gathering**- Granting intelligence agencies more autonomy in recruitment and improving information sharing to improve response times.

Role of Intelligence in National Security

- **About:** An intelligence system in internal security is a system that **collects, analyzes, and disseminates information** related to threats and risks to the internal security of a country or an organization.
- It involves **various sources, methods, tools, and actors** that work together to provide **timely and accurate intelligence** to support decision-making and action-taking by the authorities.

Objectives of intelligence system:

- **Prevention:** To identify and prevent potential threats before they materialize into actual incidents.
- **Detection:** To discover and monitor existing or emerging risks that pose a challenge to the internal security.
- **Response:** To provide timely and relevant information to enable appropriate actions to counter or mitigate the threats.
- **Evaluation:** To assess and review the performance and impact of the intelligence system

Indian Intelligence Network

- **Research and Analysis Wing (RAW):** India's primary foreign intelligence agency.
  - It specializes in collecting intelligence related to external threats and activities that can impact India's security.
  - RAW operates covertly and conducts espionage, counter-terrorism, and counter-proliferation activities.
- **Intelligence Bureau (IB):** Internal intelligence agency of India.
  - **Focus**: Domestic intelligence and counter-intelligence.
  - It gathers information related to internal security threats, including terrorism, communal violence, and subversive activities.
- **Central Bureau of Investigation (CBI):** Primarily an investigative agency, it also has an intelligence division.
  - This division assists in **gathering intelligence related to high-profile cases**, corruption, and economic offenses.
- **Defence Intelligence Agencies: It is a** Indian military intelligence agency, to collect and analyze intelligence pertaining to national defense and military operations.
- **National Technical Research Organisation (NTRO):** Specializes in technical intelligence and electronic surveillance.
  - It is **responsible for monitoring communication and electronic signals,** which are vital for national security.
- **State Intelligence Agencies:** Each Indian state has its own intelligence agency responsible for **gathering intelligence on local matters and potential threats** within the state's jurisdiction.
- **Other Agencies:** India has **various specialized agencies focusing on areas** like economic intelligence (Income Tax Department), cyber intelligence (National Cyber Coordination Centre), and nuclear intelligence (Bhabha Atomic Research Centre).

Challenges with India's Intelligence System	Recommendations to overcome Challenges

• **Lack of Coordination:** There are **14 intelligence agencies** with **overlapping mandates** and a history of turf battles.
  ○ This redundancy can be a weakness if information sharing is poor.
• **Accountability:** Agencies are not subject to parliamentary oversight, leading to concerns about **potential misuse of power and a lack of incentive** to improve performance.
• **Human Resource Issues:**
  ○ **Shortage of Qualified Personnel** in critical areas like languages, technology, and cyber analysis.
  ○ **Dependence on Deputation:** Reliance on police and military officers on deputation creates **issues with rank parity and career progression**.
• **Lacking Outsourced Expertise** for granting security clearances to private contractors, hindering potential collaboration.
	• **Strong political leadership** to streamline the bureaucratic process and prioritize intelligence reforms.
	• **Formulate National Intelligence Strategy,** outlining priorities, resource allocation, and tasking for different agencies.
	• **Independent Intelligence Oversight Body** to ensure accountability and prevent misuse of power.
	• **Intelligence Cadre:** Create a dedicated intelligence cadre with its own recruitment, training, and promotion system to attract and retain talent.
	• **Public-Private Partnerships** for specialized expertise and technological solutions, addressing security clearance concerns.
	• **Legislative Framework:** To define the authorities and limitations of intelligence agencies, while safeguarding privacy rights.
	• **Human Intelligence (HUMINT), Development:** Invest in HUMINT training and resources to improve human intelligence gathering.

• **Absence of Legislative Framework for** governing intelligence agencies creates a grey area regarding their authorities and limitations. • **Focus on Traditional Methods:** Over-reliance on TECHINT and a hesitation to invest in Human Intelligence (HUMINT) development. • **Poor State and Central Coordination on** information sharing. • **Counter-Terrorism Strategy:** National Counter-Terrorism Center's (NCTC) failure to take root hinders effective counter-terrorism efforts. • **Lack of State Police Capacity,** the resources and training to adequately handle complex security threats. • **China Focus:** Intelligence gathering has primarily focused on China's border threats, neglecting its growing presence in the Indian Ocean Region.	• **Improved Coordination:** Establish mechanisms for better information sharing and collaboration between central and state agencies. • **State Police Capacity Building:** Provide resources and training to handle complex security challenges.

Police Reforms

- **About:** Police reforms aim to transform the **values, culture, policies and practices** of police organizations.
  - **Acts as Link:** Police are the important link between the government and people. Police are also connected with prosecution and judiciary.
- **Significance:** It envisages police to **perform their duties** with respect for **democratic values, human rights and the rule of law.**
- Police come under the state list of schedule 7 of the Indian constitution.

Institutional Framework for Policing in India

- **Constitution:** 'Police' and 'Public Order' are state subjects(Schedule 7 of the Indian Constitution).
  - **State legislation on policing** is largely based on the Police act of 1861. **(Ex-** Bombay Police Act, 1951, Kerala police act 1960, Delhi police act 1978).
  - **Responsibilities of State police forces:** Primarily in charge of issues such as crime prevention and investigation and maintaining law and order.
  - First response in case of more intense internal security challenges **(Ex - Terrorist incident or insurgency-related violence).**

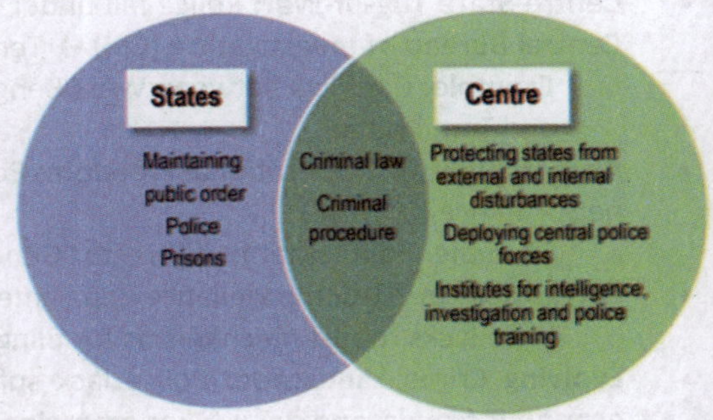

- **Role of Central Government:** Allowed to maintain its own police forces to assist the states with ensuring law and order **(Ex- CRPF, CISF)**

Areas of Concern in Policing System

- **Colonial Legacy:** The **Indian Police Act of 1861**, a colonial law, still governs the police, aiming for a suppressive rather than an enabling force.
- **Overburdened Police Force:** Police-public ratio in India stands at **152.80 per lakh person,** against the sanctioned public-police ratio of **196.23 per lakh person (UN's recommendation: 222 police per lakh persons)**
  - **Impact**: Overburdened police force + huge backlog of cases.
- **Working Hours:** Police work at **77% of sanctioned strength** and for an average of **14 hours a day [Status of Policing in India Report 2019].**
  - **Impact:** This leads to fatigue, low morale, and potentially hinders performance.
- **Absence of Incentives to Perform:** 86% of the state police are constables with limited promotion opportunities
  - **Impact:** This can lead to disengagement and a lack of motivation.
- **Lack of Diversity:** The Status of Policing in India Report (2022) highlights a lack of diversity in police forces based on caste, class, religion, and gender.
  - **Women's representation** is a mere 11.7% (as of Jan 2022).
  - **Impact:** This limits diversity of perspective and may hinder community engagement.

Need for Effective Policing Reforms

- Increasing complexity of crimes with the increase in technology enabled crimes
- The public has no corresponding obligation to help the police
- Required to help in other departments such as income tax raids, demolitions by municipal authorities etc
- Police is first responder in event of crime or any law-and-order situation
- Holding police accountable

- **Physical Infrastructure:** Many police stations lack basic equipment like radios, telephones, and vehicles (BPRD 2020).
  - **Weaponry shortage** (Rajasthan-75% shortage and West Bengal- 71% shortage, according to CAG audit report 2015-16)
  - **Surveillance vehicle shortag**e (30.5% deficiency according to BPRD)
  - **Underutilisation of Funds for modernisation** of state police forces (Just 6% of the Rs 620 crore fund for modernisation of state police forces was used in FY23)
  - **Non-functioning of POLNET** (Police Communication Network)- a satellite-based network to facilitate faster communication between police and paramilitary forces .

- **Technology:** Lack of **advancements in forensics, fingerprinting, and facial recognition** technologies.
    - **Impact:** This hinders effective investigation and crime prevention.
- **Insufficient Financial Allocation**: Only about 3% of state government budgets.
    - **Impact:** Limits resources for training, equipment, and infrastructure upgrades.
- **Police-Public Relations:** Unsatisfactory state of police-public relations, indicating a lack of trust and cooperation (2nd ARC Report)
    - **Impact:** This weakens community engagement and hinders crime prevention efforts.
- **Inter-Service Rivalry:** Centrally managed Indian Police Service (IPS) creates friction between the central government and states.
    - States view IPS officers as outsiders and prefer promoting from their own ranks.
- **Centre-State Tug-of-War:** Police fall under state jurisdiction, public distrust in state forces leads them to **favor the Central Bureau of Investigation (CBI) →** Tension between the center and states.
    - **Example:** Conflicts between West Bengal Police and CBI, withdrawal of general consent for CBI by West Bengal and Tamil Nadu.
- **Accountability vs. Operational Freedom:** Political interference hindering professional policing and leading to biased performance **(2nd ARC).**
    - **Example:** Politicization of Director General of Police (DGP) appointments.
- **Corruption:** In 2016, the vigilance department investigated 55% more cases against its own officers.
    - India lacks robust mechanisms for filing complaints against erring police officials.
- **Evolving Crime Landscape:** Police lack sufficient modern technology to deal with crimes like **organized crime, economic frauds, and deep fakes emerging.**
- **Botched Investigations:** Conviction rate below 50% for crimes under IPC (22nd Law Commission).
    - **Reason:** Lack of training in forensic science, cybercrime investigation etc

Various committees regarding Police Reforms in India (Sub-heading)

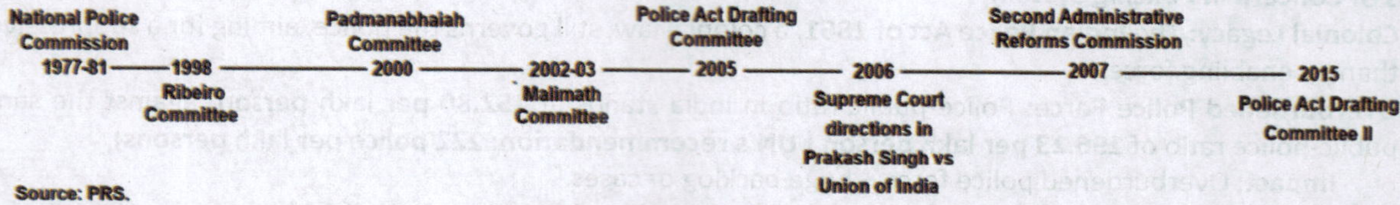

Source: PRS.

Committee	Description
Gore committee 1971-1973	• Enlarge the **content of police training from law and order** and crime prevention to a **greater sensitivity and understanding of human behaviour.**
National Police Commission 1977	• Overhauling the **training processes for constables.** • Setting up a **state security commission** in each state. • **Limiting the powers of the state government** to ensure that the police perform their duty by the law of the land. • Assured **minimum tenure for the chief of the police** in each state. • **DSP should be exclusive** to posting officers in charge of police stations. • **Internal management of the police** should be entirely within the purview of the chief of police.
Padmanabhaiah Committee 2000	• **Standardisation of recruitment procedures** for the police force & training. • Bring changes in police officers' behaviour, police investigations and prosecution. • Improve pay & perk.
Malimath Committee 2003	• A **complete revamp** of the entire criminal procedure system. • Creation of fund to compensate victims turning hostile under pressure of culprits. • Separate national level authority to deal with crimes threatening the country's security.

Soli Sorabjee Committee 2005	• A **new model police bill** to replace the colonial 1861 Police Act. • **State government is to be responsible** for the superintendence of police. • **State Security Commission (SSC)** will be set up, which would be called the State Police Board. • **DGP should be among the three senior officers** selected by the State Police Board. • All officers are to be provided with a **minimum tenure of two years, irrespective of their date of superannuation.** • A **Police Station shall be headed by a Station House Officer (SHO),** not below the rank of Sub-Inspector of Police. • Transfer is prohibited by any authority other than the one specified in law.
Second ARC, 2007	• **Separation of crime investigation** from other police functions like maintenance of law and order. • Establishment of **State police boards** for welfare and grievances redressal mechanisms for police personnel.
NHRC Recommendations, 2021	• **Burden of Proof:** Burden to explain injuries sustained in police custody rests on the authorities, presuming police inflicted the injury. • **Technology-friendly Criminal Justice System** to speed up the criminal justice system. • **Ensuring Accountability:** SC's December 2020 order to install CCTV cameras with night vision in all police stations be "implemented immediately" to ensure accountability. • **Community Policing**: Involvement of trained social workers and law students with police stations as part of community policing and incorporating community policing in police manuals, laws and advisories. • **Application of SC directives in Prakash Singh Case:** The Union Ministry of Home Affairs (MHA) and the State Governments should set up Police Complaints Authorities (PCA). o Implementation of Other Directives by SC in Prakash Singh case.

Judiciary on Police Reform

- **Prakash Singh vs Union of India (2006):** SC directive are:
  - **Constitute a State Security Commission (SSC)** so that the state government does not exercise unwarranted influence or pressure on the police.
  - **Merit based appointment of DGP** and secure a minimum tenure of two years of service.
  - **Security of Tenure of 2 years for** Police officers on operational duties (including SP+ SHO).
  - **Separate the investigation** and law and order functions of the police.
  - **Police Establishment Board (PEB):** To decide transfers, postings, promotions and other service related matters of police.
  - **Police Complaints Authority (PCA):** To inquire into public complaints against police officers of above the rank of Deputy Superintendent of Police.
  - **National Security Commission (NSC) at the union level** to prepare a panel for selection and placement of Chiefs of the Central Police Organizations (CPO) with a minimum tenure of two years.
- **Supreme Court Guidelines (On DGP), 2018**
  - **All states shall send their proposals to the UPSC** at least three months prior to the retirement of the incumbent DGP.
  - **State shall immediately appoint one of the persons** from the panel prepared by the UPSC.
  - None of the states shall ever appoint any person on the post of DGP on an acting basis, for there is **no concept of acting Director General of Police.**
    - However, **many states passed laws to circumvent** the empanelment process of the UPSC.

Implementation of the S.C Directions

- Up till 2020, **not even one state was fully compliant** with the SC directives.
- While **18 states passed their Police Acts at this time**, not one fully matches legislative models.
- **Only the North-Eastern states have followed the suggested changes in spirit.**

Pathways for Efficient Police Force

Making the Police a SMART Force: Prime Minister, at 49th DGP conference in 2014, enunciated the concept of SMART Police.

- **Thana Transformation:** Prioritize improving working conditions at police stations (thanas) → better infrastructure and support for constables.
- **Budgetary Boost:** Allocate funds for **training, technology, and infrastructure upgrades,** ensuring states fully utilize allocated modernization funds.

S for strict but sensitive,
M for modern and mobile,
A for alert and accountable,
R for reliable and responsive and
T for techno-savvy and trained."

- **Criminal Justice System Overhaul:** Implement recommendations from the **Malimath Committee report** to streamline the entire criminal justice system, fostering faster resolution of cases.
- **Investing in People: Continuous Training of** Police + adapting to the evolving criminal landscape. Specialized units like Delhi Police's cyber cell can serve as models.
- **Incorporating Technology in Policing:**

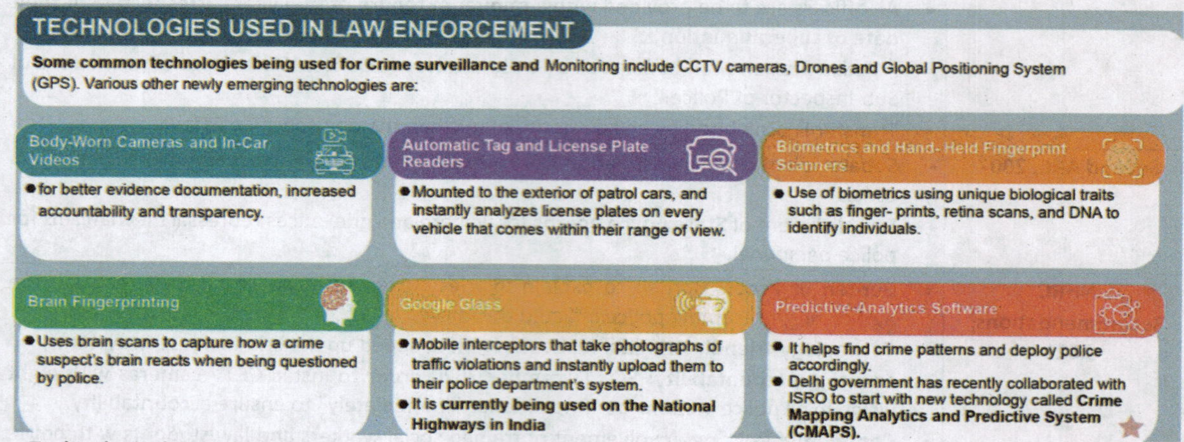

- **Technological Transformation:**
  - **BPRD Revamp:** Modernize the Bureau of Police Research and Development (BPRD) by incorporating social science expertise for better criminological research.
  - Leverage technology like **NCRB's Automated Facial Recognition System (AFRS)** for criminal identification.
  - **Data Sharing:** Facilitate seamless data exchange between agencies, aiding investigations **(National Data Governance Framework).**
- **Community Policing:** Implement successful community policing models like **Kerala's Janamaithri Suraksha Project and Assam's Meira Paibi** to bridge the gap between police and public.
- **Adapt best practices from international models** like Japan's separate police commission for recruitment and New York Police's specialization approach to make Indian police a global force.
- **Implementing NITI Aayog Suggestions on Police Modernisation**
  - **State level legislative reforms-** States should be encouraged, with fiscal incentives, to introduce '**The Model Police Act of 2015**' as it modernises the mandate of the police.
  - **Task force under MHA-** To identify **non-core functions that can be outsourced** to save on manpower and help in reducing the workload of the police.
    - **Ex:** Verification for passport applications can be outsourced.
  - **Greater representation of women** in the police force.
    - Ex: Bihar's 33% women in police force rule.
  - **Police and public order in concurrent List** to tackle increasing inter-state crime and terrorism under a unified framework.

PYQs Corner

(Write the Answer and Get Free Evaluation)

1. What are the internal security challenges being faced by India? Give out the role of Central Intelligence and Investigative Agencies tasked to counter such threats. [250 Words] [15 Marks] **[2023]**

2. Human rights activists constantly highlight the view that the Armed Forces (Special Powers) Act, 1958 (AFSPA) is a draconian act leading to cases of human rights abuses by the security forces. What sections of AFSPA are opposed by the activists? Critically evaluate the requirement with reference to the view held by the Apex Court. [200 Words] [12.5 Marks] **[2015]**

Foreign Policy

CHAPTER
08

INDIAN FOREIGN POLICY

Foreign policy is the set of goals, strategies and actions that a state or a non-state actor pursues in its relation with other actors in the international system.
Foreign policy reflects the interests, values and preferences of the nations and it guides its decisions and behaviors in the global arena.

Types of Foreign Policy

Types	Characteristics
1) Offensive	Prioritizes aggresive pursuit of a nation's interests, potentially using military force or coercion against others
2) Defensive	Safeguarding national interests and independence. • This might involve building military strength or forming alliances
3) Cooperative	Emphasizes collaboration with other countries to achieve shared goals. • Negotiations and compromise are key for mutually beneficial outcomes.
4) Isolationist	Minimizes a country's involvement in international affairs, avoiding entanglement with other nations.
5) Interventionist	Actually shaping the affairs of other countries, often promoting democracy or human rights.
6) Multilateral	Utilizes international organizations or coalition to achieve foreign policy objectives.

Core Objectives of Foreign Policy

- National Security: This encompasses ensuring the safety of citizens and territory.
  - Strategies: Military build-up, alliance or diplomacy to prevent conflict (Ex: NATO)
- Economic Prosperity: Foreign policy can be geared towards economic growth through trade agreements, attracting investments or securing resources. (Ex: RCEP)
- Political Stability: Promoting stable governance, both domestically and abroad, might involve supporting democracies, mediating conflicts, or advocating for human rights (Ex: Role of European Union)
- National Interests: Could involve territorial defense, access to resources or promoting the nation's values and ideology.
- Global Influence: Shaping international relations and the global order → involve promoting specific values like democracy or influencing other countries' actions (Ex: Bipolar world during Cold War Era)

Approaches to Foreign Policy

Foreign Policy Approach	View of the World	Key Features	Example
Realism	• World is inherently competitive and states must prepare for worst case scenario	• States act in self-interest, seeking to maximise power and security. • Anarchy prevails in international relation. • Military and economic strength are crucial. • Balance of power is essential to prevent aggression.	• George W. Bush's decision to invade Iraq in 2003.
Liberalism	• Cooperation and diplomacy are possible.	• States can collaborate on common goals. • International Institutions and norms matter. • Economic interdependence foster stability • Democracy and human rights are important.	• Multilateral efforts like the United Nations reflect liberal ideals.

Idealism	• Ethical and moral values should guide international behavior.	• Prioritizes ethical and philosophical values. • Aims for a more just and peaceful world. • Associated with Woodrow Wilson's vision for the League of Nations.	• Promoting democracy and human rights globally.
Marxism	• Capitalism perpetuates inequality and conflict.	• Focuses on economic relations and exploitation. • Sees international relations as shaped by class interests. • Advocate for a socialist transformation.	• Marxist analysis of imperialism and capitalist exploitation

INDIAN FOREIGN POLICY

Evolution of India's Foreign Policy

India's foreign policy has undergone significant transformations since independence.

Nehruvian Era (1947-1964):

- Non Alignment: Defined India's position as independent from major power blocs (Cold War) – crucial for establishing its identity as a newly independent nation.
- Panchsheel: Five principles for peaceful coexistence – important for guiding diplomatic relations.
- Focus on UN & NAM: Actively participated in international organizations to promote peace and cooperation.

India's foreign policy has Four Important goals:

→ Protect India from traditional and non-traditional threats.

→ Create an external environment which is conducive for an inclusive development of India.

→ Ensure that India's voice is heard on global forums and that India is able to influence world opinion on issues of global dimensions.

→ Engage and protect Indian Diaspora.

Shastri's Era (1964-1966):

- 1965 Indo-Pak war: Highlighted the need for stronger military and strategic alliances.
- Improved Relations with USSR: Secured vital military and economic assistance.

Indira Gandhi's Era (1966-1977, 1980-1984):

- 1971 Indo-Pak War and Bangladesh Liberation: Established India as a regional power.
- Indo-Soviet Treaty: Strengthened military and economic ties with the USSR.
- Nuclear Test (1974): Demonstrated India's self-reliance in defense but strained relations with some western countries.
- SAARC founding: Promoted regional cooperation in South Asia.

Nehru	Changing security dynamics →	Indira Gandhi
• Focus = Economy over Military = Led to problems in 1962. • Pakistan Policy = Dialogue • Nuclear = Had nuclear programme but no testing or PNE. • Moral goodness with no aggression. • Non alignment movement • Idealism	1) Indo-China war 1962 2) Indo-Pak war 1965 and 1971 3) India tests PNE-I in 1974	• Focus = Military and economy → Garibi Hatao and Self sufficiency. • Pakistan = Aggression led dialogue. • Nuclear = Tested PNE in 1974. • Sharpness and alertness with aggression. • 'Equality' as basis of engagement • Realism.

Rajiv Gandhi's Era (1984-89)

- Economic Liberalisation: Opened India's economy for growth and foreign investment.
- Sri Lankan Intervention: A complex issue showcasing India's involvement in regional security.

1990s:

- LPG Reforms: Increased focus on economic diplomacy and global integration.
- Gujral Doctrine: Established principles for peaceful relations with South Asian neighbours.
- Look East Policy: Diversified partnerships towards Southeast Asia.
- WTO Participation: Increased global trade oppurtunities.

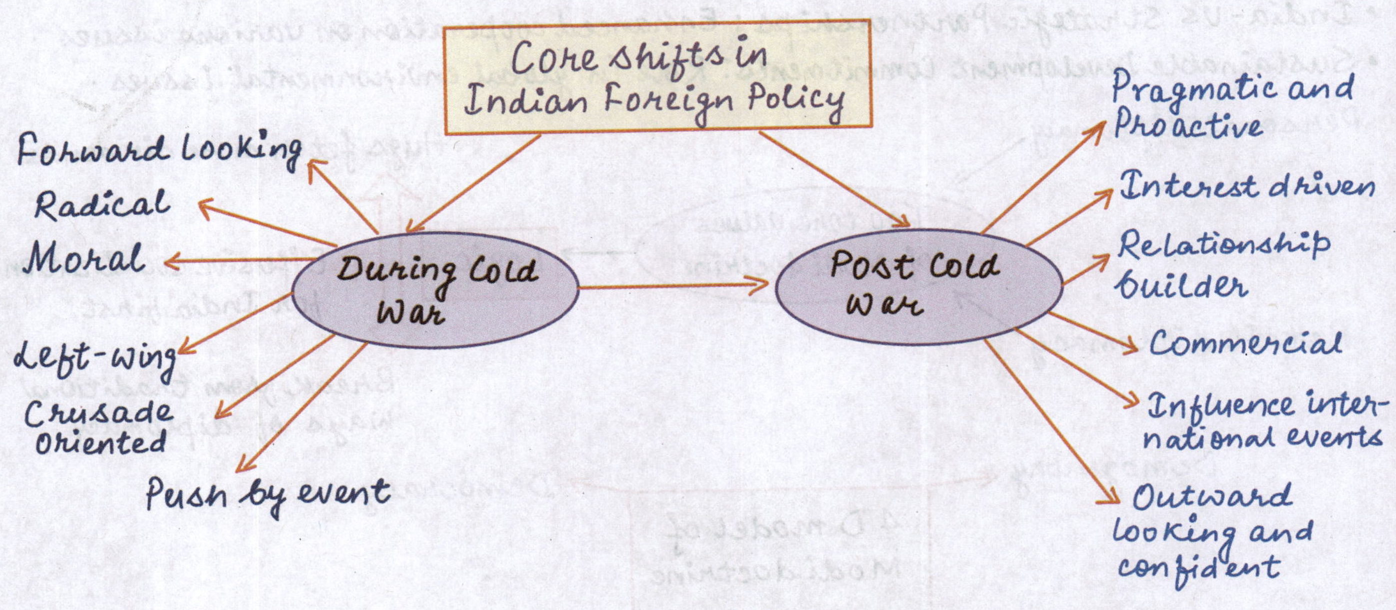

NDA-I (1998-2004):

- Nuclear Tests (1998): Solidified India's nuclear power status but led to international sanctions.
- Kargil War (1999): Highlighted the need for border security and strategic partnerships.
- Improved US Relations: Increased cooperation on various fronts.

UPA-I and II (2004-2014)

- Indo-US Nuclear Deal: Ended India's nuclear isolation and opened doors for civil nuclear cooperation.
- Engagement with China: Balancing act between cooperation and competition
- Look East and ASEAN Free Trade Agreement: Deepened economic ties with SouthEast Asia.
- UN Security Council Reforms: Advocated for a permanent seat on the council.

NDA-II (2014-Present):

- Neighbourhood First Policy: Prioritizes strengthening relations with South Asian neighbours.
- Act East Policy: Expands strategic and economic partnerships in the Indo-Pacific region.
- Strategic Autonomy: Charting an independent course in the world affairs.
- Bangladesh Land Border Agreement: Resolved a long standing border dispute.
- SCO Membership: Increased regional security cooperation.

- India-US Strategic Partnerships: Enhanced cooperation on various issues.
- Sustainable Development Commitments: Role in global environmental issues.

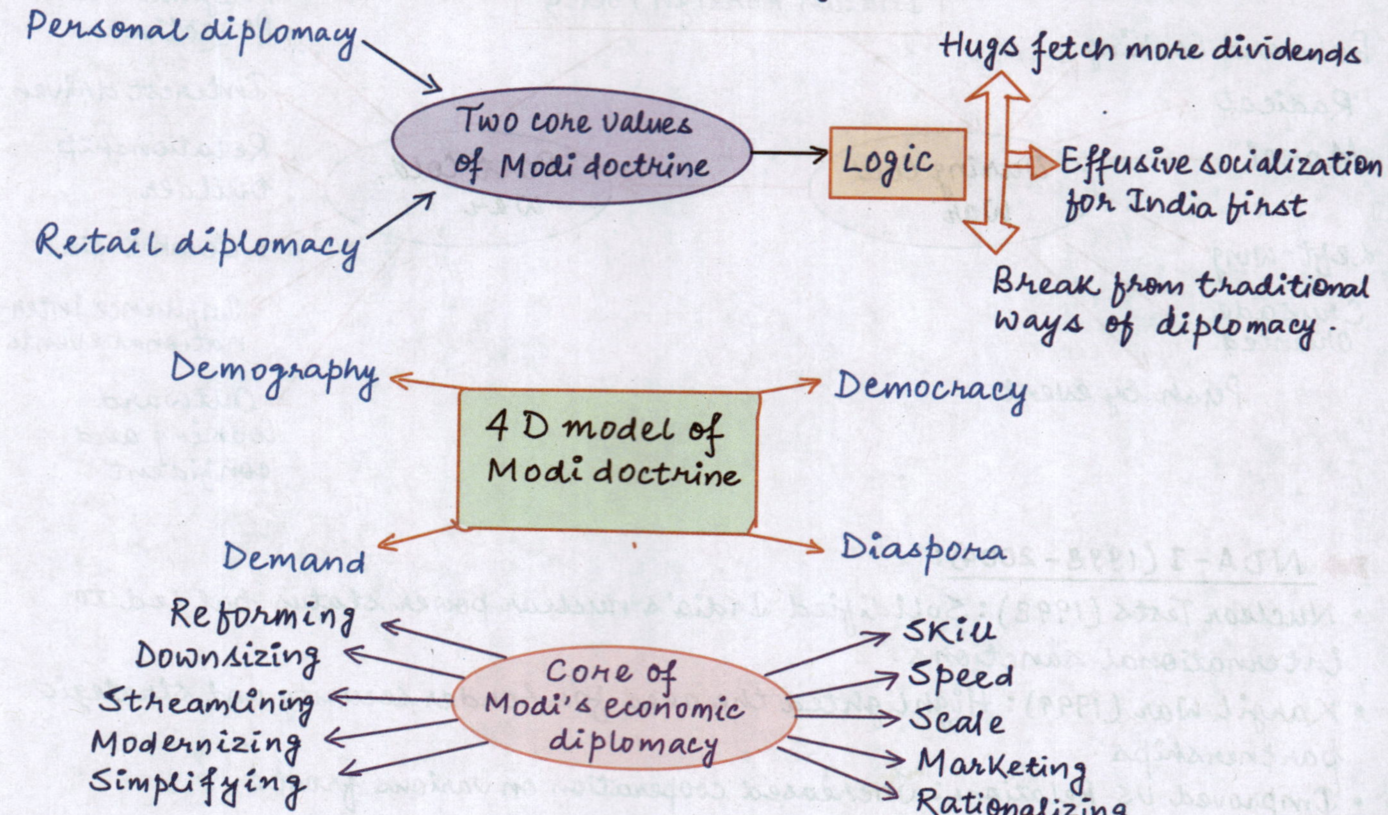

India's Foreign Policy	
Core Values	**Key strategies**
• Non-Aligned and Neutral: India charts its own course, avoiding alliances. • Respect for sovereignity: India opposes meddling in other's affairs and supports territorial integrity (Opposes unilateral sanctions/military actions) • Peaceful Coexistence: Dialogue and cooperation over conflict ("Constructive Engagement") • Global Cooperation: India advocates for international consensus and contributes to peacekeeping (UN Peacekeeping Forces).	• Capacity Building: Assisting others to strengthen democracy (Ex: Afghanistan) • Selective intervention: Protecting national interests when necessary (Ex. Bangladesh, Sri Lanka, Maldives) • Strategic Partnerships: Issue based collaborations, not military alliances (Abstaining from UN vote against Russia) • Active Diplomacy: Building strong bilateral ties and global cooperation.

Guiding Philosophy:

- Vasudhaiva Kutumbakam (One World Family): Promote global interconnectness and a human-centric approach.
- Tradition of the Middle Path: Seeking balanced solutions in international relations.

INDIA'S GUIDING PRINCIPLES OF FOREIGN POLICY

Background:

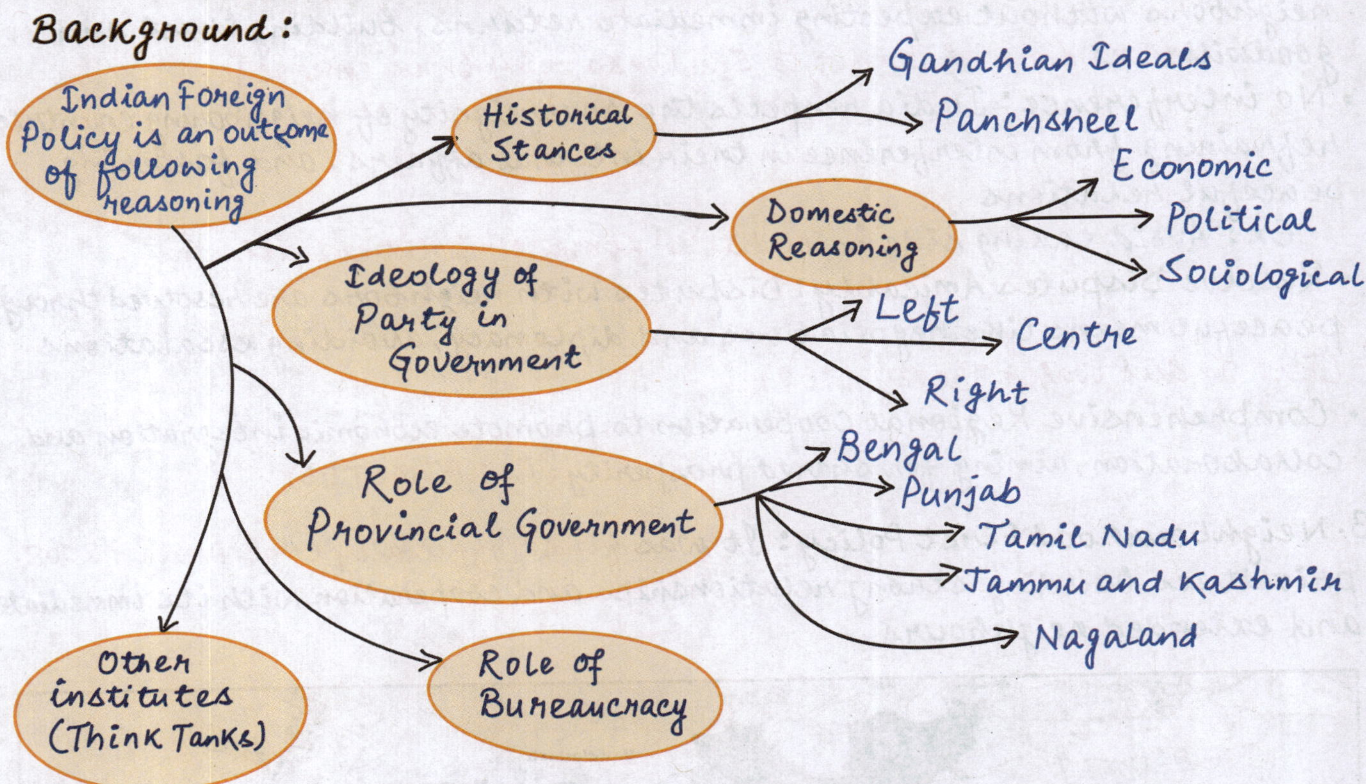

1. Panchsheel Principle

- About: They are five principles that were established to guide peaceful relations between countries.
- Origin: By India's Prime Minister Jawaharlal Nehru in 1954, in the context of establishing diplomatic relations with the People's Republic of China.

Panchsheel Principles:

1) Mutual respect for sovereignity and territorial integrity
2) Mutual non-aggression
3) Peaceful coexistence
4) Equality and mutual benefit
5) Mutual non-interference in internal affairs

- Aim : To promote peace and cooperation between countries, particularly in the context of decolonization and the Cold War.
    - They have been influential in shaping India's foreign policy and have been adopted by other countries as well.

2. Gujral Doctrine (by I.K. Gujral in 1996): It outlines India's approach to foreign policy with its South Asian neighbors.
- Non-reciprocity: India provides assistance and concessions to smaller neighbors without expecting immediate returns, building trust and goodwill (Ex: Line of credit to Sri Lanka – $4 bn in emergency).
- No interference: India respects the sovereignity of neighboring countries refraining from interference in their internal affairs, and fostering peaceful relations.
    - Ex: Avoid taking side in Nepal's domestic political debates
- Resolve Disputes Amicably: Disputes with neighbors are resolved through peaceful means like negotiations and diplomacy, avoiding escalations. (Ex: Indus Water Treaty 1960)
- Comprehensive Regional Cooperation to promote economic integration and collaboration, aiming for shared prosperity (Ex: BIMSTEC)

3. Neighbourhood First Policy: It was first officially conceived in 2008, prioritizes building strong relationships and cooperation with its immediate and extended neighbours.

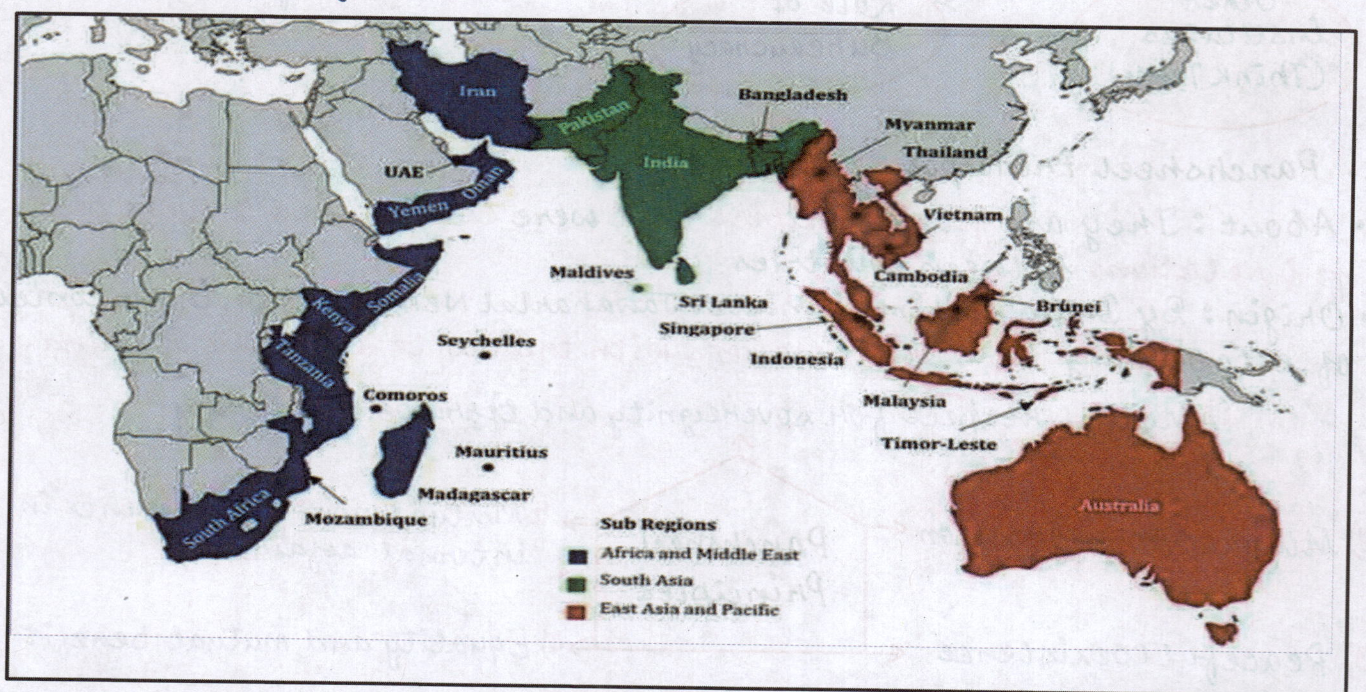

- Immediate Neighbourhood: India shares its civilizational relations, geographical land and maritime boundaries with its immediate neighbours in the South Asian region – Afghanistan, Bhutan, Bangladesh, China, Maldives, Myanmmar, Nepal, Pakistan and Sri Lanka.

- Extended Neighbourhood: Countries that are geographically distant from India, such as those in the Indian Ocean Region, Southeast Asia or West Asia, but maintain significant political, economic, cultural, and strategic ties with India.
- NFP Aim: To create a more stable, secure and prosperous region for India and its neighbours.

- NFP focuses on:
  - Consultation: Working together with neighbours to find solutions.
  - Non-reciprocity: Offering assistance to neighbours without expecting immediate returns.
  - Tangible Outcomes: Focuses on achieving practical results in areas like infrastructure, development and security.

Evolution of India's Neighbourhood Policy

- Colonial phase: Anti-colonialism, anti-imperialism, anti-racism (Asian Relation Conference of 1948) cemented India's relations with its neighbours
- 1950s and 1960s: India chose to deal with its neighbourhood by engaging in bilateral talks and treaties and not in a regional framework.
- 1960s-1990s: Phase of regional assertion and establishing sub-continental hegemony
- 1990s-2000s: Gujral Doctrine attempted to assure India's support to neighbours through unilateral concessions.
- 2008 onwards: With growing footprint of Chinese in neighbouring region conceived 'Neighbourhood First Policy (NFP)
- 2014 onwards: Revamping NFP to strengthen ties through economic cooperation, development etc.

- 5S's of Neighbourhood First Policy

Significance of NFP	Challenges to NFP
• Regional leadership: Cooperation with neighbours strengthens India's position in South Asia and the Indian Ocean Region (IOR), a Key global competition zone. • Countering China: A united neighborhood helps India counter China's influence and solidify its role as a regional security provider (SAGAR initiative) • Multilateral Cooperation: Collaboration with neighbors bolsters India's leadership in global forums like the UNSC (Permanent Membership), representing the interests of the Global South. • Security Concerns: ◦ Territorial Integrity: India seeks cooperation to prevent neighboring countries from harboring separatist groups (Ex: Myanmmar for North-Eastern insurgency) ◦ Maritime Security: Cooperation with coastal neighbors (Maldives, Myanmar Sri Lanka, Bangladesh) is crucial for effective maritime policing and preventing future Mumbai-like attacks. • Economic Interests: ◦ Energy Security: Collaboration with Nepal and Bhutan for hydropower development and with IOR nations to secure oil and gas import routes. (Over 80% of India's oil and 50% of gas come via sea).	• Policy Issues: ◦ Lack of Comprehensiveness: India manages rather than shapes relationships due to a poorly defined policy. ◦ Strained Bilateral Relations: Disputes between regional countries hinder broader cooperation (Ex: Pakistan blocking SAARC agreements) • Security Concerns: ◦ Cross-Border Terrorism: Porous borders, support from some neighbors (Pakistan), and rising extremism pose a terrorist threat. ◦ Drug Trafficking: India's location near the Golden Triangle and Golden Crescent drug routes fuels trafficking. Piracy and terrorist use of waterways are additional threats. • China's Influence: ◦ China's Belt and Road Initiative increases trade with South Asian countries, potentially undermining India's influence. ◦ Playing China Card: Some neighbors (Sri Lanka, Maldives, Nepal) leverage China to gain concessions from India. (Nepal during border blockade) • Trust Deficit with Neighbours: ◦ Military Interventions in Bangladesh, Sri Lanka and Maldives create regional suspicion. ◦ Big brother attitude: Some neighbors feel India prioritizes its own interests over theirs. (Ex: Nepal often accuses India for its big brother attitude.

- Bridging Developmental Gap: Utilizing neighboring ports (e.g., Bangladesh) for trade and promoting North-Eastern development through connections to Southeast Asia (via Myanmmar)
- Soft Power Diplomacy: Leveraging cultural and historical ties (e.g., Buddhism) to strengthen people-to-people bonds and regional influence.

- Socio-Economic Challenges:
  - Economic Crisis: Neighboring countries' economic instability (e.g. Sri Lanka) affects Indian exports.
  - Poor Connectivity: Limited infrastructure hinders trade and investment.
  - Domestic Politics and ethnic ties can negatively impact policy (Ex. Teesta Waters agreement delayed due to West Bengal).
  - Slow progress on Line of Credit projects funded by India can breed frustration and mistrust.
  - Environmental Challenges: Region's vulnerability to natural disasters and climate change can disrupt development and trigger migration.

Pathways for Strengthening India's NFP

- Enhancing Regional Cooperation: Actively utilize SAARC, BIMSTEC and IORA for continuous engagement, dispute resolution and regional integration.
- Addressing Security Challenges:
  - China: Negotiate a clear Line of Actual Control (LAC) and firmly oppose border incursions.
  - Pakistan: Counter terrorism + Economic Cooperation + people-to-people interaction.
  - Internal Security: Strengthen India's Internal Security architecture to encourage proactive responses from neighbors on terrorism.
- Global Partnerships:
  - Strategic Partnerships: Forge partnerships with the US, Russia and the EU to counter China and Pakistan.
  - Multilateral Engagements: Actively participate in the UN, BRICS and G20.
- Tailored Approach to Neighbors:
  - Understanding Concerns: Attune diplomatic efforts to the needs and anxieties of smaller neighbours.
  - Individualized Strategies: Develop customized plans for each country through improved domestic coordination between foreign and security ministries.

- **Boosting Connectivity:**
  - Infrastructure Investments: Invest heavily in regional infrastructures like roads, railways, waterways, ports, energy grids and digital customs.
  - Economic Openness: View regional connectivity as an economic advantage, not a security threat.
  - Regional Development Fund: Explore establishing a fund under BIMSTEC for infrastructure development.
- **Promoting People-to-People Ties:** Invest in medical and religious tourism to strengthen bonds and regional integration (Ex: Medical tourism+ Religious tourism).
- **Addressing Environmental Issues:** Collaborate on water sharing, resource management and environment protection through data and research exchange.

Strategic autonomy Posture of India in 21st Century:

Strategic autonomy is the ability of a state to pursue its own national interests and preferred foreign policy without being constrained by other states.

- It has to be formulated as per the security environment to ensure India's sovereignity and territorial integrity are maintained.

Characteristics of India Strategic Autonomy Posture

Multi-Alignment Approach:	• Shifting focus: India transitioned from a "US-China" (P2) mindset to a "P5+2" approach, engaging major powers (US. China, Russia, Japan, France) and regional groupings (ASEAN, SCO) to solidify its global position
Balancing Diplomacy:	• RIC and JAI Meetings: India showcases its ability to balance relations by participating in both Russia-India-China (RIC) and Japan-America-India (JAI) meetings on the sidelines of G20 summits
Issue-Based Cooperation:	• Broadened Partnerships: India has engaged with Saudi Arabia, Israel and Iran in the middle east, even attending the Organisation of Islamic Cooperation (OIC) for the first time. • S-400 Deal: India pursued the S-400 missile deal with Russia despite US sanctions. • RCEP Exit: India opted out of Regional Comprehensive Economic Partnership (RCEP) due to concerns about China domination.

De-hyphenation Policy:	• "Look West" policy is no longer tied to India's relationship with the Palestinians, allowing for independent ties with Israel
Hard Power and Military Expansion:	• Strong Response: Response to Pulwama terror attacks, including the Balakot airstrikes, demonstrates its willingness to use military power. • Logistics Agreements with the US, France, Australia, Singapore, South Korea.
Soft Power Initiatives:	• International Yoga Day, International Solar Alliance, Vaccine Diplomacy etc.

Jaishankar Doctrine

About: Articulated by Dr. Subrahmanyam Jaishankar, India's Minister of External Affairs. It outlines a pragmatic approach to India's engagement with the world, focusing on multiple key aspects:

- Pragmatism Over Ideology: It emphasizes practicality and flexibility over rigid ideological stances
  - India seeks to engage with other nations based on its national interests rather than dogmatic principles.
- Realism and National Security: National security is a central consideration, and India aims to protect its interests while navigating global challenges.
- Global Engagements: It encourages active participation in global affairs.
  - India seeks to expand its influence, build strategic partnerships and contribute to global stability.

Specific Thrust Areas of India's Foreign Policy in the Present Time

- Prioritizing an integrated neighbourhood through Neighbourhood First Policy and Outreach towards extended neighbourhood.
- Leveraging international partnerships to promote India's domestic development which includes Strategic Balancing of relations between major powers, Outreach to middle powers, etc.
- Ensuring a stable and multipolar balance of power through its commitment to multilateral and plurilateral solutions and emphasising on a rules-based international order.
- Advancing Indian representation and leadership on matters of global governance with its ethos of Vasudhaiva Kutumbkam.
- Leveraging Soft Power Potential in fields like spiritualism, yoga etc to advance India's global influence.

- Balancing Act: India aims to balance relations with major powers, including the United States, China and Russia.
  - It seeks to maximize the benefits while minimizing risks.
- Economic Diplomacy: Recognizes the role of economic strength in foreign policy.
  - Line of Credit + Big Market Potential are Key to economic diplomacy.
- Multilateralism: India actively engages in multilateral forums such as the United Nations, G20 and BRICS.
  - It advocates for reforms in global institutions to reflect contemporary realities.

India's Foreign Aid Strategy

- Government of India's approach to development partnership has been shaped by India's struggle for independence and solidarity with other colonized and developing countries
- India's approach to development is mainly human centric and is marked by Respect, Diversity, Care for the Future and Sustainable Development.
- Most fundamental principle: Respecting development partners and be guided by their development priorities.
- Other reasons behind giving a foreign aid:

1. Fostering regional cooperation and stability by providing a significant amount of aid to its South Asian neighbours like Bhutan, Nepal and Bangladesh. Ex - India's grant assisted construction of Tala Hydro-electric Project in Bhutan.
2. Strengthening political and economic ties: Lines of credit offered to resource rich countries in Africa can secure access to critical raw materials for India's own industries. Ex - Indian government pledge of $1 billion line of credit to Zambia for various infrastructure development projects.
3. Projecting India's technological advancements and establishing itself as a leader in the developed world. Ex - One Sun, One World, One Grid
4. Huminitarian assistance in times of natural disasters or emergencies. Ex - India extend a USD 75 million for the reconstruction of infrastructure in Nepal Earthquake (2015)
5. Countering China's Influence of Belt and Road Initiative (BRI) through the increased foreign aid to Indian Ocean countries and strengthening its ties.

6. Projection of soft power and enhancing its image as a responsible and benevolent global power. Ex- India's promotion of Yoga.
7. Directed towards countries with significant Indian diaspora communities, fostering goodwill and strengthening cultural ties.

- Types of Foreign Aid: Grant-in-aid, line of credit, capacity building and technical assistance and trade concessions.

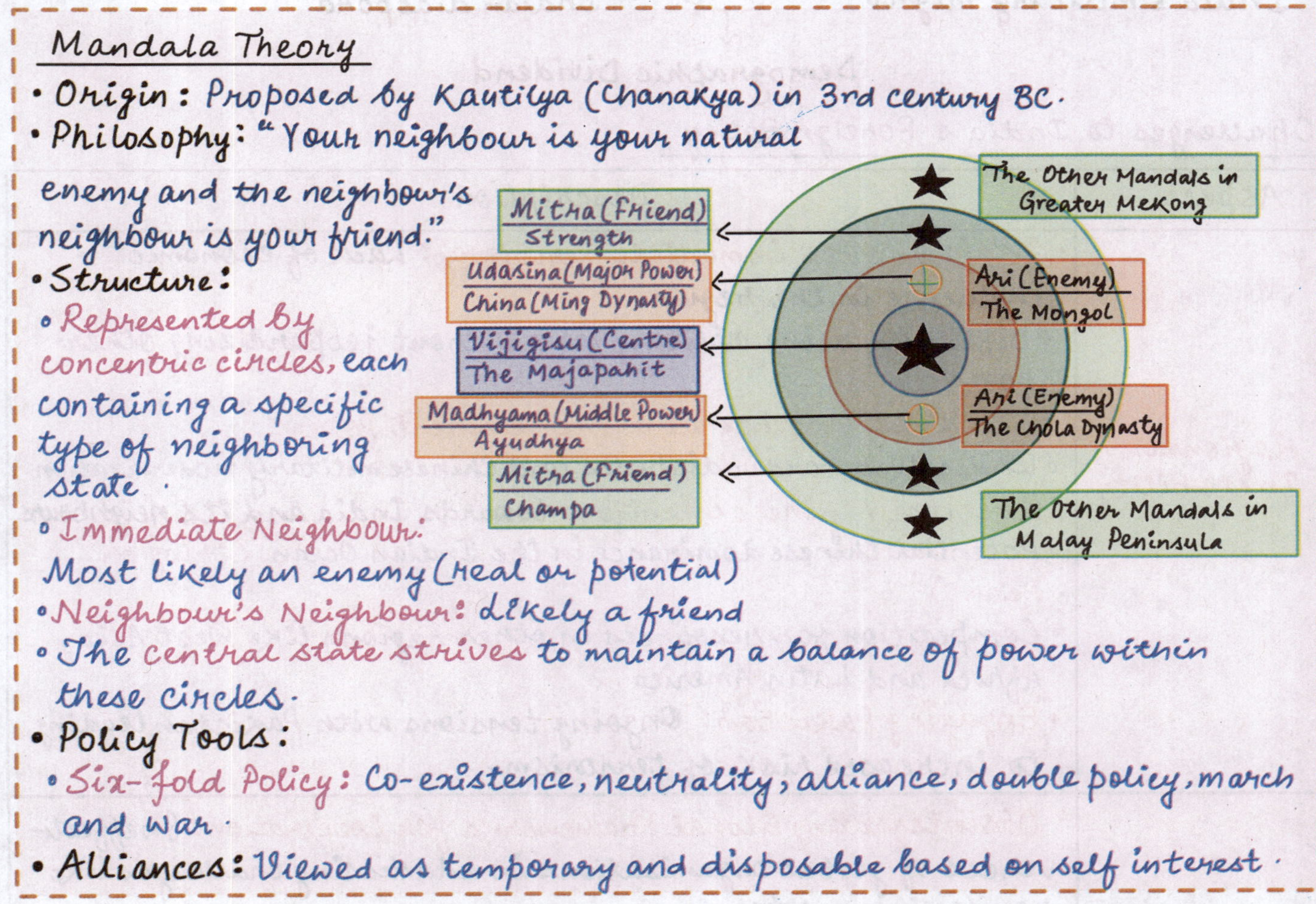

Mandala Theory

- Origin: Proposed by Kautilya (Chanakya) in 3rd century BC.
- Philosophy: "Your neighbour is your natural enemy and the neighbour's neighbour is your friend."
- Structure:
  - Represented by concentric circles, each containing a specific type of neighboring state.

  - Immediate Neighbour: Most likely an enemy (real or potential)
  - Neighbour's Neighbour: Likely a friend
  - The central state strives to maintain a balance of power within these circles.
- Policy Tools:
  - Six-fold Policy: Co-existence, neutrality, alliance, double policy, march and war.
- Alliances: Viewed as temporary and disposable based on self interest.

Stability and Dynamism in India's Foreign Policy Domain

Static factors which contribute to stability in India's foreign policies are:

1) Political stability
2) Socio-religious balance
3) Reduction and elimination of poverty.
4) Strategic independence.
5) The continuity provided by the Indian Foreign Service (IFS)

Factors that make India's Foreign Policy process dynamic and responsive:

- Digitization
- China's aggression
- India's geopolitical potential
- Indian diaspora
- Demographic Dividend
- India's military might
- Crisis situation like covid-19
- Growing Indian market

Challenges to India's Foreign Policy

Aspect	Description
Regional Instability	• India and its immediate Periphery: Lack of economic influence in the region. ∘ Difficulty using military force without jeopardizing other goals. • China's Emergence as a Pre-eminent Power: ∘ Unresolved border disputes and Chinese military modernization. ∘ Uncertain Chinese intentions towards India and its neighbours ∘ Potential Chinese dominance in the Indian Ocean (String of Pearl) ∘ Competition for resources in other regions like West Asia, Africa and Latin America. • Engaging Pakistan: Ongoing tensions with Pakistan leading to increased risk of terrorism.
Global Order	• Disintegrating Global Frameworks for Cooperation: Ineffectiveness of global organizations in addressing challenges like pandemics and trade. • Balancing Act as a Swing Power: Maintaining military ties with Russia while balancing ties with China and strategic relations with the U.S. • Churning in Europe (Ukraine Conflict): Potential emboldening of China due to Russia's success. ∘ Strained US-China relations due to differing approaches to the conflict. • Reshaping the Middle East: Securing Indian interests in the region including energy supplies and maritime security.

Internal Weakness:	• Systematic Constraints: State interference in foreign policy decisions. • Economic Challenges: Slow economic growth, lack of competitiveness and insufficient investment in human capital. • Diaspora Engagement: Lack of resources for effective engagement with the Indian diaspora.
Non-Traditional Threats:	• Evolving Maritime Geopolitics: Issues like climate change, piracy and transnational crime in the Indo-Pacific. • Resource Security: Concerns about water and food security due to population growth and resource limitations • Global Security Issues: Nuclear proliferation, pandemics, drug trafficking and human trafficking. ◦ Uncertainities with US-Russia nuclear programs and the Iranian nuclear deal. • New Technologies: Sub-conventional security challenges like infodemics (spread of misinformation.
Economic Factors:	• Stressed Economic Situations: Slow economic recovery and global trade slowdown (China-USA trade war) ◦ Vulnerabilities in global supply chains exposed by the COVID-19 pandemics. • Dependence on Energy Imports: Reliance on fossil fuels and vulnerability to price fluctuations.

Paradiplomacy

- About: Para diplomacy refers to the use of sub-national actors and organizations to further the interests of a state in the international arena.
- Importance: Para diplomacy can play an essential role in complementing the efforts of traditional diplomacy by leveraging the resources and expertise of sub-national actors.
    - NGOs, religious leaders, cultural organizations and the Indian diaspora.

Significance of Paradiplomacy
• Strengthens the federal structure as it places greater emphasis on states acting as equal partners in the development. • Propels the competitive advantage of sub-national government.

- Facilitates globalisation of location by bringing regional issues on the global stage and finding local solutions to global problems
- Strengthen public leadership.
- Allows exchange of best practices at local levels.
- Facilitates resources and cost sharing of foreign policy making with the federal governments.
- Rising global importance of cities necessitates city level diplomacy.
- Improves country's image as it widens choices, deepen connections with foreign partners, extends the home country's reach.

Paradiplomacy in India

India has witnessed a swift boost in its para diplomatic activities in the last few years.

1) Constitutional Provisions:
- Foreign affairs is exclusively a "union" subject under item 9-20 of the Union List in the 7th Schedule.

2) Emerging trends:
- Vibrant investment summits by Gujarat, Goa, Punjab.
- Greater cross border trade through border haats.
- Rising foreign collaborations in Andhra Pradesh, Telangana and Tamil Nadu.
- High-powered ministerial delegations.
- Chief Ministerial presence in international bodies and summits.

3) Contributing factors:
- Historical factor like contested borders, shared cultures and economic ecosystem.
- Emergence of coalition and regional political parties since 1967.
- Economic liberalisation and Globalisation.
- Government initiatives like Digital India, Make-in-India.
- Creation of State Division in the MEA and Sister-City agreements.

Pathways for Strengthening Indian Foreign Policy

Aspect	Description
Neighbourhood First	• Balancing with China ◦ Maintaining dialogue: Regular Special Representative dialogue address border issues (e.g., 29 rounds held to date)

	◦ Engage in BRICS and SCO forums for cooperation on climate change. ◦ Develop a robust strategy: Modernize military along the Line of Actual Control (LAC) (e.g., Project Dhruv) ◦ Strengthens partnerships with QUAD nations (U.S, Japan, Australia) for regional security. • Mindful Engagement with Pakistan ◦ Promote stability and prosperity: Offer economic cooperation through regional projects like SAARC (South Asian satellite for disaster management) ◦ Prepare for any contigency: Maintain strong military deterrence (e.g., SIPRI Yearbook 2024, India has a nuclear inventory of 172) • Feminist Approach: Promoting gender equality for regional stability and development. ◦ Support women's empowerment initiatives in neighboring countries (e.g., providing training for female Afghan diplomats)
Expanding Strategic Autonomy	• Reorient Foreign policy: Partner with IBSA (India, Brazil, South Africa) to advocate for developing country interests at the WTO (e.g., joint push for fairer agricultural trade rules) • Strengthen Multilateral Institutions: UN Security Council reform to reflect contemporary realities (e.g., India as a major troop contributor to UN Peacekeeping Missions) • Pursuit of Multi-Alignment: Building a network of relationships to advance national interests. ◦ Cultivate positive relationships: Deepen strategic partnerships with US through military exercises like Malabar Exercise. ◦ Maintain economic ties with China (FY23: Bilateral Trade at US$ 113.83 billion)
Engaging the Diaspora:	• Maximize benefits (e.g., estimated 18 million strong diaspora). Encourage investments in key sectors and leverage skills and expertise. • Protect their interests: Ensure safety and advocate for rights in host countries (Kafala system).

Shifting from Risk Aversion to Realism	• Proactive Diplomacy to achieve strategic objectives. ◦ Pursue bolder initiatives: 1998 nuclear tests established India as a nuclear power, leading to engagement with Nuclear Suppliers Group (NSG) ◦ Build Alliances: Partner with like minded countries for maritime security cooperation in the Indo-Pacific (e.g., joint naval exercise)
Securing National Interests	• Protect Territorial Integrity: Invest in border infrastructure development (Strategic roads along the LAC) and modernize military. • Counter terrorism: Dismantle terror networks, improve border security and strength counter-terrorism cooperation with regional partners (SCO) • Ensure Energy Security: Diversify energy imports, invest in renewable energy sources and secure long term LNG contracts with major producers (India-Qatar LNG deal) • Advocate for fair trade, environmental responsibility (e.g., setting ambitions clean energy targets) • Promote disarmament (e.g., advocating for the extension of the NEW START treaty with Russia and the US). • Foster regional stability (e.g., playing a mediatory role in conflicts). • Promote international peace (e.g., contributing peacekeeping forces to UN missions)
Role in shaping a new world order:	• Strengthen International law: Advocate for peaceful resolution of disputes based on international law (e.g. India's role in the Law of the Sea negotiations. • Indo-Pacific Leader: Championing a free and open Indo-Pacific through regional forums (Quad, ASEAN) • Maritime Strength: Collaborating with like-minded nations to enhance maritime security. • Re-Globalisation Champion: Diversifying partnerships and building domestic capabilities. • Equitable Global Voice: Advocating for a reformed global governance system. • G20 Leadership: Showcasing vision and building consensus on key issues during the G20 summit

Focusing on Self-Development	• Accelerate economic reforms: Implementing policies to attract foreign investment and improve ease of doing business. • Strengthen Institutions: Tackling corruption and improving judicial efficiency. • Prioritize social development: Increasing spending on education and healthcare. • Enhance India's global standing through internal progress (e.g., becoming a $ 5 trillion economy by 2025)

PYQs Corner

(Write the Answer and Get Free Evaluation)

1. What is meant by **Gujral doctrine?** Does it have any relevance today. Discuss. **[2013]**
2. In respect of India — Sri Lanka relations, discuss how domestic factors influence foreign policy. **[2013]**

India's Neigbourhood

CHAPTER

09

INDIA-CHINA RELATIONS

- **Political:** On 1 April, 1950, India became the first non-socialist bloc country to establish diplomatic relations with the People's Republic of China.
- **Economic Ties:** Bilateral trade has grown significantly reaching US $ 118 billion by 2023.
- **Historical Ties:** Conceptual and linguistic exchanges existed in 1500-1000 B.C between the Shang-Zhou civilization and the ancient Vedic civilization.
  - Several Buddhist pilgrims and scholars travelled to China on the historic "Silk Route".
- **Multilateral cooperation** at Shanghai Cooperation Organisations (SCO) and BRICS groupings reflecting common agenda for growth & development.
- **Informal Summits:** Both countries have initiated the

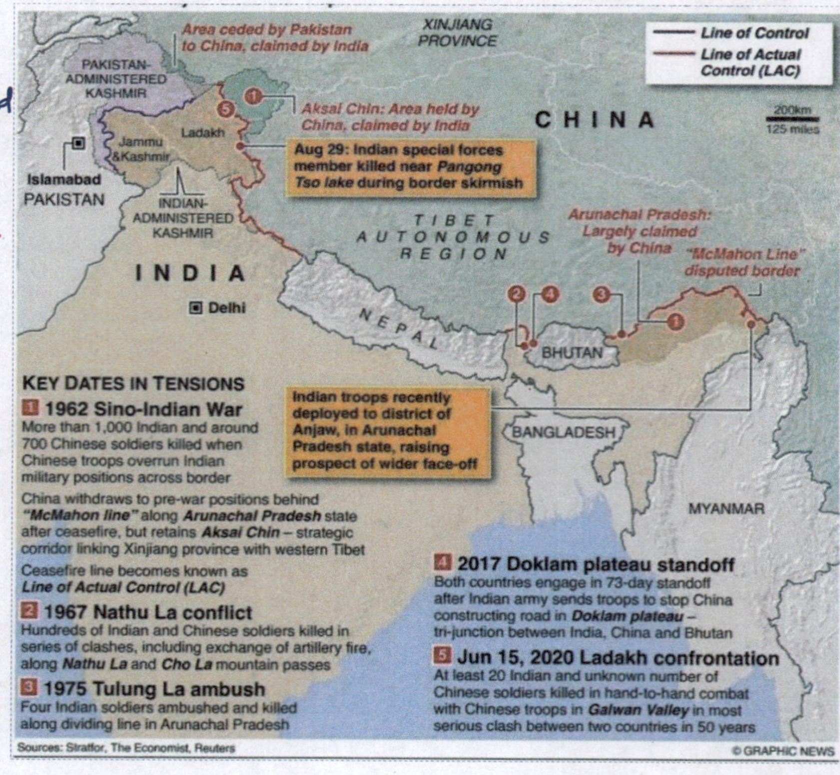

"hometown diplomacy", held two informal summits in Wuhan and Mamallapuram respectively.

Evolution of India China Relations:

India China Relations – Early Years (1950s–1960s):

- 1950: India recognizes the People's Republic of China and establish diplomatic relations.
- 1954: Signing of Panchsheel Agreement emphasizing peaceful coexistence.
- 1962: Sino-Indian War over border disputes, China wins decisively.

India China Relations – Post-war Scenario:

- 1959–1962: Unilateral changes to the Line of Actual Control, leading to conflict.
- China claims Arunachal Pradesh as an integral part, straining ties.

India China Relations – Strategic Distance (1970s–1980s)

- Limited diplomatic and trade engagements due to mutual distrust.
- India's closeness with Soviet Union and China's stance against the USSR heighten tensions
- Deng Xiaoping's reform from 1978 paved the way for economic growth and openness.

India China Relations – Efforts for Normalization (1980s):

- 1988: Indian PM Rajiv Gandhi's visit to China marks significant advancement.
- Agreements signed to maintain peace along the border.

Post-Cold War Era (1990s onwards):

- Economic cooperation rises as focal point, significant increase in trade and investment

India China Relations (2000 onwards):

- Working Mechanism for Consultation and Coordination on India-China Border Affairs (WMCC) was established in 2012.
- Occasional military standoffs over region like Aksai Chin and Arunachal Pradesh.

India China Relations – Recent Developments:

- 2017: Doklam standoff leads to significant strain
- June 2020: Galwan valley clash results in casualities on both sides, intensifying tensions.

India-China: Areas of Conflict

- Five Finger Policy: China considers Tibet to be the right hand's palm of China with Ladakh, Nepal, Sikkim, Bhutan and NEFA (Arunachal Pradesh) as its five fingers.

- Policy describes Tibet as the palm, with China aspiring to control or influence the five surrounding regions, referred to as fingers.

Ladakh: Direct land route to Pakistan
Nepal: Exert pressure on India's northern flank.
Sikkim: Isolating India's northeastern states (Siliguri Corridor)
Bhutan: Bring China closer to Bangladesh and the Bay of Bengal.
Arunachal Pradesh: Strengthens China's military presence and influence in India's northeast

- Salami Slicing Strategy: It is a divide and conquer strategy involving incremental threats and alliances to overcome opposition and acquire new technologies.
  - China is undertaking small geopolitically unlawful steps to achieve a larger gain.
  - Ex: Doklam standoff in the Himalayas + New infrastructure in the border areas (628 villages along India's borders with Tibet Autonomous Region).
- Border Dispute: McMohan Line (1913–14) proposed by British India, rejected by China.
  - Tibetan Annexation (1950): Created a long, undefined border.
  - Line of Actual Control (LAC) (1959): China's proposal rejected by India.
  - Sino-Indian War (1962): China seized territory later withdrew.
  - LAC Established (post-war): Informal ceasefire line, disputed location.
  - Ongoing Disputes: Disagreements over McMohan Line, Aksai Chin, Arunachal Pradesh.
- Aggressive Policies in India's Neighbourhood:
  - Belt and Road Initiative (BRI): India boycotted the BRI due to concerns over sovereignity, as the China-Pakistan Economic Corridor (CPEC) – a key part of the BRI – passes through Pakistan-Occupied Kashmir.
    - Concerns over transparency and potential debt burdens assoiated with BRI
  - String of Pearls: Refers to a geopolitical and strategic initiative that involves building a network of Chinese-funded owned, or controlled ports and other maritime infrastructure facilities in strategic locations across the Indian Ocean.
    - Aim: Encircle India which would allow China to influence and control key maritime routes in the Indian Ocean.
    - Ex: Gwadar Port in Pakistan, Hambantota

Port in Sri Lanka, Chittagong Port in Bangladesh and Djibouti Port in Horn of Africa.

- Debt Trap Diplomacy: China extends loan to developing countries, often for infrastructure projects, with the intention of creating economic dependence.
  - Outcome: China may gain strategic leverage or control over key assets if the debtor is unable to fulfill its financial obligations.
  - Ex: Hambantota Port in Sri Lanka is leased to China for 99 years + China owns around 70 percent of the Maldives debt (Recent Maldives hostility to India).

- India's import dependency: China has emerged as India's largest trading partner in the FY 2023-24 with $118.4 billion (trade deficit of $85 billion)

Reasons for India's dependency on China	Impact on India's domestic industry.
• Low share of manufacturing in GDP vis-a-vis domestic needs. • Liberalised trade and FDI regime. • Highly competitive Chinese goods in comparison to domestic products (in terms of price, utility, design etc). • Ineffectiveness of trade remedial measures and enforcement. • Absence of quality control and standardisation of products in domestic market.	• Chinese imported goods are labour intensive and negatively affect domestic employment. • Chinese products dominate the unorganised retail thus affecting MSME Sector. • Increase in fragility of supply chains as seen during COVID pandemic. • Threatens viability of price sensitive industries like solar industry. • Poor quality Chinese products have negative impact on human health and local environment.

- Water Dispute: No formal treaty has been established for the sharing of the Brahmaputra River water has been a significant source of tension with China constructing numerous dams in the upper reaches of the river on which India has raised objections.
- Geopolitical Rivals: Both countries are attempting to assert their global influence, and they have competing interests in a number of regions, including the Asia-Pacific and the Indian Ocean.
- South China Sea (SCS) and India: India is not a party to the South China Sea Dispute and its presence in the SCS is not to contain China but to secure its own economic interests.
  - India demands rule based order in SCS and has been critical of China's increasingly assertive behaviour.

Rising China

- **Economic Rise:** China's GDP reached US$ 17.7 trillion and is estimated that it will surpass the US by 2028.
  - China was the only major economy to have avoided a contraction during the COVID Pandemic.
- **Technological Rise:** China is driving technological innovations in emerging areas such as A.I, robotics, space technology etc.
- **Military Rise:** China's defense expenditure has rapidly increased over the years and is now the second largest military spender in the world.
- **Geo-strategic Rise:** China now has presence across the continents through its Belt and Road initiative (BRI).
- **Rise as a political powerhouse:** China has also created quasi-institutional initiatives such as the Asian Infrastructure Bank, thereby assuming a bigger role on the multilateral stage.
- **Rise as an overseas influencer:** China's interest in sectors such as energy, transport, information and digital technology.

- **Tibet Issue:** India hosts the Tibetan government-in-exile and spiritual leader Dalai Lama.
  - China accuses India of supporting Tibetan separation.
- **India-Taiwan Relation:** India maintains unofficial economic and cultural ties with Taiwan.
  - Officially India adheres to "One-China Policy", acknowledging a single Chinese government and considering Taiwan, Tibet, Hong Kong as a part of China.
  - Shifting Technology: India has moved away from explicitly using the term "One-China Policy" since 2010.

India's Response to China's Assertiveness

- **Strategic Alliances:**
  - **QUAD:** Partnering with democracies like the US, Japan and Australia to ensure a free and open Indo-Pacific region.
  - **I2U2:** A new grouping with Israel, the US and the UAE strengthens India's regional position.
- **Alternative Connectivity Corridors:**
  - **India-Middle East Europe Economic Corridors (IMEC):** Alternative trade route to China's Belt and Road Initiative (BRI), fostering ties with the Middle East and Europe.

- International North-South Transport Corridor (INSTC): Bypassing Pakistan and strengthens India's strategic presence in the Arabian Sea.
- Regional Organizations:
  - Indian Ocean Rim Association (IORA): Economic cooperation among Indian Ocean nations, countering China's influence in the region
- Necklace of Diamond Strategy: Counter response to China String of Pearl Strategy.
  - Goal: To strategically encircle China by establishing and expanding naval base in key locations
  - Acquiring access in strategically important countries like:
    - Singapore (Changi Naval Base)
    - Indonesia (Sabang Port)
    - Oman (Duqm Port)
    - Seychelles (Assumption Island)
    - Iran (Chabahar Port)
  - Developing New Bases and upgrading existing ones to strengthen its presence in the region

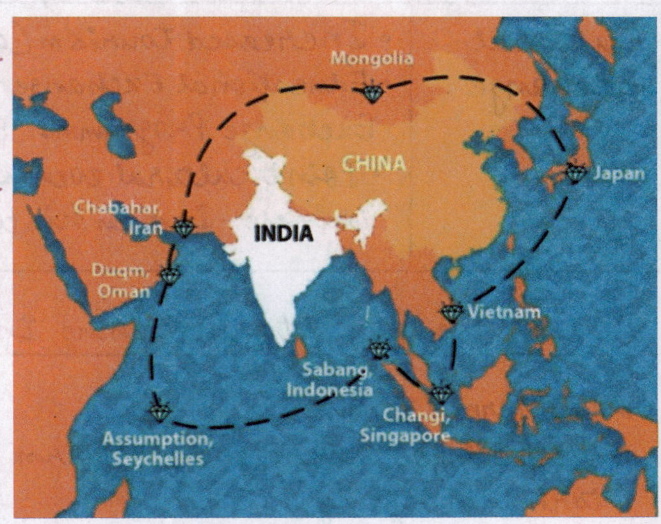

India-China: Area of Cooperation (21st century as the Asian century)

Aspect	Description
Economic Integration	• Trade: Mutually beneficial trade exceeding $136 billion FY23 (e.g., India imports electronics, China imports pharmaceuticals) • Investment in Indian startups (PayTm, Ola, Swiggy etc) • Regional Cooperation: Collaboration in BRICS promotes regional economic ties (New Development Bank)
Global Governance	• G20: Addressing global challenges like climate change and financial stability. • International Organisations: Shaping global trade rules (WTO agricultural subsidy reforms) • Emerging Markets Voice → fairer global financial architecture (AIIB)
Security and Stability	• Border management mechanisms to prevent misunderstandings (hotlines, protocols) • Cooperation in fighting terrorism → SCO RATS • Maritime security collaboration (joint naval exercises → Hand in Hand)

Technological Innovation	• Knowledge Sharing: Collaboration in IT, biotech and space exploration. • Joint Research: Partnering on clean energy solutions (solar cells) • Startup Collaboration: Fostering innovation across Asia by connecting startups.
Cultural Exchange	• Increased tourism (despite visa restrictions) • Educational Exchange Programs for future leaders (Education Exchange Programme (EEP) in 2006) • Joint cultural events (film festivals, exhibitions): Xuanzang (2016) Chinese-Indian historical adventure film.

Pathways for Strengthening India-China Relations

- Long Term Vision:
  - Respect for Sovereignity: Affirm mutual respect for sovereignity and territorial integrity.
  - Long-Term Vision: Prioritize peace, stability and mutual respect for the region.
    - Build trust, understanding and common ground for a positive future.
- People-to-People Relations:
  - Track Diplomacy: Alternative channels for dialogue by facilitating personnel exchanges at all levels and in all fields of society.
    - Track One diplomacy: Formal negotiations between nations conducted by professional diplomats.
    - Track Two diplomacy: Conflict resolution efforts by professional non-governmental conflict resolution practitioners.
- Adhering to Wuhan and Malappuram Spirit of Peace and Cooperation (8 Broad Principles)
- Cultural Diplomacy: Harness

Eight broad principles for Cooperation of India and China

1) Strict adherence to all agreements on border management.
2) Fully respecting the LAC
3) Making peace and tranquility along the frontier on basis for overall ties.
4) Recognizing that a multipolar Asia is an essential constituent of a multipolar world.
5) Showing sensitivity to each other's interests.
6) As rising powers, each will have their own set of aspirations and their pursuit cannot be ignored.
7) Managing differences effectively
8) Civilisational states like India and China must always take the long view.

the soft power of culture, tourism and people to people ties to strengthen bilateral elections.

- Student exchange programs + Language exchange programs + cultural festivals + joint research projects

- Reinforcing India's Security:
  - Military Deterrance (To Secure Peace): Bolster military capabilities (Parliamentary Recommendation: 3% of GDP defense allocation)
    - Develop border infrastructure (roads, bridges) for better access and reduced misunderstandings.
    - Establish buffer zones in contested areas, building on existing protocols.
    - Adapt the principle of "mutual and equal security" to the current situation.
    - Implement Confidence-Building Measures (CBMs) to prevent escalation.
  - Strategic Autonomy in Foreign Affairs: Maintain independent foreign policy engaging with both US and China.
  - Conflict Resolution Mechanisms for addressing border disputes and other issues.
- Economy:
  - Reduce Dependence on China: Address trade imbalance with China.
    - Diversify imports (Vietnam, South Korea, Japan, Taiwan, Indonesia)
    - Boost exports to China (high value products like engineering goods, electronics)
    - Develop domestic industries to reduce reliance on imports (PLI Scheme)

INDIA-PAKISTAN RELATIONS

India and Pakistan share linguistic, cultural, geographic and economic links, yet their relations has been mired in complexity due to a number of historical and political events.

India Pakistan Relations Timeline

India Pakistan Relations: Phase of Hostility (1947-2001)

- Partition fallout and Kashmir Conflict: Massive migration and violence.
- First India Pakistan War (1947) → Karachi Agreement (1949): Cease-fire line overseen by UN military observers.
- India Pakistan Wars and Agreements: Subsequent conflicts in 1965 and 1971 led to UN interventions and agreements like the Tashkent Agreement and Shimla Agreement.

- **Terrorism and Nuclear Tests:** Pakistan's support for insurgency in Kashmir successful nuclear tests in 1998, Kargil War (1999) + Attack on Indian Parliament (2001).

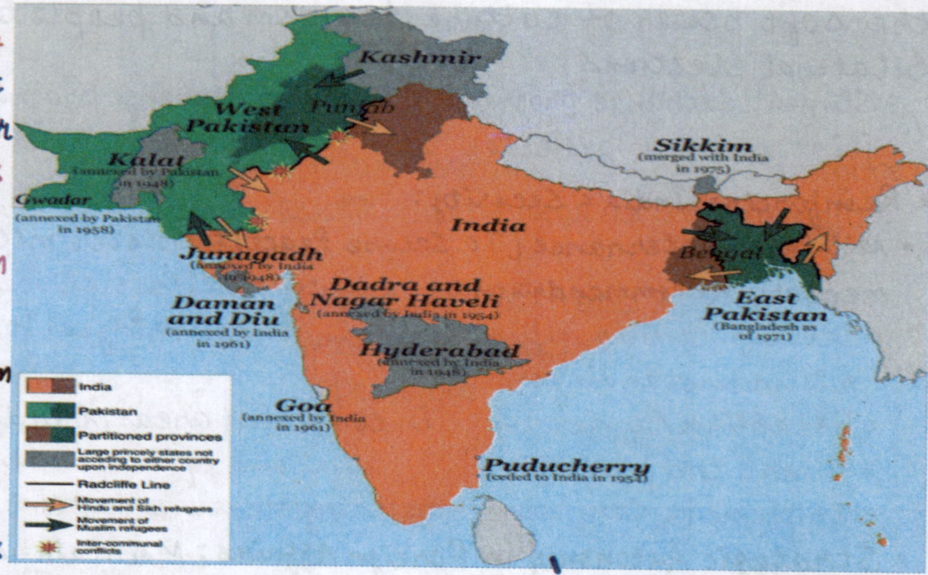

India Pakistan Relation: Pacification Phase (2001-2008):

- **Peace Efforts:** Lahore Declaration and Vajpayee's principles aimed at improving relations.
- **Composite Dialogue (2004):** Agreements on trade and gas pipeline.

India Pakistan Relations: Phase of Passive Relations (2008-2015):

- **Low Key interactions** and efforts to establish trust, with discussions often stalling.
- **Neighbourhood First Policy** + India prioritized regional cooperation (SAARC platform: SAARC university, SAARC satellite)
- **2015:** Indian PM visits Pakistan.

India Pakistan Relations: Phase of Renewed Hostility (2015 - current)

- **Escalating Hostilities:** Ceasefire violation + China-Pakistan Economic Corridor (CPEC)
- **Series of Attacks:** Uri attack (2016), Pulwama attack (2019), Lone wolf attack in Kashmir, Online Radicalisation Module etc.

Reasons for Conflict: India and Pakistan

1. **Border Dispute and Legacy**

- **Partition Trauma (1947):** The violent division of British India based on religion left a deep scar, shaping national identities and fostering suspicion.
- **Kashmir Sovereignity Dispute:** Both India and Pakistan claim Kashmir in its entirety, leading to:
  - **Armed Conflicts:** Wars in 1947, 1965, 1971 and ongoing skirmishes along the Line of Control (LOC)
- **Sir Creek Dispute:** It is a 92-kilometer marshy land separating Gujarat from Sindh (Pakistan)
  - **Interpretation of Boundary:** The disagreement centers around the interpretation of the maritime boundary line between Kutch and Sindh

- Indian Claim: India claims that the boundary lies mid-channel as depicted in a 1925 map and the installation of mid-channel pillars in 1924.

- Gilgit Baltistan Issue: Pakistan has given "Provincial status" to Gilgit Baltistan making it 5th province of Pakistan.

2. Proxy War

- Pakistan's Alleged Support and backing militant groups like Lashkar-e-Taiba and Jaish-e-Mohammed.
  - Terrorist Attacks on India: Mumbai (2008), Pathankot (2016), Pulwama (2019), Poonch-Rajouri (2023)
- Revocation of Article 370: India's decision to revoke Jammu and Kashmir's special status angered Pakistan leading to:
  - Downgraded Diplomacy: Pakistan downgraded diplomatic ties and suspended bilateral trade.
- Line of Control (LOC) Violations: Frequent transgressions along the LOC leads to:
  - Casualities: Loss of life on both sides, escalating tensions.
  - Military Build-up: Increased militarization of the border region

3. Missed oppurtunities:

- Limited Trade Cooperation: Low volume of bilateral trade hinders economic growth and people-to-people connections.
  - In 2021, India exported goods worth $ 535 million to Pakistan, while Pakistan exported goods worth $ 2.08 million to India.
- External Influences:
  - China's Role: China's growing closeness with Pakistan adds another layer of complexities.
  - Internationalisation of Kashmir at international forums further complicates resolution efforts.

Initiatives to Normalize Relations	Dynamic Challenges in Relations
1. Confidence-Building Measures (CBMs): • Military: 1965 Tashkent Declaration → Ceasefire agreement and troop withdraw. • Cross-LOC Contact: 2004 Srinagar-Muzaffarabad Bus	• Border Tensions: internal crisis can lead to unpredictable actions by Pakistan's government or military, potentially triggering violence along the Line of Control in Kashmir. • Refugee Crisis: An economic collapse in Pakistan could trigger

Service allowed families to reconnect, but remains suspended.

- Ceasefire Agreement (2021): Significant reduction in border tensions.

2. People-to-People Contact:

- Cultural Exchanges: Sporadic cultural events and film festivals have been held, but consistency is needed.
- Religious Tourism: Limited pilgrimage visits → Kartarpur Sahib in Pakistan, have Occured.

3. Economic Cooperation: Talks on regional projects like gas pipelines have not materialized (TAPI gas Pipeline)
4. Track-II Diplomacy: Backchannel communication and workshops have happened, but haven't translated to official policy changes (Neemrana Dialogue)
5. Addressing Core Issues:

- Simla Agreements (1972): Established diplomatic relations and peaceful resolution framework but failed to address Kashmir definitively.
- Composite Dialogue Process (1997-2001): Tackled various issues but ultimately stalled due to lack of progress on core concerns.

6. Indus Water Treaty (1960): It's one of the most successful water treaties in the world.

a mass influx of refugees into India.

- Regional Instability: Pakistan's instability could lead to wider regional tensions.
- Nuclear Proliferation: Weak control over Pakistan's nuclear weapons is a potential security concern.
- Unpredictable Terrorism: Evolving tactics and targets of Pakistan backed terror group can inflict heavy casualities and social unrest in India.
- Cyber Warfare: Pakistan's growing cyber capabilities threaten critical infrastructure and information systems causing sudden economic disruptions.
- Ideological Infiltrations: Radical ideologies promoted by Pakistan can exploit societal divisions within India, leading to potential violence.
- Disinformation Warfare: Pakistan can manipulate public opinion and undermine Indian government through fake news campaign on social media.
- Water Wars: Tensions over shared rivers like the Indus can escalate due to factors like drought, making water cooperation a dynamic issue.
- Shifting Criminal Networks: Pakistan can be a base for drug, weapon and human trafficking, impacting India's security with constantly evolving smuggling routes.

Indus Water Treaty (1960)

The Indus Water Treaty was signed in 1960 after nine years of negotiations between India and Pakistan with the help of the World Bank, which is also a signatory.

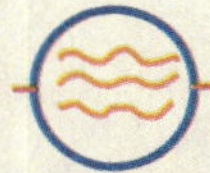

At current usage, India utilises a little over 90% of its quota of Indus water

Recently, Pakistan has raised concerns regarding Kishanganga dam in Kashmir and the Ratle hydroelectric power station on the Chenab.

About the treaty

- Sharing of water
  - Eastern rivers (Ravi, Beas, Satluj) were allocated to India for unrestricted use.
  - Western rivers (Indus, Jhelum, Chenab) were allocated largely to Pakistan.
    - India is permitted for certain agricultural uses, to build 'run of the river' hydropower projects with limited storage.
- Permanent Indus Commission (PIC): Commissioners are appointed by both the countries for cooperation and information exchange regarding their use of rivers.
  - The treaty provides a 3-tier dispute resolution mechanism of which PIC is the first stage, neutral expert is second stage and then Court of Arbitration.
- IWT does not have a unilateral exit provision, and is supposed to remain in force unless both the countries ratify another mutually agreed pact.

Issues with the IWT

1. Dissatisfaction over water apportionment: Since 80% water is allocated to Pakistan.
2. Ambiguous and room for conflict: Technical nature of the treaty and the western rivers flow through the conflicted region of Jammu and Kashmir that paves the way for conflict.
3. Lack of mutual trust: Lack of trust building mechanism between India and Pakistan.
4. Suboptimal data sharing due to diplomatic tensions.
   - Also, the quality of shared data is questioned many times and there is no mechanism for the research community to get access to it.

5. Limited role of the Guarantor: For example, in the current disputes of Kishanganga and Ratle Hydroelectric Projects, the World Bank had to appoint the Neutral Expert and chairman of COA simultaneously.

- Such concurrent appointments may pose practical and legal risks.
- However, the World Bank lacks the power to decide which one should take the precedence.

6. Lack of adequate environmental safeguards.

Reforms needed to make IWT more effective

- Ratification of the UN Water Convention: To ensure the sustainable use of transboundary water resources by facilitating cooperation
- Global forum on transboundary rivers: For solving water conflicts can assist in comprehensive policy making.
- Promoting open data policy to international supervisory bodies and other stakeholders for promoting transparency and applied scientific research.
- Optimisation of the treaty: Since unilateral exit is not possible, India should ensure full utilisation of all accessible water of the rivers.
- Renegotiate the treaty: Both the countries should undertake joint research on the rivers to study the impact of climate change for "future cooperation" (underlined in Article VII of the IWT)

Pathways for India-Pakistan Relations

1. India's Initiatives:
   - Neighbourhood First Policy: Prioritizes peaceful dialogue with Pakistan, emphasizing terrorism elimination.
   - National Security: Maintaining strong deterrence.
   - Religious Diplomacy (Kartarpur Corridor) can foster people-to-people contact.
2. Capitalizing on Oppurtunities:
   - Supporting democratic movements in Pakistan-Occupied Kashmir (PoK) to address instability.
   - SAARC Revival can counter China's Belt and Road Initiative.
   - Counterterrorism: Engaging the international community to pressure Pakistan to dismantle terror networks.
3. Strengthening Regional Connectivity: Promoting projects like Chabahar Port and INSTC to boost India's access to Central Asia and enhance regional influence.

4. Economic Leverage: India's economic growth can attract foreign investment and foster closer economic ties with other nations.

5. Diplomacy and Soft Power:

- Hydro Diplomacy: Utilize the Indus Water Treaty for hydro diplomacy, ensuring non-consumptive use of western rivers.
- Cultural Diplomacy: Promote Urdu poetry, music and art to foster people-to-people connections.
- Cricket Diplomacy: Expand cricket engagements between India and Pakistan to promote peace and cooperation (e.g., 1999 Chennai – Pakistan match)
- Economic Diplomacy: Deepen economic ties through bilateral trade and reduce import tariff to ease tensions and foster prosperity.
- Cultural and Geographical Similarities: Leverage cultural similarities through food fairs and festivals to strengthen bonds.

INDIA- BANGLADESH RELATIONS

India and Bangladesh share 4096.7 Km of border, the longest land boundary that India shares with any of its neighbors. Assam, West Bengal, Mizoram, Meghalaya and Tripura share borders with Bangladesh.

India and Bangladesh Relation

- Background
  - Cultural and Linguistic heritage binds the two nations
  - Historical Solidarity: Partition in 1947 and the subsequent separation of families forged a sense of shared pain and understanding.

- Liberation War: India played a pivotal role in Bangladesh's liberation in 1971, being the first nation to recognize its independence.

> ⋙ The foundation of India's relationship with Bangladesh was laid in the 1971 Bangladesh Liberation War. India provided critical military support in its independence.
>
> ⋙ India-Bangladesh relations soured within a few years as military regimes took control after the assassination of Sheikh Mujibur Rahman in 1975. There was anti-Indian sentiment.
>
> ⋙ After the return of Parliamentary democracy in 1991 and Sheikh Hasina coming to power in 1996, there has been deepening of India-Bangladesh relations

Signifance of Bangladesh for India

- Geostrategic Importance:
  - North-East Gateway: Bangladesh provides land access for India's North-east, boosting connectivity and development.
  - Maritime Security: Bangladesh's Bay of Bengal location is crucial for securing sea lines of communication.
- Geopolitical Importance (Act East Policy)
  - Southeast Asia Bridge to facilitate ties with Southeast Asia.
  - BBIN & BIMSTEC: Collaboration is essential for BBIN (Bay of Bengal Initiative for Multi-Sectoral Technical and Economic Cooperation) and BIMSTEC Initiatives.
  - Bangladesh's support India's UNSC bid.
- Economic Benefits: Bangladesh has emerged as India's largest trade partner in South Asia ($15.9 billion in 2022-23)
- Cultural Links: Shared heritage and religions sites bind the two nations together.
- Cultural Ties: Bangladesh's large Hindu Bengali population and shared religious sites like Ranbir Bunglow Temple and Bhoj Vihara strengthen cultural bonds with India
- Security Cooperation: Stability in Bangladesh is crucial for India's security fostering cooperation on counter terrorism and border security.
- Defence and Security: Military exercises such as MILAN and SAMPRITI, intelligence sharing and India's supply of military equipment and technology transfer and also for ensuring security in northeast.
- Traditional Sectors such as tourism, healthcare, education etc as well as Frontier technologies like Nuclear, Space, Information Technology etc.

Areas of Cooperation

- Political Cooperation – Indian PM's visit to take part in their golden Jubilee celebrations of Bangladesh Independence, Gandhi Peace Prize 2020 to Sheikh Mujibur Rehman.
- Land Boundary Agreement (2015) – Swapping of the disputed enclaves.
- Economic cooperation – India is the second-biggest trade partner of Bangladesh, bilateral trade between India-Bangladesh reached $15.9 billion in 2021-22, duty free quota access to Bangladesh under SAFTA and joint feasibility study on Comprehensive Economic Partnership Agreement (CEPA)
- Infrastructure Cooperation – India as a 'major development partner' of Bangladesh, extended Lines of Credits worth over $ 7 billion, Ahaura-Agartala rail link, Maitri Setu.
- Energy cooperation – Bangladesh importing 2,000 MWs of electricity from India, India-Bangladesh Friendship Pipeline for high speed diesel supply.

Challenges in Relationship

- Border Disputes: Unresolved demarcations (Assam, Tripura) fuel tensions.
- Immigration: Migrant flow from Bangladesh strains resources in bordering Indian states (Rohingya issue).
- Economic Hurdles: Non-Tariff Barriers (Bureaucratic red tapism)
- Connectivity Issues:
  - Undemarcated Borders: Unresolved land and maritime boundaries create friction.
  - Limited Infrastructure hinders economic development.
- Security Concerns: Cross-border terrorism and infiltration are threats to internal security.
  - Insurgent Activity: Indian insurgent groups reportedly operate from Bangladesh.
  - Drug Smuggling and Trafficking: Humans (especially children and women) are trafficked and various animal and bird species are poached through these borders.
  - Chinese Growing Influence: China's economic investment (BRI, Chittagong port) is a strategic concern for India
- Energy Tensions:
  - Water sharing disputes: Disagreements persist over sharing water from 54 shared rivers.

- Shared River Water Distribution: Distribution of water from the Brahmaputra and Ganges remains a source of tension.
- Teesta River Dispute: Unimplemented water sharing agreement creates friction.
- Farakka Barrage: Bangladesh objects to India's water diversion project.

Pathways for Strengthening India-Bangladesh Relation

- Teesta River Dispute Resolution: Forming a tripartite committee with India, Bangladesh and West Bengal can expediate an agreement.
- India-Bangladesh FTA before Bangladesh loses LDC status will benefit both nations. Safeguards to prevent misuse by China are crucial.
- Security:
  - Joint Task Forces with law enforcements agencies from both countries can effectively combat cross-border crimes like drug smuggling, human trafficking and illegal immigration.
  - Smart Border Management: Utilizing AI and data analytics can streamline border movement while ensuring security.
- Digital Connectivity: Developing a corridor focusing on high-speed internet, digital services and e-commerce can create new avenues for trade and collaboration.

Other Important Areas:

- Improved Global Image for Bangladesh: India can collaborate with Bangladesh to address human rights concerns and counter negative perceptions.
- Enhance Connectivity: Strengthening cooperation in coastal connectivity, roads, railways and waterways can improve regional connectivity.
- Energy Security: Cooperation in clean and green energy can make South Asia energy Self Sufficient.
- India-Bangladesh Friendship Pipeline: Fast tracking this project can provide critical energy supplies to Bangladesh.
- Comprehensive Economic Partnership Agreement (CEPA): Shifting focus towards CEPA negotiations can further strengthen economic ties.
- Countering China's Influence: India can assist Bangladesh with technology and finance to solidify their relationship.
- SAARC Refugee Declaration: Developing a regional framework for refugee status determination can be a joint initiative.

INDIA-MYANMMAR RELATIONSHIP

- **Stability:** India and Myammar shared Border (1643 Km)
- **Geopolitical Location:** Bordering China, India, ASEAN and the Bay of Bengal, Myanmmar is strategically significant.
    - Internal Security: Myanmmar helps contain insurgency in India's northeast.
    - Countering China: Myanmmar is Key for India's "Neighbourhood First", "Act East" and "Indo-Pacific" policies.

Evolution of Relations

➤ **Ancient times:** Cultural, religious and trade links established between India and Myanmmar

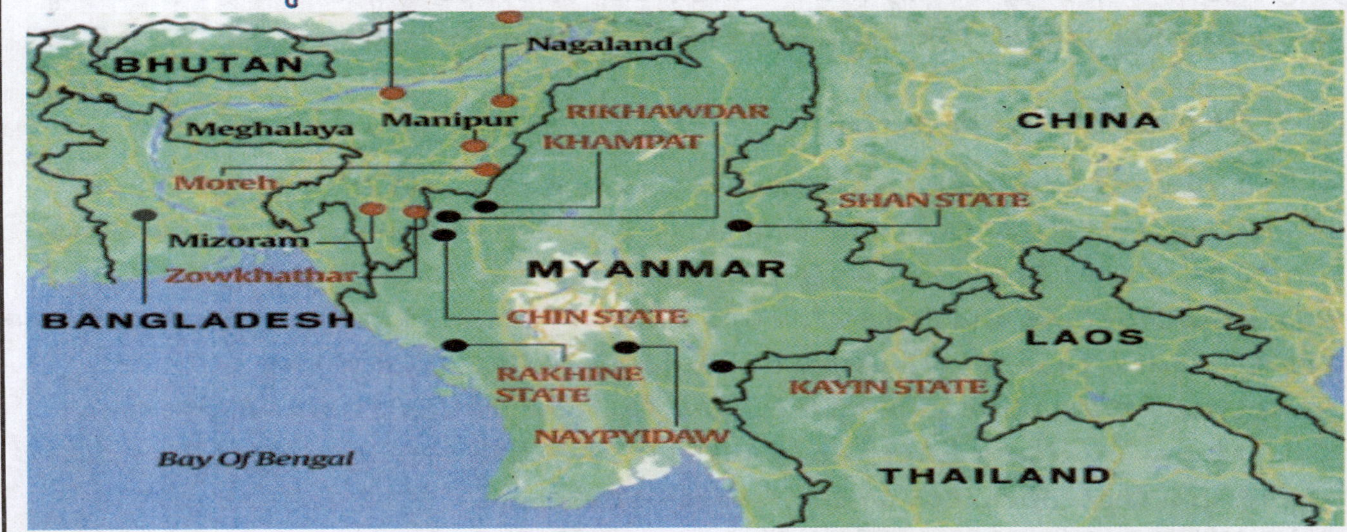

➤ 1935: Both India and Myanmmar gain independence from British rule.

➤ 1951: India and Myanmmar sign a Treaty of friendship.

➤ 1987: Prime Minister visit strengthens India-Myanmmar relations

➤ 2002: India Consulate reopens in Mandalay, Myanmmar Consulate established in Kolkata.

➤ 2014: Myanmmar becomes part of India's "Neighbourhood first" and "Act East" policies.

Myanmmar Military Coup

- Military coup in 2021 — Aung San Suu Kyi's National League for Democracy (NLD) landslide victory in the 2020 elections sparked concerns among the military. The military (Tatmadaw) alleged electoral fraud and staged a coup in February 2021.

⊗ Anti-Junta Armed Struggle – Various Ethnic armed organisations (EAOs) and People's Defence Forces (PDFs) intensified their resistance against the military regime. This has resulted in huge infiltration in India.

Significance of Myanmmar For India

⊗ Geo-strategic – Myanmmar is an important pillar of India's "Neighbourhood First" policy and "Act East Policy". For ex – India-Myanmmar-Thailand (IMT) trilateral highway, Kaladan Multi-Modal Transit Transport.

⊗ Tackling insurgency in Northeast – Insurgent groups such as ISCN-K, ISCN-IM have operational bases inside Myanmmar.

⊗ Countering China – India is developing the Sittwe port in Myanmmar's Rakhine state to counter the Chinese fronted Kyaukpu port.

⊗ Reduction of illegal migration in India – A stable Myanmmar is necessary to reduce the illegal Rohingya and Chin migration in India.

Areas of Cooperation

- Trade and economy :- Bilateral trade has increased from $12.4 million in 1980-81 to $2.18 billion in 2016-17. Myanmmar is the beneficiary of India's duty-free tariff preference scheme for LDCs.
- Infrastructure and Connectivity :- Tamu-Kalewa-Kalemyo highway, Kaladan Multimodal Transit Transport and Asian Trilateral Highway.
- Defence cooperation: Joint Military exercise, called India-Myanmmar Bilateral Military Exercise (IMBEX). Operation Sunrise target the militant groups that operates in the border states.
- Multilateral partnership: Myanmmar is a key component of India's strategy to bridge South and South-East Asia through ASEAN, BIMSTEC and Mekong Ganga Cooperation (MGC).
- Humanitarian Aid and Disaster Relief: India has provided Humanitarian aid and disaster relief in natural calamities in Myanmmar like Cyclone Mora (2017), Komen (2015), earthquake in Shan State (2010) and COVID 19

Challenges

⊗ India's Policy Paradox with respect to Myanmar coup – India faces a dilemma in the form of its commitment to democracy vs its internal security concerns (for which it cooperates with Military.

⊗ Misue of Free Movement Regime – Being exploited by militants and cross-border criminals for drugs, arms smuggling.

- Refugee Influx – Rohingyas, Chins refugees pose grave security concerns for India.
- China Inroads in Myanmmar – Steadily increasing like the China-Myanmmar Economic Corridor.
- Delays in regional connectivity Projects – Like the Kaladan Multimodal Project.

Pathways for Strengthening Ties

- Border Fencing: A 300 Km fence is planned. with a tender process underway.
- Regulatory Revisions: Experts recommends refining the Free Movement Regime (FMR) to improve movement regulation while preserving cross-border ties.
- Infrastructure and Trade: Enhancing infrastructure and formalizing trade at designated entry points can lessen negative impacts.
- Community Engagement: Involving border communities in decision making is crucial for sensitive and effective border management.
- Democracy and Human Rights: Advocate for releasing political prisoners and ending the junta's repression. Cease arms supplies to uphold India's democratic values.
- Regional Cooperation: Collaborate with ASEAN for a unified Myanmmar peace plan.
- Economic Engagement: Continue economic ties for sustainable development, while expediting Kaladan and Trilateral Highway Projects
- Security Cooperation: Strengthen intelligence sharing and joint efforts against insurgencies and drug trafficking.

INDIA-NEPAL

- Nepal is a landlocked country, and India provides its closest access to the sea.
- Border: The 1751 Km long border, shared by five Indian states, is governed by the Sugauli Treaty of 1816.
- Open Border and unrestricted Movement by the 1950 Treaty of Peace and friendship → free movement of people and goods between the two countries.
- Strong Social Bonds: Marriages and familial ties known as Roti-Beti Ka Rishta, further strengthen the relationship between the two nations.

Areas of Cooperation

- Trade: Bilateral trade of over US$ 11 billion.
  - India is Nepal's largest trade partner and source of largest FDI.
  - India's export to Nepal has grown over 8 times in the past 10 years.
- Defence: India assists the Nepal Army in its modernization, Military exercises like Surya Kiran to boost interoperability.
- Water resources: Kosi Treaty, Mahakali Treaty to discuss issues relating to cooperation in water resources, flood management etc
- Energy: Power Exchange Agreement for meeting the power requirements in the border areas, Cross border oil product pipeline from Motihari (Bihar) to Amlekhganj (Nepal), hydroelectric projects in Solu corridor.
- Connectivity projects: Raxaul Kathmandu Railway Project, BBIN
- Education: India provides scholarships to Nepalese students for various courses.
- Culture: Strong historical and cultural links in terms of religion, language, cuisine, movies etc (Roti-Beti Ka Naata)

Significance of Nepal for India	Significance of India for Nepal
• Strategic Location: Nepal acts as a buffer state for India's security. • Connectivity: Crucial land route for India to connect with neighboring countries (BBIN) • Religious Tourism: Like Pashupatinath • Energy Cooperation: Nepal's hydropower potential can contribute to India's energy security. • Regional Stability: A stable Nepal is essential for India's overall regional influence.	• Economic Dependence: Nepal relies on India for trade, transportation & access to sea routes. • Shared heritage strengthens social bonds. • Crisis Assistance: India provides substantial aid during disasters. • Infrastructure Development: Development assistance to Nepal, focusing on the creation of infrastructure at the grass-root level. • Security Cooperation: Gorkha Regiments of the Indian Army.

Challenges in relationship

- China's rising influence in Nepal's economy, politics and society impacting India's traditionally dominant influence.
  - Anti-India rhetoric is running high in Nepal.
  - Nepal's aggressive stance over border disputes (Kalapani boundary issue)
  - Nepal has joined China's BRI.
- Nepal's discontent in bilateral trade due to high trade deficit that it incurs.
- Distrust towards India as a result of India's big brother attitude, lackadaisical approach towards revisiting the Treaty of Peace and Friendship of 1950 and approach of dealing with river treaties.
- Unrestricted cross-border movement of people particularly impacting Nepal's domestic industry, local livelihood oppurtunities, Law and order, and national security during COVID.

Indo-Nepal Border Dispute

Kalapani, Limpiyadhura & Lipulekh	Susta (West Champaran):
• Claimed by Nepal but administered by India (Uttarakhand) • Disputes centers on the sources of the Kali River (boundary marker). • Strategic location for India (Observation Post).	• 145 sq km claimed by Nepal but belongs to India due to river course change. • Treaty of Sugauli assigned Land based on original river position.

Pathways for Strengthening relationship

- Focussing on multimodel connectivity between India and Nepal.
- Setting up appropriate bilateral mechanisms to discuss contentions issues (boundary dispute resolution between India and Bangladesh should serve as a model)
- Multilateral forums such as BBIN, BIMSTEC, NAM, SAARC etc must be utilised to serve common interests.
- Sustained engagements and limited interference with Nepal across the political spectrum.
- Strengthening economic cooperation
- Leverage people-to-people links to ensure a stable and mutually productive state-to-state relationship.
- Revisiting Peace and Friendship Treaty of 1950 as recommended by Eminent Person's Group set up jointly by the two countries.

INDIA-BHUTAN

- **Location:** Landlocked country in the Eastern Himalayas, between India and China.
- **Border:** Shares a 699 Km open border with four Indian states (Assam, Sikkim, Arunachal Pradesh, West Bengal)
- **Geography:** River flows south into India's Brahmaputra River.
- **Uniqueness:** First carbon-negative country in the world.
  - Promotes Gross National Happiness (GNH) over GDP.

Areas of Cooperation

- **Strong Partnership:** Treaty of Friendship and Cooperation (1949, renewed 2007) forms the foundation.
- **Trade:** India is Bhutan's top trading partner (import and export)
  - Free trade Regime established through 2016 agreement.
  - India is the leading source of foreign investment.
- **Development:** Bhutan is the largest recipient of India's foreign aid
  - India supports Bhutan "high income nation" goal by 2034.
  - Connectivity: Bhutan plans an "international city" (Gelephu) on the border with Assam.
- **Hydropower:** India built four major hydroelectric projects in Bhutan, supplying power to India.
  - 720 MW Mangdechhu project was recently handed over to Bhutan
- **Cultural Relations:** Buddhism fosters shared ideologies.
  - India-Bhutan foundation promotes cultural exchange.
- **Security:** Indian Military Training Team assists and trains Bhutan's Royal Army.
  - India's Border Road Organisation built most Bhutanese roads ("DANTAK" project)

- New initiatives: Launched RuPay and BHIM digital payment apps in Bhutan.
  - Collaborating on "Digital Drukyul" tech initiatives.
  - Jointly developed the "India-Bhutan SAT" satellite.
  - India supports Bhutan in filling STEM teacher shortages.
  - Provided Bhutan with 5.5 lakh Covishield vaccine doses under "Vaccine Maitri"

Signifance of Bhutan for India

- Geostrategic Importance: Bhutan's strategic location, sharing border with both China and India, makes it essential to India's national security.
- Energy security: Abundance of hydropower resources to meet India's energy requirements.
- Environmental Cooperation: Conservation, disaster management and climate change adaptation (Shared Himalayan ecosystem)
- Regional Integration with SAARC and BIMSTEC.

Major challenges in India-Bhutan Relationship

- Issues in hydropower trade: India's past changes in power purchasing policy, not able to fairly negotiate power tariff delay in completion of projects (E.g., Punatsangchhu I & II) by India.
- Hideout for Militants: India's North-East Militant outfits like the United Liberation Front of Assam (ULFA), National Democratic Front of Bodos (NDFB) etc uses Bhutan for the hideout.
- BBIN Initiative: The Bangladesh Bhutan India Nepal (BBIN) Motor Vechile Agreement is on by Bhutan due to environmental concerns.
- Increased financial burden on Bhutan as India moved away from 60:40 model (60% grant, 40% loan) to 30:70 model.
- Trade Issues: India is Bhutan's largest trading partner, accounting for over 80% of Bhutan's total imports and exports. So, there have been some concerns in Bhutan for growing trade deficit.
- China's presence: Bhutan's border disputes with China like Doklam raises security concerns for India.

China's Rising Influence in Bhutan	Implications for India
• Economic Grip: China accounts for over 25% of Bhutan's trade. ◦ Chinese state-owned companies dominate infrastructure projects and telecom sectors. • Territorial Assertions: China claims disputed areas like Jakarlung, Doklam, Pasamlung and parts of Sakteng Wildlife Sanctuary. ◦ China's village construction near Doklam raises concerns. • Political Maneuvering: Bhutan's foreign Minister's first visit in China in 2023 and a signed cooperation agreement suggest potential normalization of relations.	• Security Threat: A negotiated Doklam border deal could compromise India's security due to Doklam's proximity to the Siliguri corridor. • Geopolitical Imbalance: China's growing presence disrupts the regional balance, potentially leading to India-China tensions (similar to 2017 Doklam standoff) ◦ Access to Doklam could give China leverage over India's northeast. • Eroding Influence: Closer Bhutan-China ties could weaken Bhutan's traditionally pro-India foreign policy.

Way Forward

- Diversifying economic engagements: Strengthening collaboration in fields such as fintech, space tech and biotech can led to a stronger leadership.
  - India will need to sustainably invest in Bhutan's services sector in line with its philosophy of Gross National Happiness (GNH)
  - India shall leverage the Gelephu project as an oppurtunity to deepen its partnership with Bhutan and counter Bhutan's growing engagement with China.
- Initiating Trilogue with China: Opening such communication channels can minimize uncertainities with regard to border disputes.
- Improving people-to-people ties: Soft power diplomacy can be induced through Buddhism and by encouraging more tourist activisits.
- Security measures: Establish contact points between two countries and mechanisms for information regarding military outfits.

INDIA - SRI LANKA RELATIONS

India is Sri Lanka's closest neighbour. The relationship between the two countries is more than 2,500 years old and both sides have built upon a legacy of intellectual, cultural, religious and linguistic interaction.

Areas of Cooperation

- Cultural Connection: Buddhism introduced by Mahinda, son of Emperor Ashoka laid the foundation for a strong cultural and religious bond.
  - Chola dynasty's conquests of Sri Lanka → Art, architecture and language.
  - Colonial Legacy: India and Sri Lanka gained independence in 1947 and 1948 respectively.
- Economy: India-Sri Lanka Free Trade Agreement (ISFTA) in 2000 boosted bilateral trade.
  - India remains Sri Lanka's top trading partner, with bilateral trade reaching a record of US$ 5.5 billion in 2022.
  - Indian aid of USD 4 billion to Sri Lanka during economic crisis.
  - Sri Lanka has adopted India's UPI service + Rupee is used for trade settlement.
  - Developmental Assistance: India's total commitment surpasses US$ 3.5 billion with grants alone exceeding US$ 570 million.
  - Developmental projects at Kankesanthurai + Tricomalee ports + East Container Terminal at Colombo harbour

- Security Cooperation: India and Sri Lanka conduct joint military (Mitra Shakti) and naval exercise (SLINEX)
- Multilateral Cooperation: Collaborate in regional organizations like SAARC, BIMSTEC and IORA + members of UN, WTO, WHO, IMF and World Bank.
- Tourism: 60% people come from India.

Significance of Sri Lanka for India

Geostrategic Importance:

- Regional Development: India's prosperity is linked to regional growth and Sri Lanka's integration with South Asian economy aligns with this goal.
- Strategic Location: Sri Lanka's proximity to India and position on major shipping lanes.
- Indian Ocean strategy: Sri Lanka's strategic location is important for India's naval movements and Indian Ocean security + Indian Ocean region and Indian Ocean Rim cooperation.

Maritime Security:

- Sri Lanka's Ports: Potential to become maritime hubs, enhancing regional security and trade.
- Balancing China's Influence: China's growing presence in Sri Lanka necessitates India's involvement to maintain regional stability.

Areas of Conflict

- Tamil Issue: Sinhala Buddhist majority allegedly discriminates against Tamils regarding religion, language, education and employment oppurtunities.

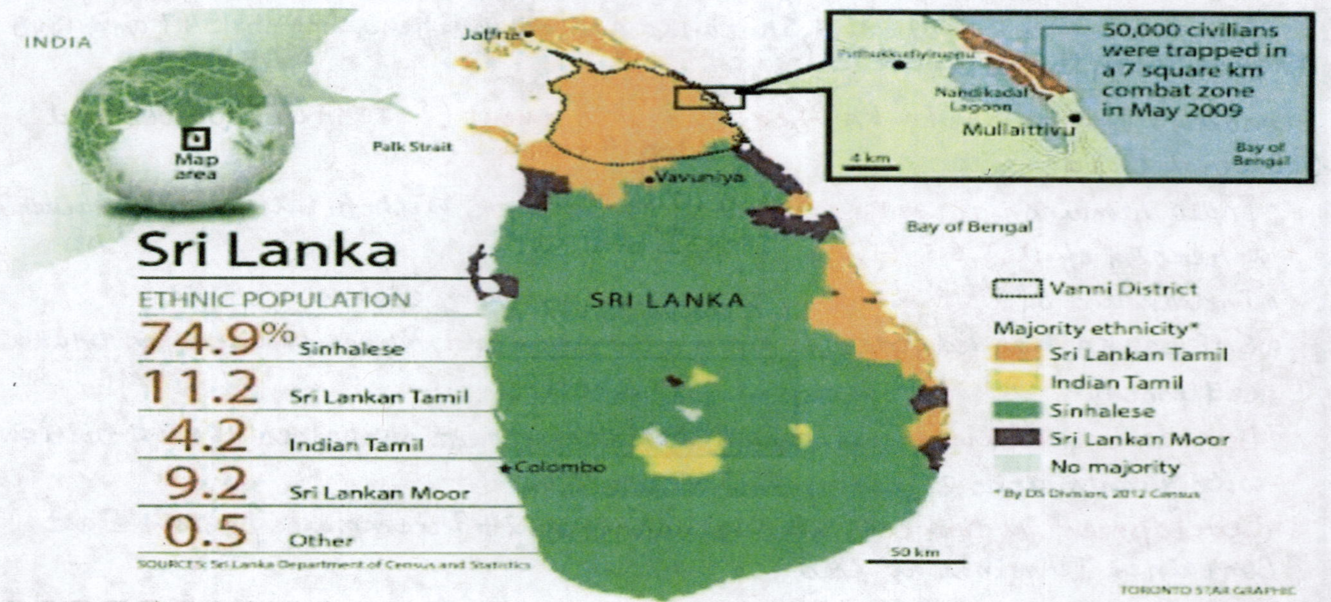

- Citizenship: Many Tamils lack citizenship, hindering their access to basic rights and economic oppurtunities.
- Civil War (2009) between Sri Lankan government and Liberation Tigers of Tamil Eelam (LTTE) resulted in human right abuses + grievances among Tamils.

- Fisheries Dispute: Indian fisherman are frequently arrested by Sri Lankan authorities for allegedly crossing the maritime border and fishing in Sri Lankan waters.
  - This leads to tensions and violence between fisherman.
- Katchatheevu Island (1974 agreement): Katchatheevu Island to Sri Lanka + Indian fisherman allowed access to Katchatheevu for rest, drying nets and festivals.
  - 1976 Agreement: Defined maritime boundary near Kanya-Kumari (India) + Gave India control over Wedge Bank Resources + Restricted Sri Lankan fishing in Wedge Bank (with exceptions).

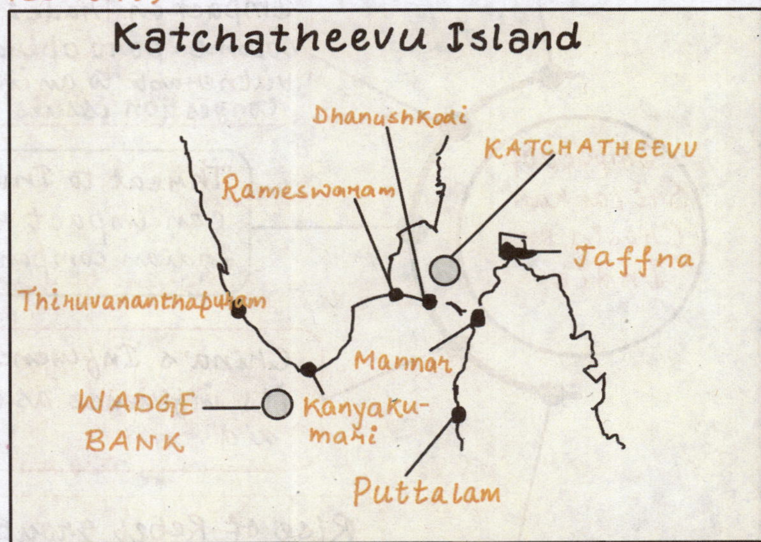

- Border Security: The maritime boundary facilitates smuggling of narcotics, goods and illegal immigration.
- China's Growing Influence: China's economic investments and infrastructure projects in Sri Lanka particularly Hambantota Port, raise security concerns for India.

Sri Lanka Crisis

Reasons for Sri Lankan Crisis:

- Debt trap Diplomacy: Sri Lanka was caught in a vicious cycle of money lending by China for infrastructure projects (Hambantota Port)
- Fall in tourism:
  - The rise in COVID-19 pandemic
  - Easter bomb blast 2019
- Agriculture Crisis: In 2020, due to ban on chemical fertilizers and switching overnight to make agriculture organic.
  - Negatively impacted economy especially rice and sugar production.

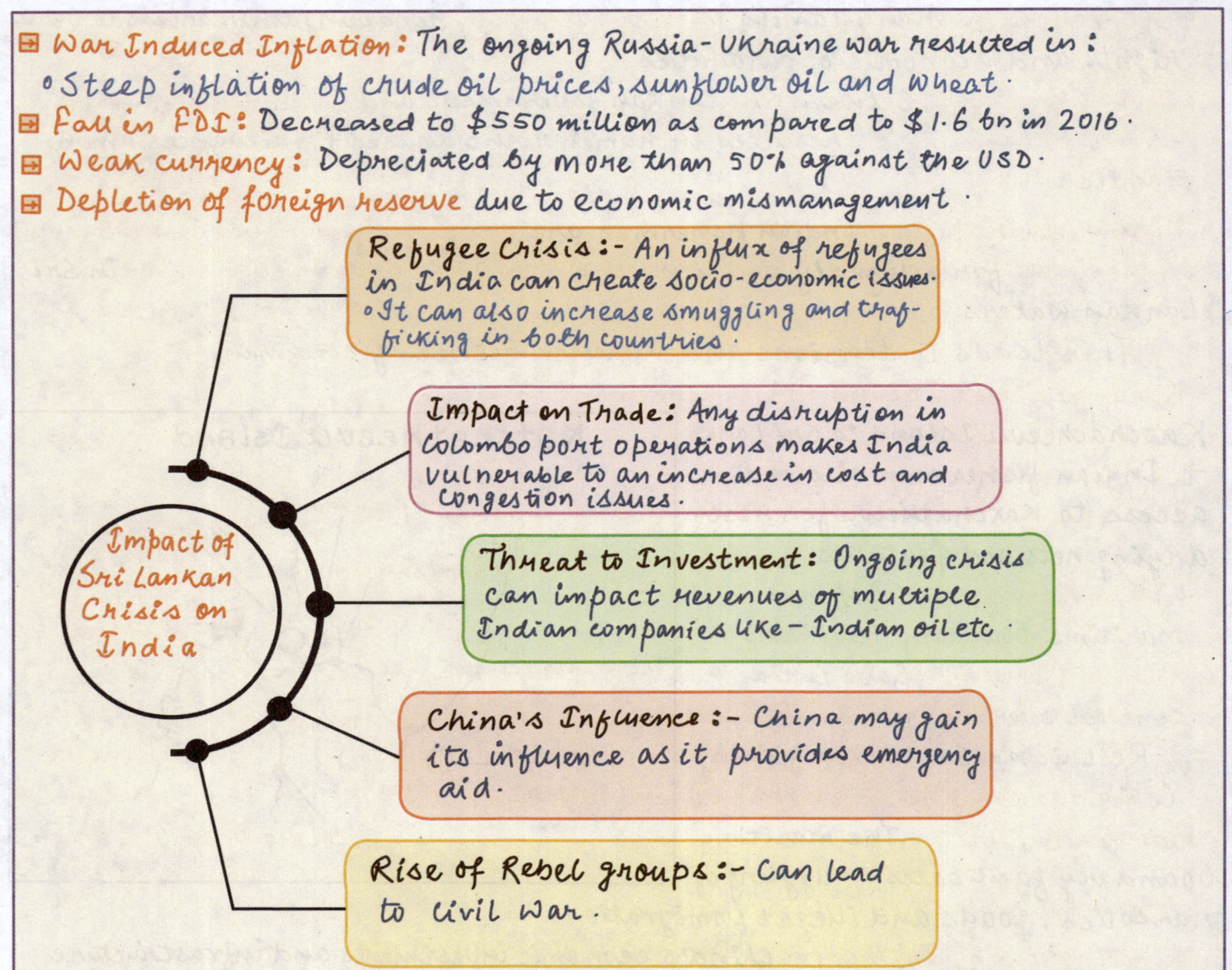

Pathways for Strengthening Relations

- **More Indian Investment:** Indian businesses can invest in Sri Lanka's infrastructure, energy and transportation systems, creating jobs and boosting both economies.
- **Ocean Oppurtunities:** India, Sri Lanka, Japan and Australia can work together to develop Sri Lanka's ports and ocean resources creating a 'Blue Economy'.
- **Trade Deal Talk:** CEPA can be signed to make it easier for businesses in both countries to sell goods and services to each other.
- **Helping Fisherman:** Indian government departments can provide support to fisherman in the Palk Bay to help them find new ways to make a living if needed.
- **Economic Integration Roadmap (EIRM):** It is based on Sub Regionalism and aims to connect 5 southern states of India with Sri Lanka to tap a total of 300 million population and $ 500 billion GDP.

INDIA - MALDIVES

India and Maldives have shared diplomatic, defence, economic and cultural relations. Located in a crucial geographical position in the Indian Ocean, Maldives is vital to India's strategy for the Indian Ocean and its neighbourhood.

- Geographical Proximity: Maldives' location near India allows the Indian Navy to monitor the region and provide security.
- Early Recognition: India's acknowledgement of Maldives' independence in 1965.
- First Responder: India has been a first responder during various crises including the
  - 1988: Military intervention (Operation Cactus) to prevent a coup.
  - 2004: Assistance after the tsunami,
  - 2014: Aid during the water shortage.
  - 2020: Comprehensive help during the COVID-19 pandemic (Operation Sanjeevani)
- India as a "net security provider" and plays a significant role in India's Security and Growth for all in the Region (SAGAR) initiative.

Significance of Maldives

- Neighbourhood First: Strong cultural, economic and trade ties for centuries make Maldives crucial to India's regional policy.
- Strategic Location: Maldives situated near key shipping lanes (Gulf of Aden, Strait of Hormuz, Malacca Strait) vital for India's trade (95% by volume, 68% by value).
- First Line of Defence: Maldives proximity makes it buffer against maritime threats like piracy and terrorism.
- Countering China: Maldives' shift towards China is a concern for India's strategic interests in the Indian Ocean Region (IOR).
- Indian Community: Large Indian diaspora contributes to Maldives' health and education sectors.

Areas of Cooperation

- Flourishing trade ties: India is Maldives' 3rd Largest partner (US$ 323.9 million by 2021).
- Security and Defence: Strong cooperation through "Comprehensive Action Plan for Defence."
  - India meets 70% of Maldives' training needs, supplies equipment (hospitals radars), builds infrastructure (coast guard bases) and conducts joint military exercises (Ekuverin) and disaster relief efforts.
  - Colombo Security Conclave (CSC) promotes regional maritime security.
- Development Cooperation: India supports Maldivian development through:
  - Educational institutions (hospitals, technical institutes) + Law enforcement training (National college) + Community development projects (HICDPs)
- Infrastructure Projects: India plays a key role in Maldives' infrastructure development:
  - Airport redevelopment (Hanimaadho International Airport) + Roads and land reclamation + Greater Male Connectivity Project (bridge and causeway connecting capital to islands)
- Tourism: Open skies agreements and visa facilitation agreements boost tourism, medical travel and business interactions.
- Soft Power → Cultural Ties
  - Expatriate Community: Indians being the second largest expatriate community.
  - Roughly 25% of doctors and teachers in the Maldives are Indian nationals.
  - Indian Cultural Center (ICC): Promotes Indian culture through yoga, music etc.
  - Entertainment Popularity: Hindi movies, TV shows and music.

Evolution of India-Maldives Relations

- 1965 - 1978: Maldives gains independence from Britain + India recognize Maldives'.
- Strategic Partnership (1978 - 1988): Maritime Boundary Agreement defines maritime boundaries between the two countries.
- Political Turbulence (1988 - 2008): Coup attempt in Maldives leads to Indian military intervention (Operation Cactus) to restore stability.
  - Interventions strain relations but is later resolved.

2008-2013 (Cordial beginning)	2013-2018 (Strained Ties)	2018-2023 (Renewed Engagement
• The first democratic government elected in 2008. • Friendly begging was underpinned by enhanced security cooperation with India including the provision of Dornier aircraft and patrol boats for maritime reconnaissance and surveillance.	• PPM won the election and the elected President Abdulla Yameen pursued crack downs on democracy, growing proximity to China and the use of Anti-India rhetoric for domestic political purposes. • During this period Maldives-China FTA was also signed.	• MDP won the election implemented an "India First policy, emphasizing economic and defence cooperation with India while addressing Indian concerns related to Chinese investments in the Maldives. • This policy aimed to mend the strained ties with the two nations.

2024 Present: 2024 Maldivian election → Victory of Mohamed Muizzu ("India Out" campaign).

- Withdrawl of Indian military personnel stationed + Non Renewal of hydrography agreement.
- Participation in a defence pact with China.

Areas of Conflict

Domestic Instability:

- **Maldivian Civil Society:** A young civil society facing issues like religious extremism and drug abuse could hinder India's effort to build goodwill.
  - More than 200 Maldivians have joined ISIS.
- **Anti-India Sentiment:** New pro-China government's willingness to cancel India backed agreements creates uncertainty.
  - Misunderstanding of India's UTF Harbour Project Agreement.

China's Growing Influence:

- **String of Pearls:** Maldives' role in China's strategic "String of Pearl" initiative could threaten India's regional security interests.
- **Expansionist:** China's growing economic investment and potential military cooperation with Maldives raise security concerns for India.
  - China Maldives Friendship Bridge.

- **Other Challenges:**
  - Project Delays: India's reputation for slow project completion could undermine its efforts in the Maldives.
  - Skewed trade relationship between India and Maldives (in India's favour)
  - Climate Change: Both nations are vulnerable to rising sea levels and other climate change impacts, requiring a coordinated response.

Strengthening India-Maldives Relations

- **Building Trust and Goodwill**
  - Increase Development Assistance: Focus on impactful projects that directly benefit the Maldivian people, addressing concerns behind "India Out" sentiments.
    - Ex: Vaccine Maitri
  - Open Communication: Engage with the Maldivian government at all levels, addressing concerns and building trust through regular dialogue (IORA Platform)
  - People-to-People Ties: Promote cultural exchange programs and educational collaborations.
- **Addressing Challenges**
  - Ensure timely completion of Indian Infrastructure projects like the Greater Male Connectivity Project to offer credible alternatives to China.
  - Youth Engagement: Include youth employability and entrepreneurship programs in India's development projects to counter radicalization risks.
  - Anti-India Perception: Improve communication strategies to highlight the benefits of Indian assistance like "Vaccine Maitri"
- **Long Term Cooperation:**
  - Common Interests: Prioritize cooperation in maritime security, climate change and economic development.
  - Respect for Sovereignity: Both nations must respect each other's internal affairs and avoid interference in domestic politics.
  - Regional Cooperation: Collaborate on common platforms like the Indian Ocean RIM Association and Indian Ocean Naval Symposium.

PYQs Corner

(Write the Answer and Get Free Evaluation)

1. India is an age-old friend of **Sri Lanka.**' Discuss India's role in the background of recent crisis in Sri Lanka in the light of the preceding statement. [150 Words] [10 Marks] **[2022]**

2. **China** is using its economic relations and positive trade surplus as **tools to develop potential military power status in Asia**', In the light of this statement, discuss its impact on India as her neighbour. [150 Words] [10 Marks] **[2017]**

3. "Increasing **cross-border terrorist attacks in India** and growing interference in the internal affairs of member-states by **Pakistan** are not conducive for the future of **SAARC (South Asian Association for Regional Cooperation).**" Explain with suitable examples. [200 Words] [12.5 Marks] **[2016]**

4. Terrorist activities and mutual distrust have clouded **India-Pakistan relations.** To what extent the **use of soft power like sports and cultural exchange** could help generate goodwill between the two countries. Discuss with suitable examples. [200 Words] [12.5 Marks] [2015]

5. **Project 'Mausam'** is considered a unique foreign policy initiative of Indian government to improve relationship with its neighbours. Does the project have a strategic dimension? Discuss. [200 Words] [12.5 Marks] **[2015]**

6. With respect to the **South China sea**, maritime territorial disputes and rising tension affirm the need for safeguarding maritime security to ensure freedom of navigation and over flight throughout the region. In this context, discuss the bilateral issues between India and China. [200 Words] [12.5 Marks] **[2014]**

7. In respect of **India-Sri Lanka relations**, discuss how domestic factors influence foreign policy. [200 Words] [10 Marks] **[2013]**

8. What do you understand by **'The String of Pearls'**? How does it impact India? Briefly outline the steps taken by India to counter this. [200 Words] [10 Marks] **[2013]**

9. Discuss the **political developments in Maldives** in the last two years. Should they be of any cause of concern to India? [200 Words] [10 Marks] **[2013]**

India's Extended Neigbourhood

CHAPTER

10

INDIA'S EXTENDED NEIGHBOURHOOD

As India strives to become a regional superpower and global leader, it prioritizes strong relationships with its extended neighbours in addition to its immediate neighbours. These extended neighbours span across various regions:

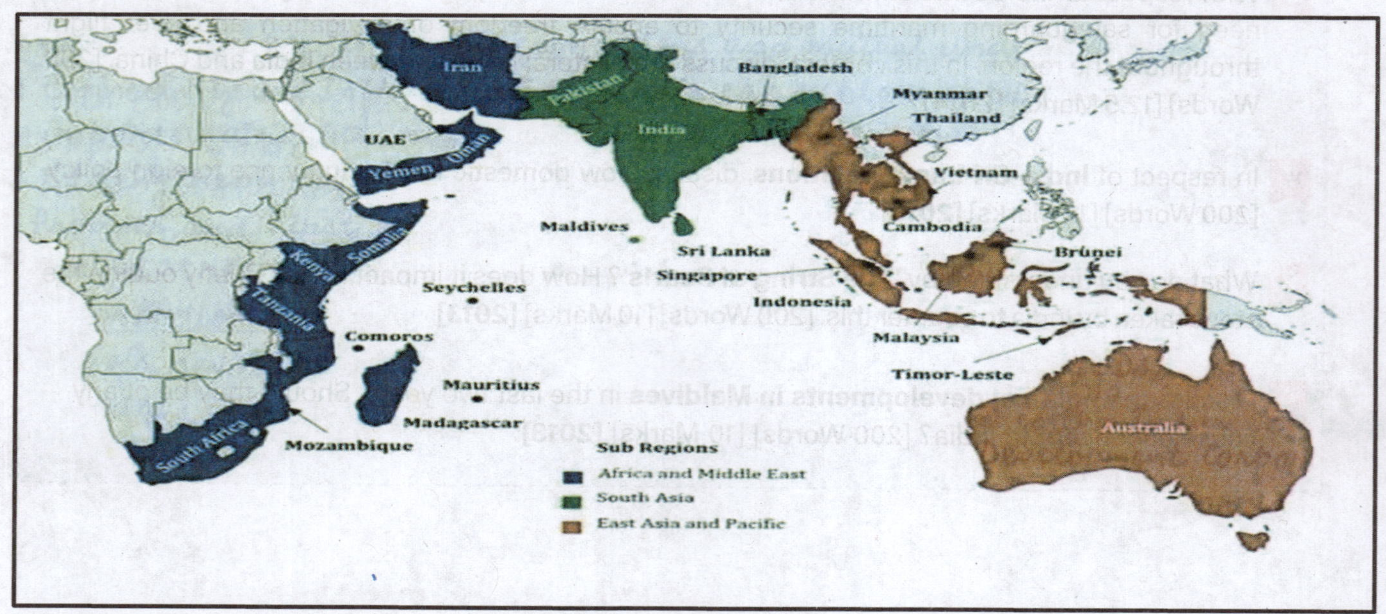

India - SouthEast Asia :

- Act East Policy : India's key diplomatic initiative to foster economic, strategic and cultural ties.
  - It focuses on connectivity, commerce, culture and capacity building.
- Institutional Support : Key organizations like ASEAN, ARF and EAS facilitate expanding bilateral engagements.

Indo - Pacific :

- Core Principles : "Inclusiveness", "openness" and "ASEAN centrality" guide India's policy in this region.
- SAGAR (Security and Growth for All in the Region) : Promotes India's geopolitical, strategic and economic interests, particularly in the Indian Ocean

Central Asia :

- Connect Central Asia Policy : Aims to establish deeper economic and cultural ties in the region (Ex : INSTC)
- 4Cs Framework : India emphasizes cooperation in commerce, capacity enhancement, connectivity and contact.

West Asia :

- "Link and Act West" Policy : It encompasses the GCC countries, Iran, Israel, and other Arab Nations.
- India - Middle East - Europe Corridor (IMEC : India's growing influence in the region.

India South-East Asia

- Longstanding ties between India and Southeast Asia (cultural exchange, diaspora, defence, economics)
- Combined population : 1.85 billion (1/4 of world)
- Combined GDP : $3.8 trillion (highlights strategic and economic importance)

Evolution of Partnership

- 1950 - Early 1960s : India supported decolonization movements in Southeast Asia.
- 1960s - 1980s : India's focus shifted inward, viewed ASEAN with distance (Cold War context)
- 1990s - 2010s : " Look East Policy

full dialogue partner with ASEAN (1995). joined ARF (1996).

- 2010s-Present: "Act East Policy" intensified cooperation. Leading to Strategic Partnership (2012) and Comprehensive Strategic Partnership (2022)

Association of Southeast Asian Nations (ASEAN)

- Member Countries: Brunei, Cambodia, Indonesia, Laos, Malaysia, Myanmar, the Phillipines, Singapore, Thailand, Vietnam.
- Objective: To promote political and economic cooperation and regional stability among member countries.
- Key Areas of Cooperation: Economic Integration + Political and Security Cooperation + Social and cultural cooperation.
- Significance: Promotes economic growth, stability and peace in the Southeast Asian region.
  - It is also a forum for diplomatic dialogue and conflict resolution.
- ASEAN Mechanisms: India actively engages in regional peace and stability through East Asia Summit, ASEAN Regional Forum (ARF) and ADMM Plus (Defense Ministers' Meeting)

Significance of South East Asia for India

- Geopolitical: ASEAN is central to India's Act East Policy, encompassing political, strategic, cultural and economic aspects.
  - India participates in ASEAN plus Six with China, Japan, South Korea, New Zealand and Australia.
- Geoeconomic: Free trade agreement (FTA) exists between India and ASEAN, with bilateral trade projected to reach US$ 150 billion by 2023 (from US$ 9 bn in 2002)
  - Significant economic weight (7% of global GDP, 26% of world population)
- Geostrategic Cooperation: First ASEAN-India Maritime Exercise (May'23).
  - India and Singapore have a bilateral agreement for logistical support to Indian Navy ships at Singapore's Changi Naval Base.
- Shared Indo-Pacific Vision: ASEAN is central to India's Indo-Pacific focus.
  - Both sides believe in an open, inclusive, rules based Indo-Pacific with freedom of navigation and peaceful dispute settlement.
- Maritime Cooperation: India and ASEAN countries collaborate on maritime security trade and supply chains through initiatives like Australia-India Indo-Pacific Oceans Initiative Partnership (AIIPOIP) + Indo-Pacific Economic Framework (IPEF).

- Countering China: Maritime cooperation against China's South China Sea actions
  - Stronger India-ASEAN ties can counter China's regional dominance.
- Other Reasons:
  - Financial Aid: India provides funds for development projects (ASEAN-India Cooperation Fund and Green Fund)
  - Trade Benefits: India imports resources from ASEAN and exports to their growing population.
  - Cultural Ties: Large Indian communities in Southeast Asia promote cultural exchange.
  - Geopolitical Standing: Stronger relations with ASEAN raise India's global profile.

Challenges in India-ASEAN Relations

- Strategic Landscape: Competition between the US and China in the Indo-Pacific region puts pressure on ASEAN to take sides, potentially destabilizing the region.
- Unstable Geoeconomics: Geopolitical tension in Indo-Pacific is producing geoeconomic consequences where issues of trade and technology cooperation as well as supply chain resilience is at peak.
- Decentralized Structure: Unlike the EU, ASEAN lacks a central authority to manage and coordinate issues across its ten member states.
- Infrastructure Gaps: Projects like the India-Myanmar-Thailand highway haven't fully addressed connectivity challenges, hindering trade and cooperation.
- South China Sea Disputes: Territorial disputes involving some ASEAN members and China can complicate regional security and stability.
  - China's claim to territories in the South China Sea overlaps with competing claims by Brunei Darussalam, Malaysia, the Philippines and Vietnam.
- Delayed Projects: Delays and challenges in IMT trilateral highway (2002) including political instability in Myanmar and financial issues.
  - Now it is expected to be completed by 2027.
- Economic Issues:
  - RCEP Absence: India's non-participation in the Regional Comprehensive Economic Partnership (RCEP) creates an economic barrier.
  - Fragmented Markets: The lack of a unified ASEAN markes makes it difficult for Indian businesses to navigate trade.
  - Trade Imbalance India has a significant trade deficit with ASEAN, with imports exceeding exports.
  - Reciprocal Barriers: Trade and investment barriers exist on both sides such as India's CAROTAR rules.

Initiatives to Improve India-ASEAN Relations

Act East Policy Pillars

- Promote trade and investment with ASEAN and East Asia.
- Strategic Partnership: Develop closer political and security ties.
- Cultural Ties: cultural exchange + people-to-people connections.
- Northeast India Integration and ASEAN.

1. Act East Policy (2014): To promote economic cooperation, cultural ties and strategic relationships with countries in the Asia-Pacific region.

- Origins: It evolved from the earlier "Look East Policy" Launched in 1991.
- Northeastern Gateway: Developing India's Northeast as a land bridge to Southeast Asia.
- 4Cs focus: Prioritize Culture, Commerce, Connectivity and Capacity Building.
- Key Initiatives:
  - Annual Delhi Dialogue on political, security, economic and socio-cultural issues.
  - MeKong Ganga Cooperation (MGC): For cooperation in tourism, culture, education as well as transport and communications.
    - Member Countries: India, Cambodia, Lao PDR, Myanmmar, Thailand and Vietnam.
  - Cultural exchange: Historical and cultural links with India.
    - Ex: Angkor Wat Temple, Ta Prohm temple + Buddhism originated in India.
  - Connectivity Projects:
    - India-Myanmmar-Thailand Trilateral Highway: Connects Moreh (India) to Mae Sot (Thailand) via Myanmmar.
    - Kaladan Multimodal Project: Links Sittwe Port (Myanmmar) to the India-Myanmmar border offering a shorter route from Kolkata to Sittwe and bypassing the Siliguri Corridor.
    - Sabang Port Development: India's first deep sea port in Indonesia, strategically located.
  - Energy Cooperation: Development of renewable energy projects (International Solar Alliance) and the import of oil and natural gas (ONGC Videsh Ltd in the hydrocarbon-rich South China Sea).
  - Science and Technology: Dedicated ASEAN India S&T Development Fund (AISTDF) to support R&D projects and development activities.
  - Renewed Engagement: Active participation in ASEAN, ARF, EAS, BIMSTEC, ACD, MGC and IORA.

2. East Asia Summit

- EAS is an important ASEAN-led frameworks to further the objectives of regional peace, security and prosperity.
- Members: Ten ASEAN Member States, Australia, China, India, Japan, New Zealand, Republic of Korea, Russian Federation and USA
- Major contributions by India in the past:
  - India partnered with Australia on Maritime Security Cooperation.
  - India in partnership with Australia and Singapore on Combating Marine Pollution.
  - India announced the Indo-Pacific Oceans Initiative (IPOI) at the 14th EAS.

Pathways for Strengthening India-South East Asia Relation

- Deepening Strategic Partnership:
  - Connectivity: Infrastructure development, logistics and transportation links.
  - Maritime Cooperation: Joint patrols, anti-piracy efforts and freedom of navigation initiatives.
  - Digital Transformation: Knowledge sharing, interoperable payment systems (like India-Singapore FinTech collaboration) and broader digital connectivity
  - Trade and Economy: Review ASEAN-India FTA, potentially integrating with the Indo-Pacific Economic Framework (IPEF) for a robust supply chain network.
  - Sustainable Development: Prioritize policies + green growth
- Collaborative Solutions: Leverage India's initiatives like the International Solar Alliance (ISA) and Coalition for Disaster Resilient Infrastructure (CDRI) to address ASEAN's energy and infrastructure needs.
  - Leveraging cultural linkages: India's cultural diplomacy through India Government's "Buddhist Circuit" initiative, should resonate with East Asian nations.
  - Strategic Cooperation: Particularly in the maritime domain, where China has demonstrated increasingly assertive behaviour.
  - Enhancing bilateral trade through regular high-level consultation and meetings.
- Actional Steps: Maintain collective dialogue under the ASEAN Indian Plan of Action to promote shared interests.
  - Enhance maritime cooperation by aligning India's Indo-Pacific Oceans Initiative with ASEAN's Indo-Pacific Outlook.

INDIA CENTRAL ASIA RELATIONS

India and Central Asia have had longstanding historical, cultural, political and economic relations that have over the time metamorphosed into a stable, mature and transformational partnership.

• **Extent:** Central Asia Region stretches from the Caspian Sea in the west to China in the east, and from Afghanistan in the south to Russia in the north.

• **Members:** Kazakhstan, Kyrgyzstan, Tajikistan, Turkmenistan and Uzbekistan (Collectively as the Central Asian Republics (CARs)).

Historical Ties

- Since 3rd century B.C through the Legendary Silk Route.
- The route served as a Medium of exchange such as goods, silk, textiles, thoughts, ideas, religion and philosophy.
- Buddhism found inroads in Central Asian cities like Merv, Tirmiz and Bokharas etc in form of Stupas and Monasteries
- Babur from Farghana valley established the Mughal dynasties in India.
- Prominent men from Central asia - Amir Khusrau, Dehlawi, Al Biruni, Abdur Rahim Khan-i-Khanan.
- Culture, music, dance, movies and literature bound the Soviet republics closer to India.
- Relations suffered post disintegration of USSR (post 1991)

Significance for India

- **Energy Security:** Central Asian countries are endowed with commercially viable natural, mineral and hydel resources. E.g., Galkynysh gas field
- **Geostrategic Importance:** Central Asia has been an arena of "great game", the region lies at the crossroads of Russia, the Middle East, South Asia and the Far East.
- Common Challenges like Illegal Drug trade, Religious Extremism, Fundamentalism arm trafficking and terrorism.
- Agricultural Cooperation like setting up of commercial agro-industrial complexes.
- Trade and Investment in the sectors like Banking, Insurance, Power generation, IT and pharmaceuticals.

Challenges

- Poor Connectivity due to adverse geographic terrain and India-Pakistan border issues.
- Untapped trade potential due to trade regulatory hindrances and potential fragility.
- Geopolitics of energy and presence of major powers like China through its BRI.

- Volatile security scenario especially in regards to Pakistan, Afghanistan and Iran-USA dynamics.
- Internal Issues: Problems of governance, regulation of movement across borders and many inter state disputes.

Steps Taken to Strengthen the relationship

- Defence agreement with Tajikistan. E.g., Farkhor Air Base
- Civil nuclear cooperation with Kazakhstan. (Supply Uranium)
- TAPI Pipeline.
- Recently started the India-Central Asia Summit.
- Connectivity efforts:
  - Connect Central Asia Policy.
  - International North-South Transport Corridor (INSTC) agreement.
  - Chabahar Port Project.
  - India acceded to the Customs Convention an International Transport of Goods under cover of TIR Carnets to facilitate the transport of goods between India and Central Asia via Iran.
  - Ashgabat Agreement on International Transport and Transit Corridor (ITTC)

Way Forward

- Finalize FTA between India and Eurasian Economic Union (EAEU).
- Revitalizing interaction in cooperation with countries like US and Russia for stabilising the region and ensures interests of all partners
- Annual military exercises and joint manufacturing of defence related equipments.
- India can help Central Asia in strengthening their local self government
- Soft-diplomacy.
- Sub-regional alliances such as SAARC and BIMSTEC can also be formed between South Asia and Central Asia.

INDIA-WEST ASIA RELATION

- About: India has enjoyed exceptionally close, historic and civilizational ties with Middle East/West Asia, which is a part of its extended neighbourhood.
- About West Asia: It is a subregion of Asia that is bordered by Europe to the west, Central Asia to the north, South Asia to the east and Africa and the Arabian Sea to the south

Changing Dynamics of India-Middle East Relations

Past: India's need to develop economically made the Middle East increasingly important both as a source of fuel imports and for Indian labour and remittances.

Present: India is now following the same course but intensified the approach as "Look West" policy, by focussing on three main axes: the Arab Gulf countries, Iran and Israel.

India's "Look West" Policy

- It is a strategic approach aimed at strengthening its ties with countries in West Asia, also known as the Middle East.
- Aims: Ensure a stable and peaceful West Asia, which is crucial for India's security.
    - Diversify its energy sources and meet its growing energy needs.
    - Boost economic growth through increased trade and investments.
    - Enhance India's strategic influence in the region.
- Focus: Building stronger political, economic and cultural relations with this region.
- Aspects of India's "Look West" policy:
    - Target Countries: Engagement with Gulf nations like Saudi Arabia, UAE, Qatar, etc., alongwith Iran and Israel.
    - Areas of Cooperation

Areas of Cooperation

- Energy Security: crucial source of oil and gas for India.
- Defence Alliances: Building partnerships for regional security
- Counter Terrorism: Cooperation to combat terrorism is a shared concern.
- Economic Integration: Expanding trade and investment ties.

Areas of Cooperation

- Historical Links: Ancient trade between the Indus Valley Civilization and Dilmun (modern Bahrain) and the Mesopotamiam Civilisation.
  - Cradle of Civilisation: - Birthplace of Judaism, Christainity and Islam.
- Energy Security: Continued cooperation with traditional suppliers in the Gulf for oil and gas imports (over 50% of India's crude oil and 70% of gas imports)
  - Renewable energy transition with agreements signed with Saudi Arabia and UAE in late 2023.
  - 20 year LNG deal signed with Qatar in February 2024 (7.5 MMTPA)
- Geopolitical Crossroads: Strategically located between continents, West Asia serves as a critical link for trade routes.
  - Ex: Suez Canal → 12.5% of global trade.
- Conflicts and Security: Israeli - Palestian dispute, Syrian civil war, tensions between Iran and its neighbours.
- Trade and Commerce: GCC became India's largest trading partner in FY 2022-23 (15.8% of total trade)
  - Growth in bilateral trade with key countries like Saudi Arabia (US$ 52.76 billion in FY 2023) and UAE (US $85 billion in FY 2023)
- Economic Partnerships: To enhance its political and interests in the region.
  - Ex: India-UAE CEPA to boost trade and investment (target: US$100 billion by 2030)

Major Initiatives by India in West Asia

- The Middle East Quad (I2U2) initiative.
  - Economic, technological and diplomatic collaboration.
- Vaccine Maitri initiative.
  - Provide COVID-19 vaccines to countries.
- Strategic Partnership in Energy sector.
  - Oil concessions to India by Abu Dhabi
- Technological Solutions.
  - The RuPay card launched in Abu Dhabi
- Soft Power Diplomacy.
  - India inaugurated the first Hindu temple in Dubai

- Humanitarian assistance: India has provided humintarian assistance to Syria during its civil war.

- Maritime Cooperation: Enhanced Security and Collaboration:-
  - India's growing role in the Indian Ocean Region (IOR) and its "Indo-Pacific Policy" focus on the western IOR and Arabian Sea.
  - Regular maritime exercises with naval forces of Oman, Saudi Arabia, Qatar, Kuwait and UAE.
  - Increased naval presence in the Red Sea due to Houthi rebel activity.
- Connectivity: International North-South Transport Corridor (INSTC) aimed at reducing the carriage cost between India and west Asia to Europe.
  - Ashgabat Agreement: It envisages the facilitation of transit and transportation of goods between Central Asia and the Persian Gulf.
- Bilateral Relation:
  - UAE: India's 3rd largest trade partner and 2nd largest export destination (3.4 million Indian diaspora)
  - Iraq: India's 5th largest trading partner (2021-22: $34.3 billion) and major oil supplier.
  - Qatar: India's most important natural gas supplier (41% of total imports)
  - Oman: Access to Duqm Port for military/logistics and Top trading partner.

Areas of Concern

- The Palestine-Israel Conflict: Balancing support for Palestinian rights with deepening strategic ties with Israel is a major challenge for India.
- Organization of Islamic Cooperation (OIC) criticizes India's policies, particularly regarding Kashmir.
- China's Influence: China's economic clout and role as a peacemaker (e.g., Iran-Saudi Arabia) complicate India's strategic calculations.
- Modest scale of India's efforts in Central Asia and the Middle East, compared to China's Belt and Road.
- Vulnerability of Indian Diaspora in the Region: This was evident during the current COVID crisis induced protectionism with regard to employment.
- India's susceptibility to regional conflicts: Saudi-Iranian rivalry and the boycott of Qatar by Saudi Arabia and the UAE. Similarly Israel suspects Iran of sponsoring Hamas and Hezbollah against it.
- Security Concerns: Religious extremism and terrorism due to its large Muslim population and internal conflicts.
  - Rise of political Islam in some Middle Eastern countries raises concerns for India's secular democracy.

Impacts of instability in the West Asia

On India	At Global Level
• Strategic balancing due to engagement with countries with conflicting interests. ◦ Emergence of Iran-Russia-China axis. • Maritime Security: Drone strikes, hijackings (Houthis attack in Red Sea) impacting freedom of navigation in India's maritime region. • Safety and security of the Indian diaspora. • Threat to Energy Security: India imports of Crude Oil (~85%) • Delay in completion → India Middle East Europe Economic Corridor (IMEC) • Impact on Indian Economy: ◦ Disruption in global maritime trade and supply chain → Rise in fuel prices. ◦ Negative Impact on inflation rate, pharma's export, trade balance, forex reserve, stock market etc. ◦ Rise in shipping costs and insurance premiums.	• Diplomatic milestones (E.g Abraham Accords, Israel-Saudi) may get compromised. • Intensification of maritime security challenges across the Indo-Pacific region in case of attacks on ships of USA, United Kingdom. • Arms race or possession of Nuclear weapons may lead to global instability issues. • Impact on Global Economy ◦ Higher oil prices may lead to higher food prices intensifying food insecurity in many countries. ◦ Economies directly expose may get downgraded and investment across the globe may suffer due to downgraded sentiment. • International Humanitarian Crisis due to loss of lives, forced displacements and instances of War Crimes (Rafah Offensive Stance of Brazil. • Credibility of international institutions → UNSC.

Pathways for Strengthening Relationship

⊞ Enhance Diplomatic Engagements and negotiations within all parties to refrain them from further violence and seek solution through diplomacy.

⊞ Building Normative framework and Process through arms control and security negotiations declaration of regional "Weapons of Mass Destruction Free Zone" leading to demilitarization.

⊞ Resolution of the Israel Palestine issues based on the Two Nation Theory for long term security, peace and stability.

⊞ Safeguarding Fiscal and External Sustainability by countries by strengthening policy buffers.

- Opportunity for India to emerge as a net security provider and mediator for South-South cooperation.
  - Maritime Security Operations have been conducted by Indian Navy (Operation Sankalp) and USA (Operation Prosperity Guardian) in the regions of Gulf of Aden, Arabian Sea, off the East coast of Somalia to protect from various non-traditional threats present in the region.
- Mediating Role: India can help mitigate sanctions and ease the US 'maximum pressure' strategy by using its leverage with the US, Saudi Arabia and Israel.
- Humanitarian assistance for response to the after effects of pandemic in the region.
- Strategic partnership and sustained soft power diplomacy with Iran, Saudi Arabia and Israel.
- Substitutes for oil: India should be relooking at options for oil supply.
- Extending collaborations in areas like semi conductor design and fabrication and space technology with countries like UAE and Israel

INDIA AND PACIFIC

- Indo-Pacific is a geopolitical construct that has emerged as a substitute to the long prevalent "Asia-Pacific".
  - Represented the eastwards shift of global developments from Euro-Atlantic dimension.
  - It is an integrated theatre that combines the Indian Ocean and the Pacific Ocean and the land masses that surrounds them.
- Key Players: India, US, Australia, Japan, ASEAN, maritime nations and countries with overseas territories.
- From the Indian perspective, it extends from the coast of East Africa across the Indian Ocean to the Western Pacific.
  - However as per the, US National Security Strategy document in 2017, it is described as the region from the "west coast of India to the west coast of United States."

Geography of the Indo-Pacific Islands

Factors driving the global shift towards the Indo-Pacific

- Important Sea Lines of Communications (SLOC): presence of key choke points, like Mozambique Channel, Bab-el-Mandeb, Lombok Strait.
- Flourishing trade and economy: Accounts for 62% of the world GDP and contributes to 46% of the world's merchandise.
- Rise in non traditional threats (piracy, illegal fishing etc)
- Richness in Natural Resources (Offshore Hydrocarbons, Sea Bed minerals, fisheries etc)
- China factor–
  - Issues related to Belt and Road Initiative (BRI)
  - China's disregard for International Rules and Customs.
  - Increasing Militarization of Indian Ocean Region.

India's Interests in the Indo-Pacific

- Peace and security in the Indian Ocean
- Expanding its presence in the region, especially in Africa, the Middle East and Southeast Asia.
- Maintain its role as a net security provider.
- Countering China.
- Enhancing Trade and Investment Cooperation and Promoting Sustainable Development.
- Other interests: Combating marine pollution, Regulating illegal, unregulated and unreported (IUU) fishing, deep sea mineral exploration and effective disaster risk management.

Key Elements of India's vision for the Indo-Pacific (PM's Shangri La Dialogue, 2018)

- A free, open, inclusive region
- Southeast Asia is at the centre of Indo Pacific.
- A common rule-based order for the region.
- Equal access to common spaces on sea & in the air, as a right under international law.
- Circumventing power rivalries through partnerships.

India's Policy towards the Indo-Pacific Region

1. Strengthening and preserving traditional roles in IOR:

- Security provider and first responder.
- Early warning and weather forecasting services.
- Providing Developmental Assistance.
- Maintaining trade and investment flows in the region.

2. Foreign Policy:

- Separate division under Ministry of External Affairs: These include Indo-Pacific Division (IPD) and Indian Ocean Region Division (IORD)
- Utilising its soft power with the help of Indian Diaspora, cultural exchanges E.g., Project Mausam.
- Policies aligning with the vision of Indo Pacific: such as Act East Policy, SAGAR

3. Naval Strategy:

- Maritime Domain Awareness (MDA): through institutions like information management and analysis centre (IMAc) and Information Fusion Centre for India Ocean Region (IFC-IOR) and initiatives like white shipping agreements and coastal surveillance radar chains on IOR regions.
- Expanding/maintaining India's naval presence: through Mission Based Deployments (MBDs) and Joint Exercises.

4. Partnerships:

- QUAD and ASEAN
- Regional groupings: E.g- Bay of Bengal Initiative for Multi-Sectoral Technical and Economic Cooperation (BIMSTEC), Indian Ocean Rim Association (IORA), Mekong Ganga Cooperation, Forum for India-Pacific Islands Cooperation (FIPIC)
- Minilaterals: E.g. Trilateral dialogue with France and Australia.

5. Initiatives:

- Indo-Pacific Oceans' Initiative.
- International Solar Alliance.
- Coalition for Disaster Resilient Infrastructure
- Indian Ocean Naval Symposium
- Asia Africa Growth corridor.

Challenges India faces in the Region

- Limited Naval capacity and Lack of Military Bases.
- Challenges to trade: Emergence of insulating tendencies amongst economies after COVID, Tariff and Non Tariff measures (NTMs) and poor infrastructure connectivity.
- Slow pace of development of Initiatives.
- Balancing continental and maritime strategies.
- Challenges to MDA: Submarines deployment, grey shipping, dark shipping.
- Disapproval from within due to divergence from traditional positions on nonalignment.
- Barriers to fruitful partnerships: Lack of definitional consensus and differences in priorities.

Pacific Islands Forum (PIF): Regional organization to promote cooperation and dialogue between its 18 member countries and territories in the Pacific.

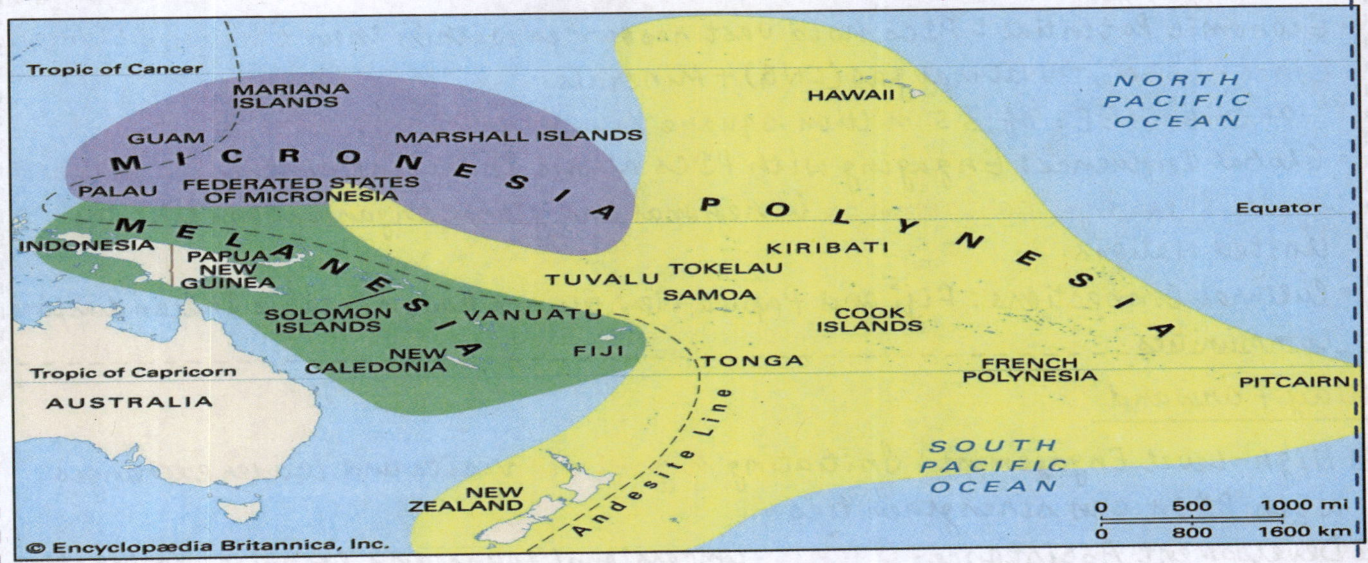

- Forum for India – Pacific Islands Cooperation (FIPIC) is a manifestation of India's Act East Policy and Indo-Pacific Policy.
- India has fostered its relationships with them through developmental aid as part of South-South Cooperation.

Region	Countries	Resources	Strategic Importance
Melanesia	Fiji, Papua New Guinea, Solomon Islands, Vanuatu	Minerals, timber, fish, gold, oil, gas copper	Natural resources, biodiversity, proximity to shipping lanes.
Micronesia	Federated States of Micronesia, Kiribati, Marshall Islands, Nauru, Palau	Fish, phosphate, coconut products	Strategic Military location control of the Pacific Ocean
Polynesia	American Samoa, Cook Islands, Niue, Samoa, Tonga, Tuvalu Wallis and Futuna	Fish, forestry, agriculture, tourism	Tourism, cultural significance, strategic military location

Significance of Pacific Island Countries (PIC) for India

- Geostrategic Significance: PIC's lie astride critical sea lanes of the Indo-Pacific, vital for global trade (central to India's security calculus)

- India's Maritime Security Strategy: As India's naval power grows, its focus extends beyond the Malacca Strait.
- Economic Potential: PICs hold vast resources within their Exclusive Economic Zones (EEZs), → Natural gas (LNG) + Minerals.
  - Kiribati EEZ of 3.5 million square Kilometres.
- Global Influence: Engaging with PICs allows India to strengthen its network of alliances and partnerships in regional and global organizations like the United Nations.
- Cultural Connections: Fiji and Papua New Guinea have sizeable Indian diaspora communities.

Way Forward

- High-Level Engagement: Initiating high-level visits and leader exchanges with PICs can strengthen ties.
- Development Assistance: Grants, concessional loans and technical cooperation.
- Combat Climate Change: Sharing best practices, providing technical expertise and supporting sustainable development projects.
- Trade and Investment: Exploring avenues to enhance trade and investment relations can benefit both sides.
- Cultural Exchanges: Promoting cultural exchanges is a valuable tool for fostering people-to-people connections and mutual understandings.
- Connectivity and Infrastructure: India can explore oppurtunities to invest in ports, airports, roads and digital infrastructure development in the PICs.
- Strengthening and preserving traditional roles in IOR such as Security Provider and First Responder etc.
- Naval Strategy: Maritime Domain Awareness (MDA) through institutions like Information Management and Analysis Centre (IMAC); Expanding/maintaining India's naval presence through Mission based Deployments (MBDs) and Joint Exercise.
- Initiatives: Indo Pacific Oceans' Initiative, Trilateral Development Corporation (TDC) fund, Indian Ocean Naval Symposium, Asia Africa Growth Corridor, International Solar Alliance, Coalition for Disaster Resilient Infrastructure etc.
- Partnerships: IPEF, QUAD, ASEAN, BIMSTEC, Forum for India-Pacific Islands cooperation (FIPIC), Minilaterals such as Trilateral dialogue with France & Australia.
- Foreign Policy: Separate Indo-Pacific Division (IPD) under Ministry of External Affairs, Utilizing Soft Power (Project Mausam), Act East Policy, SAGAR etc

INDIA AND INDIAN OCEAN REGION (IOR)

India's Presence in the Indian Ocean

Iran (construction of Chabahar Port, submarine training)
UAE (cooperation with India's oil reserves)
Oman (permission for Indian Navy use of the port of Duqm)
Seychelles (Indian base on Assumption Island (pending), provision of patrol boats, training)
Mauritius (naval communication facility, provision of patrol boats, training)
Madagascar (naval communication facility, permission for Indian Navy use of port)
Reunion Island, France (permission for Indian Navy use of base)
INDIA
Bangladesh (financial aid for Air Force)
Sri Lanka (export of patrol boats)
Maldives (provision of patrol planes and helicopters, training)
Diego Garcia island, US (UK) (permission for Indian Navy use of base)
Andaman Nicobar Islands (modernisation of bases)
Cocos Island, Australia
Myanmar (construction of Sittwe Port, export of weapons)
Thailand (joint patrol, Naval training)
Malaysia (joint patrol, Air Force training)
Singapore (joint exercises, joint patrols, leasing of training ground)
Indonesia (joint patrol, repairing of fighter jets)
Australia (joint exercises, joint infrastructure development, security cooperation with the US, Japan, France, India and Indonesia etc)

- Indian Ocean Region (IOR) broadly defines areas consisting of littoral states of the Indian Ocean.
- Geographical Extent: Sub-regions such as Australia, South East Asia, South Asia, Horn of Africa and Southern and Eastern Africa.
- IOR is vital for global trade (Straits of Hormuz, Malacca) + Rich in resources (marine life, minerals, oil/gas)
- IOR is marked by cultural, social, political and economic diversity.

Significance of IOR for India

- **Strategic Importance:** Central position of India in IOR makes it a natural maritime power, influencing sea lanes and regional dynamics
- **Energy Security:** Over 90% of India's oil depends on IOR shipping lanes, making them critical for energy security.
- **Economic Significance:** 95% of India's trade by volume and 68% of trade by value is moved through sea via Indian Ocean.
- **Resource Rich:** IOR provides resources like fish (supporting livelihoods and exports) and necessitates a secure presence for their continued access.
    - Mineral and natural resources like iron, copper, zinc, manganese, gold and silver.
- **Food Security:** About 250 million people live within 50 km of coast and dependent on sea for food and livelihood.
- **Monsoon:** Indian Ocean plays an important role in keeping Monsoon mechanism in favor of India.
    - La Nina and El-Nino phenomenon occur in Indian Ocean and affect Indian Monsoon.
- **Maritime Connectivity:** Linking major ports and cities across Asia, Africa and the Middle East

Concerns Associated with Indian Ocean Region

- **Policy Ambivalence:** India wants cooperation with democracies but avoids antagonizing China. E.g India still endorse One China Policy.
- **Net Security Provider:** Current military strength might not be enough for full regional security.
  - India needs significant investment to fulfill "net security provider" role.
- **The China Factor:** China's growing military presence (including navy) is a security challenge for India and smaller nations.
- **Resource Constraints:** India's defense spending for the navy is low compared to major powers.
  - Non traditional threats like piracy, terrorism and illegal fishing.
- **Security Concerns:** India's long coastline and past maritime terror attacks necessitate vigilance against threats from the sea.
  - Internal security issues (e.g., Kashmir tensions) divert resources from the IOR.
  - Climate change poses long term threats to coastal communities and maritime security.

Initiatives by India for Indian Ocean Region

- India's policy towards countries in the IOR is guided by the 'Neighbourhood First' policy and Prime Minister's vision of SAGAR (Security and Growth for All in the Region)
- MAUSAM, Asia- Africa Growth Corridor: These projects promote regional security, economic cooperation and development.
- Indian Ocean Naval Symposium (IONS): A forum for maritime cooperation among IOR littoral states to promote collective maritime security and combat common threats like piracy.
- Indian Ocean Rim Association (IORA): A regional organization promoting economic cooperation, sustainable development and cultural exchange among IOR countries
- Coordinated Patrols (CORPAT): Joint patrols conducted with regional partners to enhance maritime domain awareness and deter illegal activities.
- Indian Ocean Naval Symposium (IONS): Forum that seeks to enhance maritime cooperation among Navies of the littoral states of the IOR and helps to preserve peaceful relations between nations.

- Naval Exercises and CORPAT: Increased participation in joint exercises and patrols strengthens regional partnerships.
- Training and Asset Sharing: Training IOR nations' personnel and supplying naval assets builds goodwill and strengthen regional security.

Pathways for Strengthening India's Position in Indian Ocean Region

- Comprehensive IOR strategy: India needs a well-defined plan encompassing security, economic cooperation, sustainability and diplomacy.
- Strategic Partnerships: Strengthening cooperative security, intelligence sharing, and capacity building with regional allies is vital.
- Maritime Diplomacy: Active engagement in regional forums and promoting dialogue are key to fostering cooperation on maritime security.
- Sustainable Blue Economy: Supporting responsible practices in marine conservation, fisheries and renewable energy development ensures long term benefits.
- Capacity Building: Cost effective training programs for IOR nations' naval personnel, enhancing their maritime capabilities.
- Centralised Planning: To ensure a unified strategic vision, overcoming individual service biases and facilitating efficient resource allocation.
- National Defence Policy: To project India's commitment to regional security, building confidence among IOR nations and allies.
- Strategic IOR Approach to fosters positive influence and addresses concerns of smaller nations wary of a "Big Brother" image.
- Empowering Regional Partners: Investing in training and potential equipment assistance for IOR nations' navies bolsters regional security for all.
- Maritime Domain Awareness: Investments in advanced surveillance and information sharing are crucial for effective border security.

PYQs Corner

(Write the Answer and Get Free Evaluation)

1. A number of outside powers have entrenched themselves in Central Asia, which is a zone of interest to India. Discuss the implications, in this context, of India's joining the Ashgabat Agreement, 2018. [150 Words] [10 Marks] **[2018]**
2. Evaluate the economic and strategic dimensions of **India's Look East Policy** in the context of the post-Cold War international scenario. [200 Words] [12.5 Marks] **[2016]**
3. The question of India's Energy Security constitutes the most important part of India's economic progress. Analyze India's energy policy cooperation with West Asian Countries. [200 Words] [12.5 Marks] **[2016]**
4. Evaluate the economic and strategic dimensions of India's Look East Policy in the context of the post-Cold War international scenario. [200 Words] [12.5 Marks] **[2016]**

Bilateral Relations with Developed and Developing Countries

CHAPTER 11

BILATERAL RELATIONS OF INDIA

Bilateral Relations are essentially diplomatic ties between two individual countries
They are essential for countries to achieve:

- Stronger economies → trade and investment
- Improved security → cooperation on threats like terrorism.
- Greater Influence on Global Issues by working together.
- Cultural understanding → Exchange program and tourism.
- Regional Stability for peaceful coexistence.

India's strategic use of bilateral relations allows it to navigate complex geo-political situations and pursue its national interests effectively.

India's Guiding Principle	Challenges faced by India
• Strategic Autonomy: India acts independently and avoids alliances (e.g., relations with US and Russia) • De-hyphenation: Each relationship is independent (e.g., India with Israel and Palestine). • Wider Engagement: India broadens diplomatic ties (e.g., operation Ganga evacuations) • Multilateralism: India advocates for reform in global institutions (e.g UN Security Council)	• Fence Sitter Accusations: India is criticized for neutrality on global issues. • Funding wars: India is accused of financing aggression (e.g.. buying Russian oil) • New Alliances: India's US ties may create a rival China-Russia-Pakistan axis.

• Alternative Mechanisms: India creates new trade channels (e.g Rupee – Rouble trade) • Soft Power: India leverages its diaspora (e.g., lobbying for Indo-US Nuclear Deal). • Mediation: India acts as neutral negotiator (e.g., hosting G20)	Reputational Damage: Balancing with conflicting nations can strain relations. (e.g., Iran) • Import dependence limits India's global leverage. • Minilateral Groups like QUAD may hinder global Cooperation.

Way Forward

- Become an Alternative: India can represent the Global South in a polarised world.
- Strategic Hedging: Balance China by building counter-measures while maintaining ties
- Self Reliance: Reduce dependence on critical imports (defense, energy).
- Multi-aligned Foreign Policy: Build issue-based coalitions (BRICS, QUAD, G20).
- Global Leadership: Address global challenges (climate change, connectivity, terrorism)

INDIA-USA RELATIONS

- India-US relations have evolved over the last seven decades, from being described as 'estranged democracies' to 'Natural Allies'.
- The confluence of common factors like democratic values, shared areas of interests, stand against terrorism makes India and US enjoy a comprehensive strategic partnership.

Significance of Relationship

1. Defense:

⊞ Strong Growth: Indo-US defense trade has grown significantly, with US emerging as India's 3rd largest arms supplier (~11%) after Russia (~45%) and France (~29%)

⊞ Key Agreements: US recognized India as a 'Major Defence Partner' in 2016. US Defence Agreements like

- Logistics Exchange Memorandum of Association (LEMOA) in 2016.
- Communication Compatibility and Security Agreement (COMCASA), 2018
- Industrial Security Agreement 2019
- Basic Exchange and Cooperation Agreement (BECA) 2020 are signed with India.

⊞ Bilateral Military Exercises like Yudh Abhyaas, Vajra Prahar, Malabar etc are conducted between the two countries.

2. Trade Relations:

- Bilateral Trade between India and the US stood at $118.28 billion in 2023-24.
  - US was the top trading partner of New Delhi during 2021-22 and 2022-23.
- Defense Trade Rise: Defense trade is increasing alongside of imports from the US.
- Indian Service Sector Reliance on US markets.
- Investment and Job Creation: Over 163 Indian companies in the US have invested $40 billion and created around 425,000 jobs.
- Trade Deal: Both countries aim for $500 billion in trade and are working on a "mini trade deal" while FTA talks stall.

3. Energy Cooperation:

- Strategic Partnership: The US-India energy dialogue has been upgraded to a Strategic Energy Partnership (SEP).
- Initiatives:
  - US-India Climate and Clean Energy Agenda 2030 Partnership.
  - Revamped Strategic Clean Energy Partnership (SCEP)
  - Renewed India-US Civil Nuclear Energy Cooperation
  - Renaming Gas Task Force to India-US Low Emissions Gas Task Force.
- Civil Nuclear Cooperation (2008): AP 1000 reactors project underway (potentially the largest of its kind)
  - Extended MOU for collaboration on the Global Centre for Nuclear Energy Partnership (GCNEP)

Strategic Partnership:

- China Factor: The rise of China and its assertive behaviour in the Indo-Pacific has strengthened the Indo-US strategic partnership.
- Quad Cooperation: Both countries participate in the Quadrilateral Security Dialogue (QUAD) to ensure a peaceful, stable and rules-based Indo-Pacific.
- Indo-Pacific Strategy: US Indo-Pacific Strategy report identifies India as a "vital partner" in the region.
- Blue Dot Network: US initiative to certify infrastructure project with India's participation.

Challenges in the Relationship:

- **India-Russia Ties:** Russia's position as India's biggest arms supplier creates interoperability issues with US military equipment.
- **India's position on Ukraine War:** India's muted criticism of the Russian invasion of Ukraine in 2022, raised questions over India's credibility as a security partner.
- **Position on Indo-Pacific region:** The US views that the Indo-Pacific as a region where rules based liberal international order needs to be preserved vis-a-vis China's assertive rise and even the Russian threat.
  - However, India does not see the Indo-Pacific as an exclusive group of actors in a region that is against any country.
- **CAATSA:** The Countering America's Adversaries Through Sanctions Act threatens sanction on India for its S-400 missiles defense system deal with Russia.
- **US-Pakistan Relations:** Concerns from the US about human rights in Kashmir could lead to Pakistan internationalizing the issue.
- **Regional Integration:** Absence of both countries from major regional trade agreements (CPTPP and RCEP)
- **Geostrategic Divergences:**
  - US withdrawl from Afghanistan and its impact of Kashmir.
  - Different priorities in the Indo-Pacific and the Middle East.
  - Impact of Russia Ukraine war on Indian-US relations.
  - Mutual suspicion regarding potential future cooperation with China.

Trade Issues

- Pending Bilateral Investment Treaty.
- India's tariff regime
- Digital Services Tax (DST)
- Steel and aluminium tariff and retaliaratory issues.
- Generalized System of Preferences (GSP) removal by the US.
- Market access limitation for US service providers in India.
- Sanitary and phytosanitary (SPS) obstacles for Indian agricultural exports
- Intellectual Property (IP) concerns
- Disagreements on "forced" localization
- Investment reforms and limitations.

- **Climate Change:** Failure of developed countries to meet financial commitments.

Pathways for Healthy India-USA Relations

- Uphold Strategic Autonomy by nurturing ties with the US while maintaining balanced relations with other powers like Russia and China.
- Russia-Ukraine Conflict: India must respect international norms + prioritizes its national interests + contribute to peaceful conflict resolution.
- Trade with the US: Fair and balanced agreements + market access, intellectual property rights and trade deficit reduction.

- Defense Cooperation: Focussing on technology transfer and joint production to strengthen its national security.
  - Military exercises (Yuddha Abhyas, Vajra Prahar) + MQ-9B platforms.
- Regional Security: India needs to carefully manage its regional politics, particularly regarding the situation in Afghanistan.
- Leverage QUAD to promote peace and stability in the Indo-Pacific region + counter China's assertive behavior + address climate change and pandemics.
- Climate Action: India and the US can jointly tackle climate change by:
  - Developing clean energy technologies (Ex: Strategic Clean Energy Partnership (SCEP)).
  - Expanding the renewable energy use (Ex: International Solar Alliance)
  - Building Climate Resilience (Ex: CDRI)
- Science and Innovation: Leverage strengths to collaborate in:
  - Healthcare advancements (Global Disease Detection-India centre in 2014)
  - Space Exploration initiatives (Ex: NISAR)
  - Artificial Intelligence development (Ex: Initiative on Critical and Emerging Technologies (iCET)).
  - Advanced manufacturing techniques (Semiconductor + Robotics)
- Global Leadership: Work together to:
  - Strengthen Multilaterialism (Empowering WTO)
  - Reform international institutions (UNSC Reforms)
  - Address global challenges on a unified front (Freedom of Sea line of Communication).

INDIA-RUSSIA

- Recently, India and Russia held their 22nd annual summit on 8 and 9 July, 2024 in Moscow.
- Overview of the Relationship:
  - Russia has been a longstanding and time-tested partner for India and development of India-Russia relations has been a key pillar of India's foreign policy.

Timeline of India-Russia Relationship

- 1947:- Establishment of diplomatic relations.
- 1971:- India signed the Indo Soviet Treaty of Friendship and cooperation in 1971 during the Bangladesh liberation war.
- 1975:- India's first satellite 'Aryabhatta' launched on the Soviet launch vehcile 'Soyuz'

- 1988:- Kundakulam Nuclear Power Plant agreement.
- 1993:- Treaty of friendship and cooperation.
- 2000:- Declaration on Indian-Russian Strategic Partnership, leading to annual Summits.
- 2010:- Special and Privileged Strategic Partnership.
- 2021:- First India-Russia 2+2 Ministerial dialogue.
- 2022:- Revival of Rupee Ruble mechanism for trade with Russia.
- 2024: 22nd annual summit on 8 and 9 July, 2024

India-Russia Relationship

- It is driven by shared interests of multilateralism; and global peace and prosperity.
- Principles of Relationship:
  - Mutual trust
  - Respect for each other's territorial integrity.
  - Alignment on most critical international and regional issues of war and peace.
- Annual summit serves as the highest institutionalized dialogue mechanism in India-Russia partnership.

Significance of Russia for India.

- Balancing China and its assertiveness
- Emerging New Sector of Economic Engagement like mining, high end technologies. India's footprint in the Russian Far East and in the Arctic.
- Combating Terrorism: Both countries are calling for early finalization of the Comprehensive Convention on International Terrorism at UN.
- Support of Russia at Multilateral forums like UNSC and NSG.

Areas of Cooperation

Defence and Security Cooperation	• Russia is a major supplier of defense items to Indian armed forces and both nations are in joint research, development and production of advanced defence items. ◦ Bilateral projects includes the supply of S-400, licensed production of T-90 tanks and Su-30 MKI, production of AK-203 rifles in India and Brahmos missiles among others. • Cooperation is guided by the Agreement on the Programme for Military Technical Cooperation for 2021-2031. • INDRA as a tri-service bilateral military exercise.
Internation Multilateral Cooperation	• Russia supports India's bid for a permanent seat in the UN Security Council (UNSC) and membership of Nuclear Suppliers Group (NSG)

	• Also, both nations have an active engagement at: ◦ International/ Multilateral Organizations (e.g BRICS & SCO) ◦ Connectivity Projects such as INSTC (International North-South Transport Corridor) etc. • It help to act decisively against international terrorism and cooperate on matters such as drug trafficking, issues in Afghanistan etc.
Trade and Economic Cooperation	• Bilateral trade during FY 2021-22 amounted to $13.2 billion ($30 billion set for 2025) • Bilateral investments between the two countries crossed the US$30 billion target set in 2018 ($50 billion target set for 2025).
Other Areas of Cooperation	• Nuclear Energy: The impeccable non-proliferation record of India has strengthened the partnership for peaceful use of nuclear energy. ◦ India and Russia have also signed a tripartite pact with Bangladesh for civil nuclear cooperation. • Space Cooperation: Russia has supported India's space programme since its early days. ◦ Russia is supporting India's 1st manned space mission Gaganyaan. • Science and Technology: India-Russia relationship extends to the field of basic science as well including Russian-Indian Network (RIN) of Universities, Arctic and Antarctic Research, etc.

Challenges in India Russia Relations

1 India's Shifting Priorities

- Rise of US-India Ties has strained India relation with Russia especially since 2008 (Landmark nuclear deal)
  - Signing of foundational military agreements (LEMOA, COMCASA, BECA) further highlights this shift.
  - India to reduce its defence supplies from Russia to avoid USA sanctions under CAATSA
  - Countering America's Adversaries Through Sanctions Act: Allows imposition of sanctions on countries dealing with these three nations (Russia, Iran and North Korea)

- India's Inclination towards West: India shares a natural affinity towards the West (USA and major European nations) due to their democratic set up.

2. Russia Shifting Priorities

- Russia's Pivot to China by supplying weaponary like the S-400 missile system to China.
  - Russia's participation in China's Belt and Road Initiative (BRI)
- Russia's Engagement with Pakistan: Russia's military cooperation with Pakistan further complicate the relationship.
- Internal Issues in Russia: Russia's domestic challenges, including protests and economic difficulties, may limit its capacity to engage with India as effectively.
- Commercial ties with Russia are stagnant despite good political relations.
- India's concerns regarding supply and servicing of Russian defence supplies.

3. Changing World Order: US-China rivalry is shifting the world order towards a bipolar world → Against India Russia's vision for a multipolar world.

- Differing Global Views: Russia views the Indo-Pacific concept as a US strategy to counter China + underming ASEAN centrality + increasing US influence.
  - It clashes with India's strategic interests and its participation in the QUAD grouping.
- Diplomatic Dilemma for India: India faced criticism in the West for refraining from condemning the Russian invasion of Ukraine and for its continued expansion of energy and economic cooperation with Moscow.

4. Trade and Economic Challenges

- Trade Deficit: Increased oil purchases since 2022 and the strengthening of the Russian Ruble against the Indian Rupee will increase the deficit further.
- Economic Challenges: Regulatory impediments and the use of phytosanitary standards (classifies tea as fruit and vegetable) and non-tariff barriers by Russia.

Pathways for Strengthening India- Russia Relationship

- Deepening Defense Cooperation: Utilize India as a manufacturing hub for exporting Russia-origin military equipment to third countries (e.g., the BrahMos missile joint venture).
  - Upgrading Defence Cooperation through Make in India.
  - Joint manufacturing of spare parts and Logistics support.

⊟ Expanding Strategic Partnership:

- Explore oppurtunities in the Eurasian region, potentially by collaborating with the Eurasian Economic Union (EAEU) on mutually beneficial projects.
- Promoting Multipolar World Order: Cooperate in international forums like BRICS and SCO to address global issues + promote shared values.
- Technological collaboration in areas like artificial intelligence, space exploration (Gaganyaan Mission), cyber security and renewable energy.
- Strategic Autonomy: India needs to maintain a balanced relationship with Russia, China and the US, prioritizing the national interests.

⊟ Strengthening Economic Ties:

- Diversification in areas like pharmaceuticals, information technology and infrastructure development.
- Trade Facilitation: Reduce trade barriers, simplify processes and create a business friendly environment
- Rupee-Ruble Mechanism to shield bilateral trade from the effects of Western sanctions.
- Deepening economic cooperation: Operationalization of the 'Green Corridor' project: International North-South Transport Corridor and the signing of an FTA with EaEU.

4. Enhancing People-to-People Ties:

- Cultural Diplomacy through Yoga and other cultural exchanges
- Utilize media, social media and cultural events to build positive narratives.

INDIA-JAPAN RELATIONS

The friendship between India and Japan has a long history rooted in spiritual affinity and strong cultural and civilizational ties. Throughout the various phases of history, the two countries have never been adversaries and bilateral ties have been singularly free of any kind of dispute.

India Japan relation at a glance

- **1952** • Establishment of diplomatic relations
- **1991** • Japan was among the few countries that bailed India out of the balance of payment crisis.
- **2014** • Upgraded bilateral relations to 'Special Strategic and Global Partnership.
- **2017** • Agreement for cooperation in the Peaceful Uses of Nuclear Energy entered into force.
- **2021** • Agreement concerning Reciprocal Provision of Supplies and Services between defence forces of both countries came into force.
- **2022** • Celebrated the 70th anniversary of establishment of diplomatic relations.

Areas of Cooperation

1. Economic Powerhouse:

- Strong Trade Ties: India-Japan Comprehensive Economic Partnership Agreement (CEPA) making Japan India's 12th largest partner.
  - Bilateral trade: US$ 21.96 billion during FY23.
  - Exports from Japan to India US$ 16.49 billion (FY'23) and imports → US$ 5.46 billion

Significance of the India Japan relations

- Counterweights to China's growing influence in the region.
- India as Security Provider + Japan contributes to regional stability.
- Important for Act East Policy and Free and open Indo-Pacific Strategy.
- Shared Vision for a Multipolar World to avoid reminiscent of the Cold War.
- UNSC reform through India and Japan along with Germany and Brazil (G4)

- Investment and Infrastructure: Source of foreign direct investment and Official Development Assistance (ODA) for India.
  - Mumbai-Ahmedabad High Speed Rail, Western Dedicated Freight Corridor (DFC), Delhi-Mumbai Industrial Corridor etc.
- Focus on Northeast India collaborating on socio-economic development projects and connectivity initiatives (India-Japan Act East Forum)
  - Act East Forum was established in 2017 and aims to provide a platform for India-Japan collaboration under the rubric of India 'Act East Policy' and Japan's Free and open Indo-Pacific Vision.' The objective is to coordinate developmental projects in North-East India in areas of connectivity, forest management, disaster reduction and capacity building

2. Strategic Partnership:

- Defense Cooperation: India-Japan "2+2" dialogue strengthens defense ties with Japan's participation in Exercise Malabar.
- Shared Security Concern: About China's growing assertiveness, particularly in the East China Sea and along the Indo-china border
- Countering China's influence through Supply Chain Resilience Initiative (SCRI) to reduce dependence on China in the Indo-Pacific region.
- Blue Dot Network to certify infrastructure development projects worldwide.

3. Maritime Cooperation

- Indo-Pacific Vision: Both countries actively promote a "Free and Open Indo Pacific". strengthening regional connectivity and cooperation through organizations like QUAD.
- Connectivity Projects: Collaborating on initiatives like the Asia Africa Growth Corridor (AAGC)

4. People to People

- Cultural Ties: Centuries old cultural exchange, particularly through Buddhism fosters a strong foundation for the relationship.
- Broad Cooperation digital technologies, disaster management, skill development, science and technology, healthcare and even sister-city partnerships.

Challenges in Relation

- Strategic Dissonance: India's "multi-alignment" strategy and reliance on Russian arms clash with Japan's strong opposition to Russia's actions in Ukraine.
  - Objection to Russia's Vostok-2022 exercises near Kuril Islands (India participated).
- India and Japan end up on opposite sides → India's tariff structure on imports.
- Limited Economic Integration:
  - Trade: India-Japan trade remains just a quarter of trade with China; Limited Success of CEPA; entry barrier for Indian companies and products.
  - Difference on Cross-border Data Flow: While India is looking at data localization, under 'Osaka Track' Japan proposed standardization of cross border data flow.
  - Scepticism on the feasibility of the AAGC.
  - Different interests: India's exit from RCEP was disappointing from Japan's view.
  - Pending projects: Flagship bullet train project between Ahmedabad and Mumbai is still a work-in-progress with land acquisition still not complete.

• Common ground: India and Japan relation is developing in backdrop of rising China but not because of mutual grounds of development such-as trade, science and technology cooperation etc.

Pathways for Strengthening Ties

- Investment: Improved logistics, a more open, stable and consistent trade policy regime, and the establishment of a 'centralised single window clearance' system will increase India's attractiveness for Japanese investors.
- Robust trade: Both leaders must recognize the need for enhancing bilateral trade and encourage further review of the implementation of CEPA through existing mechanisms.
- Counter China: The annual trilateral Malabar exercise, which also includes United States, can give a vision where the three nations can combine militarily to counter Chinese threat in the region.
- Energy security: Develop stronger partnerships through a Green Energy Partnership and creating new innovative partnerships in Manufacturing and MSME sectors.
- Overcoming Non-Tariff Barriers (NTBs) → Improving India's sanitary and phytosanitary standards through technology transfer.
- Improved logistics, a more open, stable and consistent trade policy regime and a 'centralised single window clearance system' will increase India's attractiveness for Japanese investors.
- Attracting Japanese Investors: Improving logistics infrastructure + Open, stable and consistent trade policy regime + efforts to improve ease of doing business.
- Revitalizing AAGC to better balance regime and business interests, making it more commercially attractive.
- Clean Energy Cooperation: India's inclusion in Asia Energy Transition Initiative (AETI) strengthens cooperation in clean energy.

INDIA - FRANCE RELATIONS

India-France shared a time tested relationship. The visit of French President Emmanuel Macron to India as the chief guest for the Republic Day and PM Modi's visit at the Bastille Day Parade in France, exemplify the natural bonds of friendship between the two countries

India-France Relations

- India and France have traditionally close and friendly relations.
- Post India's Independence - Diplomatic relations were established, French aircraft like Ouragan, Mystere, Jaguar have been part of the Indian air fleet since 1960's. France stepped into supply nuclear fuel for Tarapur Plant after US backout.
- Post Cold War Era - India and France entered into Strategic Partnership in 1998 with defence, security and space being major areas of cooperation

Areas of Cooperation

- Geo Political Cooperation:- France was the first P-5 country to support Indian membership in the UNSC. France's support was vital in India's accession to the Missile Technology Control Regime, Wassennar Arrangement and Australia Group.
- Geo-strategic cooperation: Indian Air force planes have been deployed to Reunion Island. France is part of India-France-Australia Trilateral Dialogue that supports free, open and inclusive Indo-Pacific. France with India's stand on Pakistan supported cross border terrorism.
- Defence and Security: France is India's second-Largest defence supplier in 2017-2021 with Rafale, scorpene submarines. Joint exercises like Varuna (Naval), Garuda (Air Force) and Shakti (Army).
- Economic Cooperation: India-France trade $13.4 Bn in 2022-23. France is the 11th Largest foreign investor in India.
- Energy, Climate and Science and Technology: France supports India's entry into NSG, jointly set up ISA with India. CNES and ISRO collaboration on TRISHNA satellite and construction of world's largest nuclear park in Jaitapur.

Significance

- Securing the Indo-Pacific:- Counter the growing Chinese aggression. For ex - India France Joint Strategic Vision for Cooperation in the Indian Ocean Region in 2018.
- Strategic Autonomy:- Relations not constrained either by the Anglo-Saxon views (in France) nor the Anti-Western thoughts (in India). For ex - France support of India after 1998 Pokharan Nuclear Test.
- Global Stability:- Checking Russia's assertiveness in Europe and China's assertiveness in Asia.
- Horizon 2047 Agreement - Future roadmap of India-France collaboration for the next 25 years in AI, super computing and cloud computing.

Challenges

- Absence of Free Trade Agreement :- Stalled progress on the India-EU Broad based Trade and investment agreement (BTIA)
- Trade Imbalance and IPR Issues :- France exports more to India and inadequate IPR protection of French firms in India.
- Stalled Projects like the Jaitapur Nuclear project.
- Differences in geopolitical approaches - Ukraine war stand and France stand on BRI contrarian to India's.
- Emerging geopolitical scenario - Middle east crisis.

Way Forward

- Early conclusion of FTA - India - EU BTIA
- Implementation of Agreement on Migration and Mobility.
- Increased Trade and Investment via Joint Ventures.
- Expedition on stalled projects like Jaitapur Plant

INDIA-ISRAEL

India and Israel are strategic partners and share values of democracy and pluralism. The two countries have contributed to deepen their strategic partnership with a focus on innovation and research as two Knowledge-based economies

Areas of Cooperation

- Political Relations: Full diplomatic relations were established in 1992, which were upgraded to a strategic level in 2017. Both countries are members of I2U2 initiative alongwith US and UAE.
- Economic and commercial Relations: India has benefited from Israeli expertise and technologies in horticulture mechanization, micro-irrigation and post harvest management.
    - Bilateral mercandise trade stood at US$ 5.66 with the balance of trade being in India's favour.
    - India is Israel's third largest trade partner in Asia.
    - Trade in diamonds constitutes close to 50% of bilateral trade.
- Defence and Security :- India imports critical defence technologies from Israel. Joint production and development of key defence items such as Barak missile.
- Culture and Education : India is an attractive alternative tourist destination for Israel. New funding programme of joint academic research.
- Indian Community : Around 85 000 Jews of Indian-origin in Israel

India's De-Hyphenated Policy: Israel and Palestine

- In International politics, de-hyphenation means dealing with two countries having adversarial relationships between them, in an independent manner.
- Traditionally, India's foreign policy towards Israel and Palestine has been a hyphenated foreign policy. However, hyphenating the ties with Israel—linking them to ties with the Palestinian Authority—essentially prevented India from pursuing a pragmatic policy of what was in India's best interests.
- India in the recent year has been following a de-hyphenation policy between Israel and Palestine. It means India's relationship with Israel would stand on its own merits, independent and separate from India's relationship with the Palestinians. The de-hyphenation is a balancing act, with India shifting from one side to another as the situation demands.

Areas of Concerns

- Trade and Investment potential is not harnessed fully: Trade is mainly confined to diamond and defence.
  - FTA talks are stagnated for more than a decade.
- Emerging fissures in the West Asian region: Growing closeness of Israel and Saudi Arabia against Iran creates challenge for India to balance its relations with the three.
- Human Rights violation by Israel against Palestine: India has been vocal about human rights violations, however India faces strategic dilemma in dealing with the issue.
- In defence domain, Israeli companies are concerned about uncertainities related to India's protracted defence acquisition procedure.
- Israel's close ties with China.

Way Forward

- Enhancing people to people contact.
- Education: Indian Institutions of higher education could benefit from the strong culture of research and innovation that thrives in Israel.
- Learning from Israel's Water Management Technologies.
- Cooperation in Semiconductor Manufacturing.
- Mutual Learnings on community practices.

INDIA-UAE

PM Narendra Modi at the Vibrant Gujarat Summit 2024 has stated that the India-UAE relations are "stronger than ever".

India-UAE Relation-History

- India and the UAE established diplomatic relations in 1972.
- India-UAE relation was upgraded to comprehensive strategic partnership in 2017.
- India-UAE relation has entered into a phase of intense engagement. PM Modi has visited UAE six times since 2015. UAE premier has visited India four times since 2016.

Significance of Relations

- Geostrategic Significance:
  1) Security - Conflicts in the Middle East fuel ISIS recruitments from Kerala.
  2) Countering Piracy in the Arabian Sea - Through exercises like Zayed Talwar (Naval) and Desert Eagle (Air force)
  3) Energy Security - UAE is the 6th Largest exporter of crude oil to India.
- Geopolitical Significance
  1) Cooperation in international forums - India's UNSC Bid, UNFCCC, ISA
  2) Countering growing China's influence in Middle East.
  3) Crucial for India's OIC membership and India-GCC FTA.
- Geo-economic Significance:
  1) Remittances - UAE one of the top sources as home to 3.5 million Indian expatriate population (2021)
  2) Trade and Investment - India-UAE trade targeted to reach $100bn by 2030 (India-UAE CEPA), UAE is the ninth largest investor in India.

Recent Achievements

- India-UAE Comprehensive Economic Partnership Agreement - Reduced tariffs on 80% of goods and zero duty access to 90% of India's exports.
- Rupee-Dirham deal - Enables the use of local currencies for cross-border transaction.
- Launch of I2U2 and IMEC - These platforms to promote connectivity and cooperation in fields of technology, infrastructure and sustainability.
- Religious freedom - UAE allowing to open the first Hindu temple on its soil - BAPS Hindu Mandir Abu Dhabi.

Challenges

- Large Non Tariff Barriers (NTBs) in trade has dampened Indian Exports.
- China's Cheque Book Diplomacy crowing out Indian companies from the UAE.
- Inhumane conditions imposed by the Kafala system on Indian immigrants.
- Arab-Iran Conflicts puts India in a diplomatic tight spot.

Way Forward

- Establishment of 2+2 Dialogue with UAE.
- Predictability in the use of Non-Tariff Barries (NTBs)
- Reformation of Kafala System.

INDIA-EUROPEAN UNION

The relationship between India and European Union (EU) are based on shared values and principles such as democracy, rule of law, rules based international order and multilateralism. Factors shaping India-EU relations in current times include Changing geopolitical developments such as Russia-Ukraine war, Convergence of interests in the Indian Ocean and New emerging world order after COVID-19.

Significance of EU for India

- To counter China.
- Post-Brexit scenario, India recognizes that its own economic prospects depend on the continued growth and internal stability of this region.
- Economic logic: India has been a beneficiary of preferential tariffs under the EU's generalised system of preferences, European companies in India provides million of jobs, trade agreement with EU would help India in further expanding and diversifying its exports and securing the value chains.
- Potential relationship with smaller countries of EU like Denmark. Estonia and Portugal.
- FDI inflows from the EU stand at $ 101.26 bn between 2000-2022.
- EU is India's third largest trading partner and second largest destination for Indian exports after US.

Areas of Cooperation

- Blue Economy: The EU's Blue Growth Initiative, corresponds with India's call to embrace a "Blue Revolution."

- Defending multilateralism and rule based order: both sides are considering each other important partner on several reform agendas like UN, WTO and so on.
- Indo-Pacific: EU's Indo-Pacific strategy has much to complement New Delhi's goals in the region.
- Fighting Climate Change and facilitating the transition to a sustainable economy through Clean Energy and Climate Partnership.
- Connectivity: India and EU have announced comprehensive connectivity Partnership that will provide an alternative to China's BRI.

Concerns in India-EU relations

- Inadequate diplomatic relation.
- Untapped trade potential due to absence of a FTA (BTIA)
- Human rights: EU members expressed concerns about the deteriorating human rights situation in India.
- Lack of people to people ties.

Way Ahead

- Early conclusion of BTIA is crucial.
- Strengthening yearly political dialogue.
- Launching concrete trilateral / cooperation projects in pilot partner countries such as Africa, Central Asia.
- Enhancing cultural dialogue with all countries of Europe.

PYQs Corner

(Write the Answer and Get Free Evaluation)

1. "The **USA is facing an existential threat in the form of a China**, that is much more challenging than the erstwhile Soviet Union." Explain. [150 Words] [10 Marks] **[2021]**
2. What is the significance of Indo-US defence deals over Indo-Russian defence deals? Discuss with reference to stability in the Indo-Pacific region. [250 Words] [15 Marks] **[2020]**
3. The time has come for India and Japan to build a strong contemporary relationship, one involving global and strategic partnership that will have a great significance for Asia and the world as a whole.' Comment. [150 Words] [10 Marks] **[2019]**
4. "What introduces friction into the ties between India and the United States is that Washington is still unable to find for India a position in its global strategy, which would satisfy India's National self-esteem and ambitions" Explain with suitable examples. [250 Words] [15 Marks] [2019]
5. "India's relations with Israel have, of late, acquired a depth and diversity, which cannot be rolled back." Discuss.[150 Words] [10 Marks] **[2018]**
6. Economic ties between India and Japan while growing in the recent years are still far below their potential. Elucidate the policy constraints which are inhibiting this growth. [200 Words] [10 Marks] **[2013]**

Bilateral, Regional and Global Groupings

CHAPTER 12

SOUTH ASIAN ASSOCIATION FOR REGIONAL COOPERATION (SAARC)

- **About:** South Asian Association for Regional Cooperation (SAARC) is an intergovernmental organization for South Asia, founded in 1985.
- **Members:** Afghanistan, Bangladesh, Bhutan, India, Maldives, Nepal, Pakistan and Sri Lanka.
- **Objectives:** To promote the welfare of the people of South Asia and improve their quality of life and accelerate economic growth, territorial integrity, mutual trust, strengthen collective self-reliance. etc
- SAARC comprises 3% of the world's land area, 21% of the world's population and 5.21% (USD 4.47 trillion) of the global economy

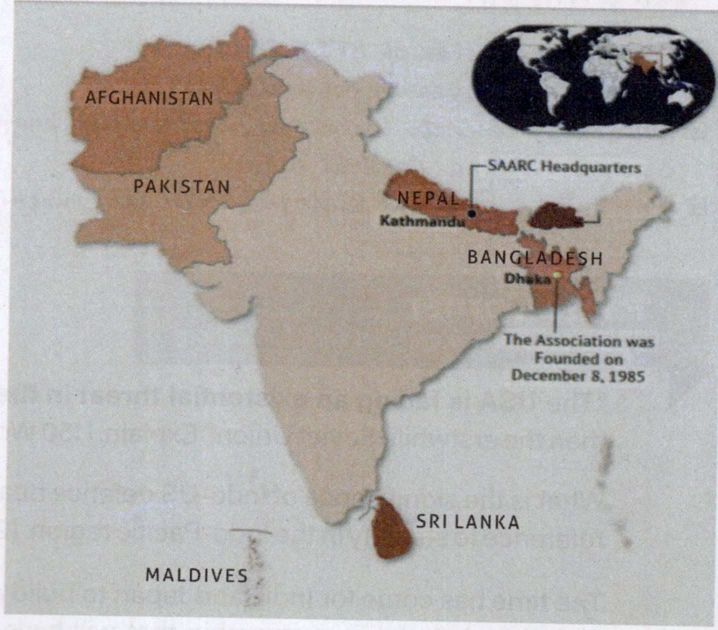

Significance of SAARC for India

- Regional Integration: Offering a middle ground between globalization and isolationism.
  - Ex: SAARC Arbitration Council to resolve disputes between members.
- Socio-Economic Development through trade and collaborative development initiatives.
  - Ex: SAARC Preferential Trading Arrangement (SAPTA) and SAFTA.
- Countering Terrorism cooperation to strengthen security and defence mechanisms.
  - Ex: SAARC Anti-Terrorism Mechanism.
- Countering China's Influence: By engaging regionally in development and economic cooperation, SAARC can provide an alternative to China's OBOR project.
  - Ex: SAARC Development Fund.
- India-Pacific and Act East Policy: SAARC can be a bridge between South Asia and Southeast Asia, fostering economic, social and political ties.
  - Ex: SAARC motor Vechile Agreement (yet to materialize)
- India's Soft Power: Platform to cultivate regional cultural, religions and spiritual connections, while offering developmental assistance to member states.
  - Ex: SAARC Development Fund, South Asian University.
- India's Global Ambitions: Active involvement in SAARC allows India to build a regional security architecture and promote stability.
  - Ex: Vaccine Maitri programme.

Challenges of SAARC

- Indo-Pak Relations: Escalation of tension and violence between India and Pakistan has significantly damaged SAARC's prospects. Pakistan has adopted an obstructionist attitude within SAARC.
  - No Summit meeting since 2014.
- Trust deficit among members.
- Unresolved Border Issues + Fear of India's Big Brotherly attitude among among small neighbours.
  - India's apprehensions of extracting undue concessions by neighbours.
- Decision Making by consensus enabled Pakistan to oppose every initiative of India on connectivity and trade.
- Lack of Dispute resolution mechanism + Lack of resources with members.
- Bilateral issues like Bangladesh's concerns over CAA-NRC, the Madhesi issue and the Kalapani Border issue between India and Nepal etc
- Rising Chinese footprint.

Need for Revival of SAARC

- Representative of the entire South Asian region: It reflects the South Asian identity of the countries.
- Dealing with common issues of the region like terrorism, energy shortage, hydro-politics, and climate change among many others.
- Critical for economic integration of the region: As per the World Bank report, with intra-regional trade at less than 5% of the total trade. South Asia is the least integrated region in the world.
- The central pillar of India's Neighbourhood first policy.
- No real alternatives: BIMSTEC cannot replace SAARC for reasons such as lack of a common identity and history among all BIMSTEC members

Initiatives for Regional / Subregional Cooperation in South Asia

- South Asia Cooperative Environment Programme (SACEP) (1982): Promotes environmental protection and enhancement in the region.
- South Asia Seas Programme (SASP): Protect and manage marine environment and coastal ecosystems in a sustainable manner
- South Asia Subregional Economic Cooperation (SASEC) programme: Enhancing cross-border connectivity + Boosting trade among countries + Strengthening regional economic cooperation.
- Bangladesh, Bhutan, India and Nepal (BBIN) Motor Vechile Agreement (MVA)

Way Forward

- Conduct of SAARC meeting, physical or virtual is quintessential.
- Resolving differences among countries: Set up a mechanism for informal discussions, formal mediation and resolution mechanisms tailored to the region's specific needs and problems.
- Economic integration is the Key to all the problems: South Asian Region must identify economic and social element as priorities rather than being marred by the security element.
- Redefining the SAARC charter, which includes removal of excessive safeguards, the inclusion of the 'SAARC Minus' concept and focus on Trade Facilitation, Energy Trade Connectivity etc.

BAY OF BENGAL INITIATIVE FOR MULTI-SECTORAL TECHNICAL AND ECONOMIC COOPERATION (BIMSTEC)

- **About:** established in 1997 with headquarters in Dhaka (Bangladesh), BIMSTEC is a regional organisation comprising 7 member countries located in Bay of Bengal region.
  - Members: Bangladesh, Bhutan, India, Myanmmar, Nepal, Sri Lanka and Thailand.

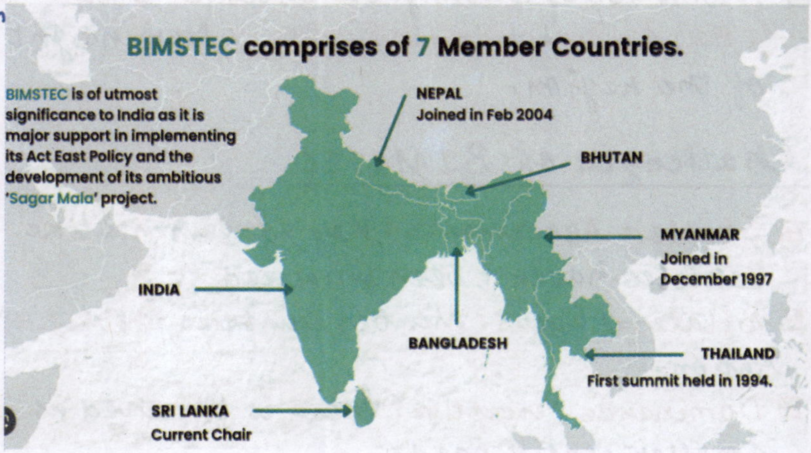

BIMSTEC comprises of 7 Member Countries.

BIMSTEC is of utmost significance to India as it is major support in implementing its Act East Policy and the development of its ambitious 'Sagar Mala' project.

NEPAL Joined in Feb 2004

BHUTAN

MYANMAR Joined in December 1997

INDIA

BANGLADESH

THAILAND First summit held in 1994.

SRI LANKA Current Chair

- **Objective:** To accelerate the economic growth and social progress in the sub-region through joint endeavors in a spirit of equality and partnership.
- **Main Sectors of Cooperation:** Trade and investment, Transport and communication, Fisheries, Agriculture, Public Health, Poverty Alleviation, Counter terrorism and transnational crimes, Environment & Disaster Management, People-to-People contact, Climate Change, Cultural Cooperation.
- **Significance:** 22% of the world's population + combined GDP of US$ 3.7 trillion.
  - Trade of India with BIMSTEC: 4% in 2020.
- **Principle of BIMSTEC:** Sovereign equality, territorial integrity, political independence, non interference in internal affairs, non aggression, peaceful co-existence, mutual respect and mutual benefit.

Importance of BIMSTEC for India

- **Strategic Location:** India's northeast borders position it as a key regional player.
  - BIMSTEC is key to fulfill the country's strategic aspirations to cater the wider concept of 'Indo-Pacific' and an Indian Ocean community
- **Act East Policy:** BIMSTEC aligns with India's "Act East" policy for deeper Southeast Asian ties.
- **Disaster Management:** India shares data through the Tsunami Early Warning System.
- **Connectivity and Infrastructure:** Improved networks facilitate trade and movement.
  - Projects: Kaladan Multimodal Project, Asian Trilateral Highway, BBIN Motor Vehicles Agreement.

- Counterterrorism and Security: BIMSTEC tackles shared security threats.
- Maritime Security: Collaboration on maritime issues and sustainable development.
- Regional Integration: BIMSTEC allows India to lead and influence regional cooperation.
- Counter Chinese Influence due to BRI.
- Promotion of Intangible Culture: India's Centre for Bay of Bengal Studies (CBS) at Nalanda University → New insight and research in intangible heritage of the region.

Challenges of BIMSTEC

- Stalled Agreements: Key agreements like FTA, coastal shipping and motor vehicles haven't been finalized.
- Bilateral Focus: Member countries prioritise bilateral ties over regional cooperation.
- Dominance Perception: India is perceived as playing dominant role, neglecting smaller states' needs.
- Slow Progress: Irregular summits (5 summits in 25 years) and slow-decision making hinder progress (e.g., 17 years for a secretariat + Charter adopted in 2024).
- Competing Interests: Some members prioritize other regional organizations like ASEAN.
- Regional Geopolitics: Reluctance to convey the impression of anti-China.
- Physical Infrastructure: Poor rail and road connectivity, insufficient last-mile links and cumbersome customs and clearance procedures.
- Absence of Strong institutional framework: Inadequacy of secretariat, negligible budget etc.

Way Forward

- Strengthening political engagement: The decision taken in Colombo to host a summit every two years is welcome if implemented.
- Increasing its membership base: Membership to Indonesia, Malaysia and Singapore etc.
- Prioritize sustained physical connectivity and high quality infrastructure.
- Prioritizing multilateralism including facilitating tourism diplomacy, academic and student-exchange programs and cross-border public health initiatives.
- Implementing the BIMSTEC Master Plan on Transport Connectivity (BMPTC): Improve physical and digital connectivity among the members and facilitate the movement of goods and people.

- Strengthening the cooperation in the energy sector, especially in the field of renewable energy and natural gas.
- Enhancing the cooperation in the security sector, especially in combating terrorism, extremism, drug trafficking and cyber crime.
- Empowering BIMSTEC to be a platform for dispute resolution among member countries.
- Concluding FTA.
- Promoting the people-to-people exchanges and cultural ties

SAARC	BIMSTEC
• Regional organisation looking into South Asia. • Established during Cold War Era. • Member countries suffer for mistrust and suspicion. • Suffers from regional politics. • Asymmetric power balance. • Intra-regional trade only 5 percent	• Interregional organisation connecting South Asia and South East Asia. • Established in post-Cold War Era. • Members maintain reasonably friendly relations. • Core objective is the improvement of economic cooperation among countries • Balancing of power with the presence of Thailand and India on the bloc. • Intra regional trade has increased around 6% in a decade.

Similarities between BIMSTEC and SAARC:

- Geographical location: Both organisations are located in South Asia, with member countries sharing cultural, historical and economic ties.
- Objectives: Both organizations aim to promote regional cooperation and integration in various areas, including trade, investment and infrastructure development.
- Membership: Almost similar, with some countries being members of both.

India's foreign policy objectives realised by prioritizing BIMSTEC:

- Reducing Dependence on SAARC: With SAARC being marred by political tensions, India formed BIMSTEC to promote regional cooperation in a more effective manner.
- Economic Integration among member countries, which can contribute to India's economic growth and strengthen regional stability. Ex: Kaladan, IMT Highway, BBIN
- Countering China's influence and maintain its strategic interests. Ex: Gateway to southeast Asia and Key for "Act East Policy."

ASEAN

- Association of Southeast Asian Nation (ASEAN) was established on 8 August 1967 in Bangkok, Thailand.
- ASEAN Declaration (Bangkok Declaration) was signed to bring ASEAN into force. 
- Aim and purposes: To accelerate the economic growth, social progress and cultural development.
    - To promote regional peace and stability.
    - To maintain close and beneficial cooperation with existing international and regional organisations.
- Members: Brunei, Cambodia, Laos, Indonesia, Malaysia, Myanmmar, the Philippines, Singapore, Thailand and Vietnam.

Significance of ASEAN for India

- Centrality in India's Act East Policy and SAGAR initiative and in Indo-Pacific policy.
- Economic: India ASEAN FTA and India's CECA with various countries of the ASEAN region.
- Common Security Threats: ASEAN-India Work Plan to Combat Transnational Crimes.
- Financial Cooperation through ASEAN-INDIA Cooperation fund (AICF), ASEAN India Green fund (AIGF) etc.
- Connectivity Projects: India-Myanmmar-Thailand Trilateral (IMT) Highway, Kaladan Multimodal Project, Maritime Transportation Agreement and a Railway link between New Delhi to Hanoi are in pipeline
- Cultural cooperation: Special Training Course for ASEAN diplomats, Exchange of Parliamentarians etc.
- Defence and Security Corporation through Joint Naval and Military exercises.

Challenges faced by India in its dealings with ASEAN

- Conflicts in priorities: India's opposition to BRI and its withdrawl from RCEP.

- Skewed trade relations: ASEAN's share in India's foreign trade and inflows of FDI is higher than India's share in ASEAN's.
- Maritime challenge: By deepening defence cooperation in the South China Sea, India risks getting embrolled in future maritime conflict between China and one or more ASEAN nations.
- China's influence: China's ability to sow divisions within ASEAN is against India's economic and security interests in the region.
- Centrality of ASEAN in the Indo-Pacific is under jeopardy due to inability to counter China, decline in the relevance of the East Asia Summits and presence of QUAD, AUKUS in the Indo-Pacific.
- Lack of a custodian and strong institutions for ASEAN.
- Divergent interests and priorities of ASEAN members.

Pathways to Strengthen Relations

- Collective dialogue to promote common interests under ASEAN-Indian Plan of Action.
- Trade facilitation: Reviewing ASEAN-India FTA, establishing supply chain networks under the Indo-Pacific Economic Framework (IPEF)
- Enhancing policy prioritization for sustainable finance and growth.
- Enhancing Maritime cooperation through convergence between India's Indo-Pacific Oceans initiative and ASEAN Outlook on Indo-Pacific.
- Capitalize in technology.
- Collaborate on energy transition through initiatives like ISA and One World One Grid

SHANGHAI COOPERATION ORGANISATION (SCO)

- Shanghai Cooperation Organisation (SCO) is an inter-governmental organization encompassing approximately 60% of the Eurasian area and 40% of the global population.
- Combined GDP → around 20% of the World GDP.
- Goals: Promote cooperation in politics, security, economics and culture
- Members: India, China, Russia, Iran, Pakistan, Kazakhstan, Kyrgyzstan, Tajikistan and Uzbekistan.
  - Belarus became the 10th member state (July 2024).

Significance of SCO for India

- Geopolitical: SCO allows India to participate in an alternative economic structure, bypassing trade hurdles caused by sanctions on Iran and Russia.
  - Neutral stand of India: SCO is considered as a counterweight to NATO.
  - Aid in balancing China's influence.
- Energy Security: Forum for India to engage with the energy-rich countries of Central Asia.
- Fostering Regional Stability:
  - Afghanistan Contact Group (ACG, 2005): Promotes regional cooperation with Afghanistan.
  - Ukraine-Russia Conflict: Forum for India to advocate for peace in the region.
- Strengthening Bilateral Relations: engagement with Central Asian nations and major regional powers like China and Russia on shared security challenges.
  - India's focus area → Startups, digital inclusion, youth empowerment, traditional medicine and Buddhist heritage.
- Cultural cooperation: Varanasi designated as first tourism and cultural capital.
- Promoting Regional Connectivity: Projects like TAPI pipeline, INSTC and Chabahar project enhance India's soft power and economic ties.
- Counter-Terrorism Efforts: Regional Anti-Terrorism Structure (RATS) provides a platform for sharing intelligence, conducting joint-exercises and operations.
- Combating Drug Trade originating from Afghanistan and Pakistan (80%)
- Access to critical resources like Uranium (Kyrgyzstan) and hydrocarbons (Turkmenistan + Iran)

Challenges with SCO

- Bilateral Issues and Trust Deficit: Internal conflicts and mistrust between members like India, China and Pakistan create challenges.
- China's strong presence creates an imbalance in power dynamics.
- Anti-West Perception hinders wider global cooperation.
- Sovereignity: SCO's support to China's Belt and Road Initiative (BRI) may violate India's territorial integrity.
- Divergent Interests: Member states with diverse interests, political systems and priorities → Difficult to reach a consensus, hindering the effectiveness of SCO.
- Russia-Pakistan-China axis: Growing closeness of Russia-China and China Pakistan creates hurdles for India at strategic level in furthering its interest in SCO.
- Weak fight against terrorism: SCO has not taken any visible counter terrorism measures against threats emanating from Af-Pak region.
- Lack of a unified approach for dealing with Taliban.

Role of India in Strengthening the SCO

- **Leveraging Multilaterialism:** During its presidency, India should utilize the SCO for the development of Eurasia.
- **Facilitating Dialogue** between Russia and the West to promote a rule based order.
- **Balanced Alliances** by engaging with various regional groupings like QUAD, BRICS, SAARC and ASEAN.
- **Constructive Approach** to transform the SCO into a platform for agreements, not disagreements.
- **Trade in Rupee:** Promote trade settlements in national currencies, lessening reliance on the US Dollar and price fluctuations.
- **Asian Ascendancy:** With East Asia emerging as the economic powerhouse, the SCO offers a strategic platform for India to strengthen regional trade ties and capitalize on Asia's growth.

BRICS

- BRICS is an acronym for the grouping of the world's leading emerging economies, namely Brazil, Russia, India, China and South Africa.
- Recently, five new members namely Egypt, Ethiopia, Iran, Saudi Arabia and the United Arab Emirates have joined BRICS as full time permanent members.

BRICS in Numbers

- Population: Approximately 3.5 billion people (45% of world population)
- Economy: 28% of the global economy (USD 28.5 trillion)
- Energy: Iran, Saudi Arabia and UAE → 44% of the global crude oil production.

Significance of BRICS for India

- Voice of developing countries against terrorism and for protection of their rights from WTO to climate change.
- Safe space to modulate rivalry: During the Doklam standoff of 2017 and the recent Ladakh standoff, both China and India remained engaged through BRICS.
- Providing a transcontinental reach with the presence of Brazil and South Africa.
- Boosting India's demand for institutional reforms such as UNSC, WTO etc.
- Contribution in creating an inclusive international financial architecture.
- Import dependency, 34% of India's total imports are from the other four BRICS nations.
- Achieving SDG goals to eradicate hunger and poverty with the help of initiatives like the BRICS Agricultural Research Platform.
- Balances India's growing partnerships with the West (such as through QVAD) highlighting its commitment to strategic autonomy and multi-aligned foreign policy.

Major Initiatives of BRICS

- New Development Bank (NDB) (HQ: Sanghai) and Contingent Reserve Arrangement (CRA) was created to provide mutual financial support.
- Medical cooperation: Ufa Declaration was adopted to prevent the spread of infectious disease.
- BRICS Science, Technology and Innovation (STI) Framework Programme (2015) helped facilitate a common response to COVID-19.
- BRICS Payment Task Force as a step towards cooperation between central banks and other financial institutions on national payment systems.
- BRICS Rapid Information Security Channel promotes exchange of information on cyber threats among their central banks.

India's contribution to BRICS

- Launching of BRICS Vaccine R&D Centre.
- Proposal of the New Development Bank.
- Urbanization Forum for tackling challenges of rapid urbanization of all members.
- Institutionalised the practice of holding BRICS Academics Forum

Significance of BRICS Expansion

- Closer Geopolitical and Geoeconomic Alignment among member countries.
  - Brazil: New Markets (Trade oppurtunities with Middle East and Africa) + Infrastructure Investment.
  - Russia: Counterweight to Western Powers + Energy Partnerships: Collaboration with oil producers (Saudi Arabia, Iran)
  - India: More balanced BRICS with strong new members + Connectivity Boost (INSTC).
  - China: New markets in Africa and Middle East + Leverage economic power within BRICS.
  - South Africa: Investment and Development + More African Nations in BRICS.
  - New Members: Access to larger market, trade and investment + Enhanced Bargaining power on global stage.
- Strategic Resources: Inclusion of major oil producers (Saudi Arabia + Iran) strengthens BRICS' position near crucial trade routes (Suez Canal and the Strait of Hormuz and Bab-al-Mandab Strait)
- Infrastructure and Connectivity: New members like India, Iran and Russia can collaborate on projects the International North-South Transport Corridor.
- Africa's Growth: Inclusion of African nations bolsters efforts towards integration and development within the African Continental Free Trade Area.
- Global Peace: Bringing together Middle Eastern players like Egypt, Iran, UAE and Saudi Arabia could foster regional stability.
- Multilateral Reform: BRICS can push for a more equitable global system that reduces dominance of western powers.
  - Increased collaboration with similarly aligned nations for a shared purpose
  - Sentiments against the West and solidarity among Global South nations.

Challenges with BRICS

- Dilution of Purpose: Rapid expansion risks diluting the original goals of BRICS, especially if China exerts undue influence.
- Still at developing Stage as the grouping is yet to evolve as an organization and needs time to develop its institutions and governance structure.
- China's Dominance: Some see the expansion as a ploy to advance China's global agenda.
- Balancing Act for India: India's participation in multiple regional groups (QUAD, SCO, IPEF) could become more complex with a more political BRICS.
- Lack of transparent criteria for membership raises questions about future inclusions.

- Geopolitical Tensions: Internal conflicts within BRICS, like Egypt-Ethiopia's Nile dispute or Saudi Arabia-Iran rivalry could create friction.
- Trade Hurdles: Sanctions on Iran and Russia's exclusion from SWIFT could hinder intra-BRICS trade.
- Minilateralism Concerns: The rise of BRICS might contribute to "minilateralism" hindering global cooperation on pressing issues.
- Disparities among the members due to a mix of democratic and authoritarian regimes.
- Approach towards institutional reforms: BRICS is interested only in selected reforms of the UNSC.
- More investment is needed in NDB.
- Low Intra-country trade, imports and exports among BRICS nations are low due to geographical distance and restrictive trade environments.

Pathways for Strengthening BRICS

- Setting up of a permanent secretariat with its expanded membership.
- Collective stand against trade protectionism, increase investments and share a global political agenda
- Socioeconomic convergence among the existing member countries.
- Following bottom-up-approach can lead to increase in participation of private sector and citizen involvement → BRICS visa, BRICS University etc.
- Members should focus on building trust by sharing knowledge, promoting trade and development and advancing developmental finance.

Pathways for India in BRICS

- Balancing Act: India must navigate ties with the West (US) while engaging with sanctioned members like Iran.
- Countering China through economic diplomacy and relations with Russia and Iran.
- India's leadership within BRICS: Advocate for universal security, prioritizing collective well being + Emphasize collaboration on issues affecting developing nations.
- Economic Initiatives: Promote intra-BRICS trade using Indian payment systems (Rupee internationalization)
  - Secure energy diversification and better pricing through cooperation with the Middle Eastern oil producers.
  - Advocate for clear membership criteria to manage future inclusions.

- Global Governance Philosophy for BRICS: Universal participation in international affairs and rule-making.
  - Public Health Leadership: Advance global health governance favoring developing countries.
  - Utilize the BRICS Vaccine Research and Development Centre.
  - Create early warning mechanisms for infectious diseases.
  - Provide high-quality public goods for global health collaboration.

QUADRILATERAL SECURITY DIALOGUE (QUAD)

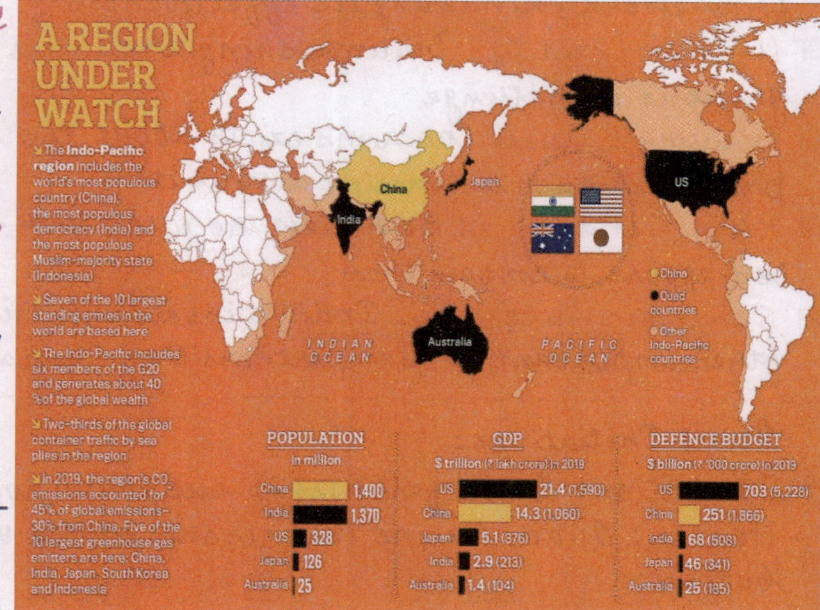

- About: Quad is an informal strategic forum among like-minded democracies across the Indian and the Pacific Ocean.
- Aim: To ensure and support a "free, open and prosperous" Indo-pacific region.
- Members: USA, India, Japan, and Australia.

Significance of QUAD for India

- Indo-Pacific Influence: QUAD allows India to play a more prominent role in the strategically and economically vital Indo-Pacific
- Aligned with Act East Policy, promoting ties with East and Southeast Asia.
- Defence Cooperation between Quad member strengthens India's military capabilities.
- Diverse Collaboration: QUAD fosters cooperation on issues like supply chain resilience.
- Strong Bilateral Ties with like minded countries through information sharing, defense cooperation and more.
- Economic Advantage: Reduced dependence on China can make India a more attractive investment destination.

Challenges of the Quad

- Unclear objectives and is perceived as an anti-China alliance.

- Implications on India's other bilateral/multilateral engagements like India-China and India-Russia relations and halted progress in the development of BRICS and Shanghai Cooperation Organisation.
- Critical Technologies and Resilient Supply chains: India is not part of the Osaka track, that includes other Quad countries.
- Conflicting signals from US: Alongwith QUAD, the US announced a new trilateral defence partnership with Australia and the UK (AUKUS).
- China's Influence: China has strong economic ties with QVAD members, especially Australia.
- Limited Institutionalization: Quad currently lacks a strong institutional framework, hindering its effectiveness.
- Unique Identity: Distinguishing the Quad's purpose from other regional group is a challenge.
- Delivery Issues: Concerns exists about the Quad's ability to deliver on its promises, such as vaccine distribution.
- Russia and China: Both view the QUAD with suspicion, criticizing it as a US-led effort to contain them (Asian NATO, Cold War Mentality).
- Strategic Autonomy: India's involvement in Quad could risk alienating other important Indian partners like Russia and Iran.

Quad Initiatives:

- Education: Quad fellowship supports doctoral studies in STEM fields.
- Health: Quad Vaccine Partnership boosts vaccine production and distribution.
    - COVID-19 Global Action Plan enhances pandemic recovery efforts.
    - Quad Vaccine Experts Group facilitates cooperation on vaccine strategies.
- Cybersecurity: Quad Senior Cyber Group promotes shared cyber standards.
- Space: Collaboration on satellite data sharing.
- Climate Change: Quad Climate Working Group focuses on adaptation and capacity building.
- Technology: Cooperation on critical technologies for digital economies.
- Non Traditional Security: The Quad tackles issues like Illegal fishing.

Way Forward

- Regional Prosperity: Quad should focus on promoting a rules-based order and regional prosperity in the Indo-Pacific.
- Complementing Existing Structures: Quad should work alongside existing regional organizations, not replace them.

- Inclusive Engagement: Quad should proactively engage with other regional players to address shared interests.
- Balancing Clarity and Ambiguity: By focusing on areas of cooperation while avoiding direct confrontation with China.
- Need for clear vision: Quad nations need to explain the Indo-Pacific Vision in an overarching framework. This will reassure the littoral states that the presence of QUAD benefits the region.
- Expanding the Quad: India can invite more countries from Indo-Pacific region like Singapore and Thailand.
- Need for a Maritime Doctrine: India should develop a comprehensive vision on the Indo-Pacific to ideate on the current and future maritime challenges.

I2U2

- I2U2 initiative is a strategic partnership of the new grouping of India, Israel, USA and UAE.
  - 'I2' stands for India and Israel, whereas 'U2' stands for USA and the UAE.
  - Also referred to as the 'West Asian Quad'.
- Background: I2U2 was initially formed in October, 2021 following the Abraham Accords between Israel and the UAE, to deal with the issues concerning maritime security, infrastructure and transport.

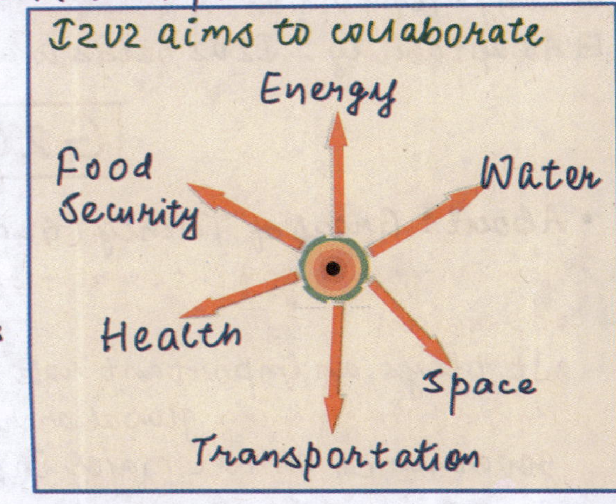

Significance of I2U2 for India

- Economic and Technological collaboration: Joint investments in water desalination, clean energy, infrastructure and critical technologies.
- Strategic Partnerships: Strengthens ties with the US, Israel (defense partner), and UAE (economic and political partner).
- Countering China's Influence: Offers an alternative to China's Belt and Road Initiative (BRI).
- Market Access: Provides access to advanced Israeli technology and UAE's financial resources.
- Food Security: Cooperation in agriculture and food processing can bolster India's food security.

Challenges:

- **Internal Disagreements:** Friction due to differences in priorities and competition for resources (e.g., Iran nuclear deal)
- **Geopolitical Tensions:** Regional conflicts impacting cooperation (e.g Israel-Palestine).
- **US Focus on Indo-Pacific:** Limited US resources and commitment to I2U2 initiatives.
- **Translating Plans to Action:** Difficulty converting plans into concrete projects.
- **Balancing Alliances:** Balancing I2U2 with other regional commitments (e.g SCO, QUAD)

Way Forward

- **Building Trust:** Mutual understanding among members is crucial for long-term success.
- **Focus on Deliverables:** Concrete results will demonstrate value and attract investment.
- **Transparency and Inclusiveness:** Open decision making processes are vital.
- **Long-Term Vision:** A strategic direction will ensure continued relevance.
- **Adaptability:** I2U2 needs to adapt to address emerging challenges and oppurtunities.

G20 Grouping

- **About:** Group of Twenty (G20) is the premier forum for international economic cooperation.
  - It plays an important role in shaping and strengthening global architecture and governance on all major international economic issues.
- **Background:**
  - 1999 (Inception of G20): Founded in 1999 after the Asian financial crisis as a forum for the Financial Ministers and Central Bank Governors.

- 2008: G20 was upgraded to the Level of Heads of State/Government in the wake of the global economic and financial crisis in 2007.
- 2009: G20 designated as the 'premier forum' for international economic cooperation.
- 2023: India for the first time held the Presidency of the G20.

• G20 Membership: 19 countries + 2 regional bodies (European Union and African Union)

• Importance of G20: 85% of the global GDP + More than 75% of the global trade + 2/3rd of the world population.

Importance of G20

1. Geopolitical Powerhouse:
   - Fairer Representation: G-20 includes developing nations (India, Indonesia and Brazil), unlike G-7's focus on developed economies.
   - Global Balance: more equitable distribution of power compared to older groups like the G-7 and P-5 (UN security council)
   - Diplomacy Platform: Facilitate bilateral meetings between leaders (India-Canada summit during G20 summit in Delhi)
   - Bridging Divides: G-20 brings countries with differing ideologies together for solutions (US and Russia on the same platform despite current disagreement)
2. Economic Powerhouse:
   - Economic: G-20's large share of global GDP shapes global financial policies (shaping World Bank and IMF guidelines)
   - Crisis Response Team: G-20 tackles major economic crisis like the 2008 crash and COVID 19 (economic stimulus effort).
   - Debt Relief: G-20 provided debt relief to developing nations during the COVID 19 recession.
   - Climate Action: Acknowledges the threat of climate change and has taken the initiatives in areas like energy efficiency, renewable energy (such as promoting solar power).
   - Gender Equality: Aims to close the gender gap in the workforce by 25% by 2025.

Challenges Faced by G-20

1. Structure:
   - Informal: No permanent set-up, agenda changes yearly (critics call it a G-7 extension).
   - Non-Binding Decisions: Guidelines on preventing terrorism financing lack enforcement mechanisms.

2. Geopolitical:

- Rising Tensions: US-China friction, post Brexit trade issues, Russia-Ukraine crisis all hinder cooperation.
- Unequal Influence: G-20 decisions (e.g ending coal funding) burden smaller nations.
- Africa's Under-representation: Raises fairness concerns.

3. Economic:

- Protectionism: De-globalization and self interest threaten G-20's credibility.
- Slowing Growth: China's slowdown, potential US/UK recession risk global growth.
- Inflation and Rates: Raising interest concerns dampen economic activity.

India and G20 Summit

India recently held the prisedency of the G20 summit for the first time at New Delhi, with the theme "Vasudhaiva Kutumbakam" or One Earth, One Family, One Future".

Key Outcomes of the G20 Summit:

1. Unanimous adoption of the G20 New Delhi Leaders' Joint Declaration.
2. Formal Inclusion of the African Union as a permanent member of the G20.

Significance of Vasudhaiva Kutumbakam Ideology for Global Unification

- Encourages human-centric progress, a shared future - One Future.
- Overcome the 'us-vs-them' mentality.
- Inclusion by accepting diversity and not imposing uniformity.
- Cooperation for resolving problems associated with Global Commons.
- Takes forward the idea of ideological harmonization on values like equality, non-violence etc.

Significance of inclusion of African Union in the G20.

For the G20	For India
• Utilize Africa's enormous potential in mitigating climate change: Africa is home to 60% of the world renewable energy assets and more than 30% of the mineral important to renewable and low carbon technologies. • Boost credibility of its policies and decisions: AU's inclusion enhances	• Championing the cause of global south: India's successful endorsement for inclusion of AU in the G20 solidifies its image as the Voice of the Global South. • Align with India's aspirations: The step aligns with India's own global aspirations to foster a multipolar world and a more equitable and representative international order.

G20's capacity to devise inclusive and equitable solutions that are truly beneficial to the global community.

- Reinvent its image: It makes G20 more representative, repurposing the G20 to be the vehicle for building a fairer, more prosperous and sustainable world.

- Permanent seat in UNSC: India is keen to garner support from AU for Permanent Membership of the UNSC.
- Resource diversification: Africa is a resource-rich continent dominated by commodities like crude oil, gas, pulses and lentils, gold and other precious metals

For Africa

- Inclusivity: It gives more leadership and voice to African countries on issues like global tax reforms, debt relief, climate change discussions etc.
- Correcting Imbalance: Africa has remained a passive receiver rather than an active contributors to discussions shaping its economic activity.
- Signal towards Growth of Africa: It signals the rise of a continent - otherwise framed as a victim of war, extremism, hunger and disaster.

India's efforts in promoting integration with the African continent

- The Pan African E network Project (PANEP): It is an information and communication technology (ICT) project that seeks to connect the member states of the Union through a satellite and fiber-optic network to India and to each other.
- India Africa Forum summit: It aims for greater cooperation between India and Africa.
- The Indian Technical and Economic Cooperation Programme: It is the leading capacity-building platform of the Ministry of External Affairs active in the African Union.
- Asia-Africa Growth Corridor: It seeks to develop infrastructure and digital connectivity in Africa through Indo-Japan collaboration.

3. Memorandum of Understanding (MoU) to establish Indian Middle East Europe Economic Corridor (IMEC)

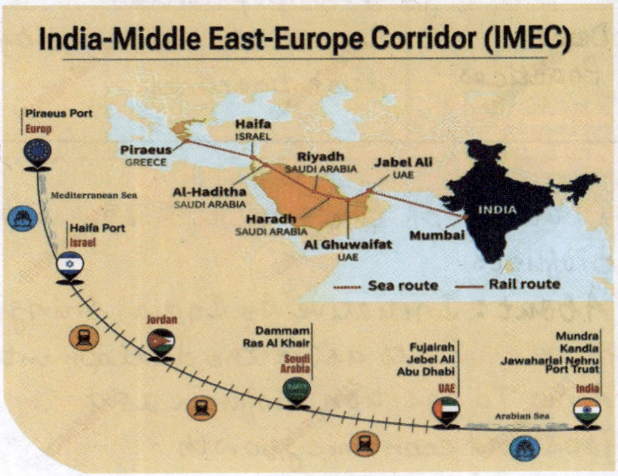

About: IMEC will consist of Railroad, Ship-to-Rail network and Road transport routes extending across two corridors,

- East Corridor: Connecting India to the Arabian Gulf.
- North Corridor: Connecting the Arabian Gulf to Europe

India-Middle East-Europe Corridor (IMEC)

Significance of IMEC

- Eurasian Shift: Signals a more balanced and connected Eurasia.
- Trade Boom: Lower costs, improves access and boosts investment.
- Regional connectivity: Enhances infrastructure, cooperation and energy flow.
- Economic Unity: Bridges India, West Asia and Europe.
- Stable Region: Closer economic ties promote security and stability
- Stronger supply chains: Makes global trade more resilient.
- Sustainable future: Aims for clean energy and improved internet access.

Significance for India

- Faster Trade: Upto 40% faster trade with Europe.
- Lower Costs: Reduced logistics costs and trade barriers.
- "Act West" Policy: Aligns with India's focus on Western partnerships

IMEC vs China's Belt and Road Initiative (BRI)

- In terms of objectives, both mega transnational projects are similar.
- China's New Silk Route is larger in terms of scale.
  - Announced in 2013, China has signed BRI cooperation documents with more than 150 countries and over 30 international organizations and created over 3000 projects.

Expected benefits of IMEC over BRI

Parameters	IMEC	BRI
Design	Based on collaborative consultations with all participants.	Centrally designed
Benefits	For common benefit of all in the region	Primarily serves China's interests
Employment	Focus on generating employment for the local population.	Mainly generates employment for Chinese companies.
Debt Practices	Proposes to follow the best international debt practices.	Criticised for putting unsustainable debt burdens on participating nations.

4. Launch of the Global Biofuel Alliance (GBA) to increase the consumption of Biofuels.

- About: Initiative by India, bringing together the biggest consumers and producers of biofuels to drive the development and deployment of biofuels.
- Aim: To position biofuels as a key to the energy transition and contribute to jobs and economic growth.

Significance of GBA :

- Knowledge Hub : GBA connects countries to share biofuel expertise, fostering innovation.
- Sustainable Practices : GBA prioritizes eco-friendly biofuel production throughout its lifecycle.
- Feedstock Options : GBA explores various biofuels sources to avoid land-use issues.
- Lifecycle Check : GBA encourages biofuel assessments to ensure environmental benefits.
- Policy Alignments : GBA works towards consistent biofuel policies for stable investments.
- Building Skills : GBA provides training to developing countries for effective biofuel industries

Benefits of GBA for India.

- Boost India's biofuels initiatives such as PM-JIVAN Yojana, SATAT and GOBARdhan scheme.
- Contribute to increasing farmers' income and create new jobs.
- Reduce oil dependency (India imports more than 80% of its crude oil)
- Achieve National Targets (National Policy on Biofuels targets to achieve 20% ethanol blending in petrol by 2025-26
- Additional oppurtunities for Indian industries (meeting global biofuel demand and exporting technology and equipment.,

Challenges

- Defining Sustainability : A lack of consensus on what constitutes "sustainable" biofuels creates hurdles.
- Technology Transfer resistance from developed countries regarding access to biofuel technologies.
- Geopolitical Concerns : Oil producing nations might oppose the GBA's goals.
- Compete with other renewable energy sources like solar and wind
- Production Challenges like limited feedstock availability, potential impact on food security and the need for cost-effective technologies.

5. Other Outcomes :
   - Proposal to launch a G-20 satellite → to help the countries of the Global South.
   - Global regulatory framework for crypto-assets and use of Artificial Intelligence responsibly
   - Consensus on G20 framework for GDPIR (Global Digital Infrastructure Repository)

INDIA AND GLOBAL SOUTH

The term "Global South" refers to countries generally considered developing or less developed. These nations are:

- Primarily located in Africa, Asia and Latin America.
- Characteristics : Lower economic output and living standards compared to the "Global North".

India and Global South:

- Diplomacy and Partnership: Engage with all nations, not just the traditional "North-South" dynamic (e.g., India's Vaccine Maitri initiative)
- Climate Leadership: Advocate for fair policies like "Common but Differentiated Responsibilities" and increased climate finance from developed nations.
- Institutional Reform in institutions like UN Security Council to ensure better representation for the Global South.
- Capacity Building: Offer training and development programs for other Southern nations (e.g India-UN capacity Building Initiative)
- Fostering Dialogue: Organize forums for collaborative discussions on shared challenges (e.g., Voice of the Global South Initiative)
- Initiatives by India for the Global South
  - Millets and other Ancient Grains International Research Initiative (MAHARISHI) for global food security.
  - Global South Centre of Excellence to conduct research on development solutions.
  - Global South Science and Technology initiative to share India's expertise in space technology and nuclear energy.
  - Global South Young Diplomats forum to synergize the diplomatic voice of the Global South.
  - Global South Scholarships for students from developing countries to pursue higher education in India.

Factors favoring India to act as a Voice of Global South

- Historical and philosophical appeal leader of the Non-Aligned Movement, philosophy of "Vasudhaiva Kutumbakam".
- Economic and geopolitical clout in global politics.
- Bridge between developed and developing world – One of the fastest growing economies in the world.
- Responsible partner – First responder in the humanitarian crises, Technical and financial aid giver etc.

Challenges Associated with Global South

- Underrepresented: Excluded from key issues (e.g UN Security Council), their voice go unheard.
- Climate Change Burden: The South suffers most despite lower historical emissions.

- Ripple Effects of Northern Conflicts: Wars in the North (e.g. Ukraine) cause food/oil prices hikes, hurting the South most.
- Value Disagreements: Clashes with the North on democracy, human rights etc hinder cooperation.
- India's Leadership Challenge: Balancing Act.
    - Balancing Interests: India struggles to balance national needs with leadership duties (e.g., rice export ban).
    - Limited Resources: Supporting other Southern nations can strain India's own resources.
    - China's growing economic and political clout challenges India's leadership aspirations.

Pathways To make Global South more Effective

- Ensuring Representation: India's "5-pillared approach" (Respect, Dialogue, Peace, Cooperation, Prosperity) offers a framework for inclusive discussions.
- Building Southern Solidarity: invest in infrastructure and technology transfer to foster cooperation among Southern nations in trade, technology, tourism and resource management.
- Reforming Institutions: (E.g WTO) to increase financial independence for the South and improve access to capital.
- India's Leadership: India proposed "4 Rs" (Respond, Recognize, Respect and Reform) framework offers a path forward.
    - It emphasizes responding to Southern priorities, acknowledging differentiated responsibilities, respecting national sovereignity and reforming institutions for greater relevance.

PYQs Corner

(Write the Answer and Get Free Evaluation)

1. Virus of Conflict is affecting the functioning of the SCO'. In the light of the above statement point out the role of India in mitigating the problems. [150 Words] [10 Marks] **[2023]**
2. How will 12U2 (India, Israel, UAE, and USA) grouping transform India's position in global politics? [250 Words] [15 Marks] **[2022]**
3. Do you think that **BIMSTEC is a parallel organization like the SAARC**? What are the similarities and dissimilarities between the two? How are Indian foreign policy objectives realized by forming this new organisation? [150 Words] [10 Marks] **[2022]**
4. Quadrilateral Security Dialogue(Quad)' is transforming itself into a trade bloc from a military alliance, in present times–Discuss.[250 Words] [15 Marks] **[2020]**

Indian Diaspora

CHAPTER
13

INDIAN DIASPORA

Diaspora

- **About:** Any person/s belonging to a particular country with a common origin or culture, but residing outside their homeland for various reasons.
  - Indian Diaspora encompasses a group of people who can either trace their origins to India or who are Indian citizens living abroad, either temporarily or permanently.
- **Indian Context:** Diaspora generally includes
  - Non Resident Indians (NRIs): Indian citizens living abroad, either temporarily or permanently.
  - Persons of Indian Origin (PIOs) - Merged with OCI (2015): Foreign citizens with Indian ancestry (except for specific countries)
  - Overseas Citizens of India (OCI): PIOs who register under the Citizenship Act.

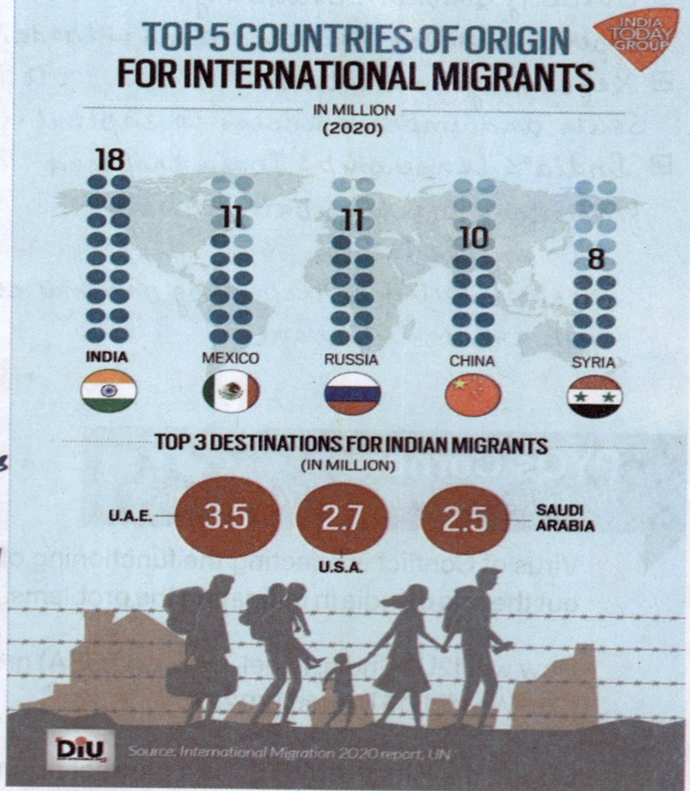

• World Migration Report, 2022: India is the largest origin countries of emigrants (18.7 million) > Ukraine (11.9 million) > China (11.1 million) > Mexico (11 million) > Venezuela (8.9 million)

 ◦ Countrywise: Highest number of Indians abroad are living in UAE > US > Saudi Arabia > Kuwait > Oman > Qatar > Nepal > UK > Singapore > Ukraine

• Remittances: India received highest remittances in 2023 at $120 billion, followed by Mexico ($66 billion), China ($50 billion), the Phillipines ($39 billion) and Pakistan ($27 billion) (World Bank).

Reasons for Diaspora Growth

Push Factors	Pull Factors	Other Factors
• Economic Hardship: Poverty, limited job oppurtunities & inequality can force people to seek better lives elsewhere. (e.g., Venezuelan exodus) • Social Discrimination: Racism, religious persecution or discrimination based on gender or sexuality can drive people to find more accepting societies. (e.g., Rohingya exodus) • Conflict and Persecution: War, terrorism or political oppression can force people to flee their homes (e.g., Jewish migration during the Holocaust) • Environmental Issues: Droughts, floods and other disasters can make an area unliveable (e.g desertification in Africa)	• Economic Oppurtunities: Job prospects, higher wages and better living standards attract people. (e.g., Indian doctors migrating) • Freedom and Tolerance: Democratic governments and religious freedom can be appealing compared to more restrictive societies (e.g., Hong Kongers migrating after the 2020 National Security Law) • Social Amenities: Quality education and healthcare system draw people to certain countries (e.g, retirees moving to Spain or Portugal). • Family Reunification: Joining family members who have already migrated is a common reason to move.	• Trade and Globalization: Trade routes and economic networks can facilitate migration and create diaspora in the commercial centres (e.g., Indian migration to Southeast Asia). • Technology: Advancements in transportation and communication make migration easier and help people stay connected to their homeland. • Cultural ties: Existing cultural connections, historical influences and shared languages can attract people to specific destinations.

Significance of the Indian Diaspora for India

Socio-cultural:

- Preserving traditions: Keeps Indian traditions alive through language schools, cultural events and artistic expressions (Carnatic and Hindustani music)
  - Fiji recognized Hindi as an official language.
- Cross-cultural Exchange: Introduce Indian culture to host countries (Diwali), fostering understanding and cultural fusion (e.g., Indo-Caribbean cuisine)
  - Ramlila is organized in Indonesia.
- Cultural Exchange: Spread of Yoga, Ayurveda, Indian cuisines, cultural events etc
- Literary writings: Sociocultural experiences voiced by writers like Salman Rushdie, Raja Rao, Amitav Ghosh etc.

Economic:

- Remittances: Money sent back home by the diaspora → Reducing poverty + help improve sovereign ratings and its ability to repay debts.
- Trade and commerce: Helps connect India with new market and opportunities in their host countries (Consume Indian products: Pickles)
- Entrepreneurship: They can invest in Indian businesses or transfer knowledge and expertise, boosting innovation and entrepreneurship.

Political:

- Informal Ambassador: Diaspora serves as a living bridge, facilitating communication and building trust between India and host countries.
- Advocacy: The diaspora lobbies local governments and international organizations on issues important to India, such as trade agreements and human rights.
  - Ex: Ghadar movement in North America during colonial times.

Significance of the Indian Diaspora for India

- Lobbying Power: Advocate for home country interests (Diaspora in executive position: Vice President of USA).
- Skilled Professionals: Fuel innovation (US tech sector and Indian diaspora)
- Entrepreneurial Spirit: Drive business creation (40% of Silicon Valley startups founded by Indian-origin entrepreneurs in 2021)
- Tourism Boost: Drive travel and revenue (Chinese New Year celebrations worldwide)
- Bridging the Gap: Facilitate knowledge sharing (India-US research collaborations)
- Philanthropic Powerhouse: Support development projects (Bills and Milinda Gates Foundation)

- Soft Power Boost: Enhance home country's image.
- Vibrant Diversity: Enrich social fabric (Diwali celebrations in the UK)

Challenges of a Growing Diaspora

Individual and Family

- Family Strain: Migration can disrupt families, leading to psychosocial issues and identify struggles.
- Cultural Strains: Generational differences within families can arise due to varying cultural ties.

India (National Level)

- Brain Drain: Migration of skilled professionals can hinder development.
- Remittance Dependence: Over-reliance on remittance income can create economic vulnerability.
- Cultural Erosion: Diaspora communities abroad may lose touch with traditions.
- Political Influence: Lobbying and activism can create internal tensions.
- Tax Revenue Loss: A large diaspora population can reduce tax revenue.
- Remittances Transfer costs: High transfer costs can push funds to unregulated channels.

Destination Countries (National Level)

- Social Strain: Large influxes can strain resources and lead to social tensions.
- Cultural Clashes: Differences in customs can create misunderstandings and discrimination.
- Security Concerns: Integration challenges can create conditions for extremism.
- Economic Competition: Diaspora workers may be seen as competition for jobs.
- Political Pressure: Diaspora lobbying can conflict with host nation's interests.

Challenges Faced by Indian Diaspora by Region

1) West Asia

- Vulnerability Conflict: Political Instability can expose Indian expats to violence (e.g Yemen Civil War).
- Uncertainties: Policies promoting local hiring ("Saudisation") can cause job losses and force unexpected returns to India, impacting low-skilled workers.
- Exploitation of migrant workers → leading to wage theft, poor working conditions or even abuse
- Legal and Visa Issues: Visa sponsorship or "Kafala" system, which binds workers to their employers, limiting their ability to seek better living or working conditions.

- Recruitment Malpractices: Exorbitant fees on migrants + risk of passport confiscation by employers or sponsors.
- Discrimination based on ethnicity, religion or socioeconomic status, leading to social exclusion and difficulty accessing services.
- Invisibilization of Migrants: Qatar → Lack of clarity and uniformity in data from different agencies made migrant workers, especially those in low-wage jobs, less visible.

Various Evacuation Operations by Indian Government
• Operation Kaveri (2023): To evacuate Indians from Sudan.
• Operation Ganga (2022): To rescue Indian students from Ukraine in the middle of a war with Russia.
• Operation Devi Shakti (2021): To evacuate people from war-torn Afghanistan.
• Operation Bharat Mission (2020): To bring back Indians stranded in foreign countries during COVID-19 pandemic.
• Operation Sankat Mochan (2016): To rescue Indians from South Sudan.
• Operation Rahat (2015): To evacuate Indians from Yemen.

- Terrorism: Presence of ISIs → Radicalization of Indian youth is a security concern.

2. Europe, North America and Australia

- Secessionist Movements: Pro-Khalistan Protests can create geopolitical tensions and threaten India's integrity.
- Racism: Members of the diaspora may face discrimination based on ethnicity, skin colour or cultural background.
- Recognition: Indian qualifications may not be readily recognized or valued.
- Work place challenges like glass ceilings, biases and stereotyping hindering career advancement.
- Immigration Issues and residency status can cause stress (e.g., H1B visa concerns under Trump Adminstration)
- Language and Cultural Barriers pose challenges in communication and integration into the local community → Social Isolation.

Indian Government Initiatives for Diaspora Engagement:

- Ministry of External Affairs acts as a central hub (formely merged with the Ministry of Overseas Indian Affairs)
- Overseas Citizenship Scheme (OCI): Simplified travel and certain residency benefits in India.
- Diaspora Welfare Program: Scholarships + Pension schemes + community welfare funds.

- Pravasi Bharatiya Diwas (PBD): Biennial flagship event to celebrate diaspora's contribution.
  - Pravasi Bhartiya Kendra: Fosters social, cultural and economic ties.
  - Pravasi Bhartiya Samman Award for outstanding achievements by NRIs, PIOs or diaspora organizations.
- Cultural Connect: Know India Program + Pravasi Teerth Darshan Yojana.
- e-Migrate System: Regulates emigration for blue-collar workers seeking oversees employment.
- Students Registration Portal: Locate and assist Indian students abroad in case of emergencies.
- Online Voter Services: NRIs can now register and vote electronically in Indian elections.
- Pravasi Rishta Portal: Bridges gap between government, missions abroad and diaspora.

International Collaboration:

- Bilateral and Multilateral Arrangements: Agreements like MMPAs, CAMM and LMAs established with countries like France, the EU and GCC nations.
- Global Compact for Safe, Orderly and Regular Migration (2018): Promoting international cooperation of migration governance.

Legal Framework and Worker Protection:

- Emigration Act (1983): Regulates emigration of Indian workers and mandates registration of recruitments agencies to prevent exploitation.
- Labor Mobility Partnerships: Labor agreements and MoUs with GCC nations like UAE, Saudi Arabia, Kuwait, Bahrain to enhance protection for workers.
- Indian Community Welfare Fund (ICWF): Emergency financial support to Indian workers in distress abroad.
- Awareness Campaign ("Surakshit Jaaye Prasikshit Jaaye") to promote safe and legal migration.

Pathways for Strengthening Ties with Indian Diaspora

1. Policy and Law

- Consolidated Policy: Establish a clear roadmap for engagement under the MEA.
- Inter Ministerial Coordination: Ensure alignment on migration policies across ministries.
- Unified Grievance Redressal to address diaspora concerns.

2. Skills and Knowledge Transfer:

- Standardized Skill Training: Upgrade domestic training and implement national curriculum.
- Financial Literacy Programs: Empower migrant and families with informed financial decision-making.

3. Safety and Security

- Social Security Agreements: Promote bilateral/multilateral agreements for migrant worker benefits.
- Mutual Legal Assistance Treaties (MLATs): Strengthen support systems. combat crime and prevent fraud.

4. Other steps

- Regulate Recruitment Agencies: Implement stricter monitoring and mandatory e Migration registration.
- Diplomatic Advocacy: Champion worker rights through dialogue and bilateral agreements (e.g Kafala system reform)
- Global Platforms: Utilize UN forums and international agreements to push for change.
- Family Reunification: Streamline visa processes to facilitate family reunification for migrant workers.

PYQs Corner

(Write the Answer and Get Free Evaluation)

1. Indian diaspora has scaled new heights in the West. Describe its economic and political benefits for India. [10 Marks] **[2023]**

2. Indian diaspora has a decisive role to play in the politics and economy of America and European Countries. Comment with examples. [150 Words] [10 Marks] **[2020]**

3. Indian Diaspora has an important role to play in South-East Asian countries' economy and society. Appraise the role of Indian Diaspora in South-East Asia in this context.[250 Words] [15 Marks]**[2017]**